András Török's

BUDAPEST
A CRITICAL GUIDE

András Török's

BUDAPEST
A CRITICAL GUIDE

Illustrated by
ANDRÁS FELVIDÉKI

The Chapter on "Drinking Wine"
was Fully Rewritten by
ANDRÁS EGYEDI

CORVINA
1997

For MÁRTA and GYÖRGY, my parents, who have never had time to enjoy their home town, and now that they do, they are reluctant to do so

Special thanks to

DR ZOLTÁN SZENTKIRÁLYI and DR BALÁZS VARGHA[†], who were kind enough to go through the manuscript as consultants of the very first edition

ANDRÁS BARABÁS who improved on the text and who could possibly write a much better book on Budapest

PETER DOHERTY who comes from Dublin and who knows best what to enjoy and laugh at in Budapest

The author and the illustrator are also indebted to a large number of people, among others, to

Márta Aczél, Judit Béres, Ákos Birkás, Éva Blaschtik, Ferenc Bodor[†], Alexander Brody, Endre Bojtár, Mária Borbás, László Darvas, Katalin Délceg, Klára D. Major, Győző Duró, Ágnes Eperjesi, Edit Erki, Zoltán Erő, Péter Esterházy, Katalin Farkas, András Ferkai, József Finta, Ádám Fischer, Doris Fischer, András Fűrész, George and Julie Gábor, Zsuzsa Gáspár, Éva Gedeon, János Gerle, Tibor Frank, József Hegedüs, Robert Hetzron, Iván Horváth, Éva Jeles, György Kassai, Mária Kemény, János Kenedi, Károly Kincses, Gábor Klaniczay, János Mátyás Kovács, László Kúnos, László Kis Papp, Pál Kövi, Endre Lábass, George Lang, Tony Lang, Alain Lombard, László Lugosi Lugo, István Margócsy, Miklós Molnár, Ákos Nagy, Ádám Nádasdy, Vilma Nádasdy, András Nyerges[†], Ágnes Padányi, Vera Pécsi, Klára Péter, Attila Pogány, Péter Polgár, Gábor Preisich, Mihály Ráday, István Rév, András Rochlitz, András Román, Róbert Sarlós, Jean-Luc Soulé, Erzsébet Szabados, György Tibor Szántó, Anna Szemere, Ákos Szilágyi, István Teplán, Lionel Tiger, Ágnes Tompa, Iván Tosics, Mihály Vargha, Benedek Várkonyi, Anna Veress, Tibor Vidos, Miklós Vincze, Júlia Váradi, Péter Virágvölgyi, Richard Saul Wurman, Zsófia Zachár.

Design by András Felvidéki
DTP by graphoman
Ground Plans by Andrea Réti
Cover Photo by Gergely Pohárnok

Original English version
    translated by Peter Doherty and Ágnes Enyedi,
    edited by Zsuzsa Gáspár
Third edition revised with the assistance of Flóra Török
This revised edition went to press on 15 February 1997
Edited by István Bart
ISBN 963 13 4387 1 (Hungary)

CONTENTS

WHAT IS THIS BOOK FOR?

Introduction to the First Edition

BUDAPEST, my birthplace, used to be compared to Vienna by visitors. "The Danube, the ring boulevards, the many eclectic and neostyle buildings — the city is a second Vienna, in a more modest edition", they would say. "True, Mother Nature has been more generous, but as regards historic buildings, it cannot even hold a candle to Vienna. On top of that, the Hungarian language does not resemble any other European language."

Budapest now has earned a higher reputation among the young who come from Paris, Amsterdam, Warsaw or St. Petersburg. There are many backpacking tourists in Budapest but the number of "non-package" independence-loving visitors, who arrive in their own car, has also much increased recently. Those friends of mine, mostly my age, whom I have shown around in the last fifteen years have usually sung the city's praises beyond the point of politeness.

They said they found Budapest to be truly cultured, truly European. They said that from certain points of view it has better preserved the old, humane qualities of days gone-by than many other cities, where development has swept the past away. They remembered staircases, badly needing renovation, locksmith's workshops with wooden floors, and the smell of oil and small suburban family-run restaurants. They were fascinated by the large, uniform riverbank, and the beauty of the three bridges in the middle. They also said that the historic buildings seemed to be familiar to them (perhaps because quite a few of them are copies?) and were very accessible.

It is not so much the grandeur but the prettiness of the buildings that captivated them. They even said that the city was like Sleeping Beauty still hidden from the eyes of Europe. My friends who have returned after two, three or more years have said that Budapest has changed a lot. New shops and restaurants have opened, and now you can even get a taxi. They noticed some nice modern buildings. They found their money still went a long way, though not as far as it had done.

"We would not have got too far without you", my friends said. And that was more than a simple compliment. The spirit of the city had revealed itself to them, a spirit which can get close to you only with the help of a native. This book was written in order to provide an invisible host for you.

THIS BOOK tries to combine three types of guides with the advantages of all three: the Baedeker type, the critical guidebook and the alternative guidebook. Obviously it will not be exhaustive in any single type.

THERE IS a Hungarian saying for things which seem impossible: "an iron ring made out of wood". Even if this book cannot overcome the language difficulties, it is designed to put the visitor at ease when making his own plans to discover the city. After all, it is easier to get help with the language from friends, business-partners, interpreters or hotel receptionists, than to get ideas for spending one's time.

THE COW AND THE SOCIAL SAFARI

Introduction to the Third, Revised Edition

Budapest, my native city has changed a lot in the eyes of the serious travellers, since this book was first published 8 years ago. I don't mean the more and more numerous luxury restaurants, the ever nicer shops, the Vienna prices in some places.

It has changed so much even for me — almost beyond recognition. The society of scarcity has changed to a society of affluence and squalor. While respect for traditional cityscape has also returned. In contrast with unbelievable visual pollution: billboards by the thousand in the city, and with the brand names of the two biggest, ever warring soft drink manufacturers on thousands of shop signs. And little, lit cigarette boxes on façades.

Even I don't really remember that meek and mellow dictatorship: melted away in front of our very eyes around 1989. Just for your education, Gentle, Serious Reader, since the good old days are here, in every cupboard, all over town, under every carpet — let me give you a short lecture.

You should know that this ancien régime was different from all the others in Eastern Europe. Most Hungarians did not cry out against it every day after getting up; on the contrary, they had to remind themselves of what kind of a regime they were living in, at the weekend. They laughed at the ignorant "politicians", and — at least my class, the egghead dissident folks — detested money.

We used to wear ragged blue jeans from twenty to thirty and our hair was reluctant to follow the Zeitgeist into a shorter and shorter style. We read a lot of books, but very few papers, always trying to read between the lines. We didn't expect this world to disappear in our lifetime. We were conditioned to irreverence and to having absolutely no responsibility outside the family.

Until one day some of us found ourselves in the government, responsible for billions of forints of budgets.

Being born in 1954, I didn't have any memories of the revolution in 1956. My best friend, a poet and scholar did. He kept on telling me the story about the Cow.

He explained that in the dark 50s his family didn't think the régime would last. They felt that a big dark cow that was grazing over a beautiful meadow (i.e. Hungary) suddenly sat down. But that darkness, they thought, cannot last forever: it is the very nature of cows that one day they get up. And the Cow did get up. For only twelve days — a glorious but short time. After that nobody thought that she would ever leave. Some people — including me — thought it was not a cow, just a cow-shaped piece of solid rock. And it is possible to live under a rock — if you are some species of fungus.

Around 1982 the government decided to introduce some "reforms": after inventing lukewarm water they opted for inventing hot water. Letting small businesses start and flourish was going to erode the remaining ideological features of the system. Earlier, a district hall official could turn down a permission for a shoemaker's shop just by saying that there are enough shoemakers in a given neighbourhood.

That made a slow but dramatic impact on Budapest. There were better and better shops. The gentrification of the Inner City started again, first making the tourist reservation just a bit bigger, later spreading throughout within the Grand Boulevard. That slowly changed my generation as well. Some of us felt that it was worth earning money so as to spend it in an intelligent way. Some of us were not interested in money at all — we published the half a dozen underground papers, for a couple of thousand people. Some were interested in both. Some in nothing. But everyone thought that the régime cannot become more liberal than it had become. Common sense was infiltrating everyday life more and more, though. Not so much, though, that one of the stupidest laws — my favourite — was abolished. Until the autumn 1989(!) if you had a car younger than three years old, you could only sell it to the state, at a depressed price. Thus, a three-year-and-one-day-old car was much more expensive than a three-year-old car...

Bur who remembers these days? Suddenly, to our astonishment, the Cow started fidgeting, and slowly, very slowly it was getting up. It was a slower and less dramatic event than in the countries around Hungary; nobody was killed and there were hardly any demonstrations, the world press showed much less interest.

There is a free Parliament, free business, even a free press. In a couple of years' time Hungary might become one of those smaller, prosperous, boring countries. Not yet though.

When the Cow left, we hoped the grass to recover overnight. Alas, no. There happened to emerge new Cows from our very own barns. Some swore they spotted some new Cows coming in from the West. Some patches of the grass recovered wonderfully by now. Some others are in worse shape than ever before.

You should come and check it out from time to time. It can easily amount to a Social Safari for the Discerning Traveller.

(October 1988 — January 1997)

A CITY

A CRASH COURSE IN BUDAPEST

An Exercise in Civic Boosterism
(The Absolute Minimum You Should Know if you Aim at Being Called
Well-Informed by Locals On Your First Day.)

Budapest is the overgrown capital of the Republic of Hungary, inhabited by about 2 million restless inhabitants — most of them readers, and not only of the telephone numbers in the television commercials. It was established in 1873, out of Buda, Pest and northern Old Buda (Óbuda). It consists of 23 municipal districts.

Roughly two-thirds of the territory is in almost completely flat Pest on the eastern bank of the Danube, the rest in the hilly part called Buda, originally a much older settlement.

The following tries hard to list places where Budapest eggheads go to, meet at, or point out to foreign egghead friends they desperately try to impress.

WEATHER is far from boring in Budapest. It is pretty predictable: can be very hot in the Summer, and can theoretically be very cold in the Winter: the latter happens every five-six years. In Hungary we celebrate name-days which are usually the feast days of a saint of that name. The name-days of Sándor, József and Benedek fall between March 18th and 21st and, according to the saying, they "bring the warm weather in their bags". Indeed this is usually the time when Spring allows us to shed our Winter topcoats — a good time for a visit too. A really heavy fall of snow is somewhat rare, but it is followed by slush and filthy piles of frozen snow pushed to the edges of the pavement. Dusk falls early in Winter, between 3.30 and 4.30 in the afternoon and the sun is rarely seen. However, the other three seasons make up for this. Stormy days total about 30. Summer is warm, temperatures of 30° C (86° Fahrenheit) are by no means unusual. Nevertheless raincoats or umbrellas should not be left behind, especially if it rains on Medárd Day (June 8th). Tradition has it that the next forty days will also bring rain. $(X° \ Celsius = (9X \ / \ 5) + 32 \ ° \ Fahrenheit)$

NOT AN EXOTIC COUNTRY ANY MORE As an associated country to the European Union, there are no special, unusual visa, customs or registration regulations in Budapest. Visas are not required for citizens of European countries. The exception, at the time of going to press is the countries of the former Soviet Union (if you are not a packaged tourist). They (and citizens of the non-European countries, with the exception of the USA and Canada) should obtain a visa from a Hungarian consulate abroad. A visa is valid for six months and entitles the holder to a stay of up to thirty days. For a longer stay, you must extend the visa at the local police station. Visas can also be obtained at road frontier crossing points or at Budapest Ferihegy Airport. There visas cost somewhat more. Passengers arriving by train or boat must buy their visas in advance.

If you are in doubt, you can always call Tourinform Budapest: (361) 1179-800.

TRANSPORT Budapest has a proverbially good public transport

which has become increasingly foreigner-friendly to use. Maps are to be found at more and more tram stops, ticket vending machines now tend to speak in several languages. If I were you, I walked and walked and walked, then used the underground and tram lines. They are never blocked by the insane amount of cars. Bus routes are more difficult to find out about.

You should remember — apart from the three underground lines — Tram 2 (on the Pest riverfront) and Tram 4/6 on Grand Boulevard, you can get to pretty everywhere you are unwilling to walk to.

You are likely to find very useful *The Budapest Citymap for Tourists* from Budapest Transport Ltd, from human ticket vendors in larger underground passages. (There is a yellow tram and a pink tram ticket on the cover, and 'Budapest 1997' in large lettering.)

The average Budapest citizen tends to have a car, usually over seven years old, but they often walk and rarely resort to the ever more expensive taxis. If they do, yes, then they order it from home, and do not hail one in the street. They try to call a CityTaxi (211-1111), a Fótaxi (122-2222) or a Yellow Pages Taxi (155-5000).

The real Budapest patriots often use the underground and admire the lamps in the carriages on line 2 (the Red Line). These lamps reflect the thirties in Russia. No Budapest citizens are surprised if caught in a hurricane on one of the endlessly long escalators. (That's how the metro is ventillated.) And they beware of pickpockets.

PHONES, FAXES Budapest people love the recent changes for

the better. They are about to forget that once upon a time there was a scarcity of phone lines. Waiting for installation literally lasted years, sometimes a dozen or more. In the early 80s an MP in the all-communist Parliament made an ironic suggestion that telephone applications should be made inheritable...

They fancy the big blue coin-operated telephones imported from South Africa, but almost all of them have a telephone card.

The card-operated phones are imported from France, and they "speak" in Hungarian and English, alternately. Phone cards are sold at newsagents' all over the town. The proper way to ask for one is "Kérek egy telefonkártyát" (Keeh-rek edy telefon-kaahr-tyaaht). Then comes the inevitable question about the kind. There are two kinds, one of fewer units and the more substantial one. Find your way with writing the number on a piece of paper.

Faxes are to be found everywhere in businesses, but you have to queue up for them in post offices. And if you want to receive a fax, you have to browse among dozens of other faxes for strangers with the same initials as you. Or you can go to the elegant business centre of Kempinski Hotel, downtown.

The first floor of Inner City Telephone Centre (Belvárosi Telefonközpont) is a place where you can personally browse in all the printed directories of the world, and can sit down in reasonably comfortable boots. (V. Petőfi Sándor utca 17-19.)

Various services are provided by the telephone company called MATÁV: they include alarm calls, jokes and bedtime stories — in Hungarian, of course. The only service for which you don't need the local dialect is an "A" for tuning: 117-1822.

MONEY
The Forint (Ft) became the Hungarian currency in August 1946, after a period of extremely high inflation was brought to an end.

The denominations of notes are brown 5,000 Ft with Count Széchenyi, the early 19th-century aristocrat and reformer on it, the green 1,000 Ft with Bartók, the composer, the purple 500 Ft with Endre Ady, the poet, and the red 100 Ft with Kossuth. (See them in more detail in the Chapter "Who Was Who".) You can occasionally spot brown 50 Ft with Ferenc Rákóczi II, who led an unsuccessful struggle for independence against the Habsburgs in the early 18th century. The blue 20 Ft note has the picture of György Dózsa, the leader of a 15th century peasant revolt and the green ten-forint-note, with Sándor Petőfi, the poet, are collectors' items now. Instead, there are oversize coins.

Coins come in denominations of 200, 100, 50, 20, 10, 5, 2 and 1 Ft. You may find some fillér coins in your change, but there is now nothing you can buy for less than 1 Ft. There is a ridiculous quagmire in the front of coins, since an autocratic President of the National Bank in the early 90s (who is the final say in money design) decided to merge two separate designs after a competition and an opinion poll. That's why the recto and the verso of the coins are so different. The 1 forint coin is said to be too small (mocked as "shirt buttons" by Budapest people. The 100 Ft coin is too large, and was recently replaced by a two-metal smaller coin. This one will be soon withdrawn, since the inner part tends to fall out, if you put them into a freezer, as a recent TV programme found out. (Why should the coins be resistant to freezers? Don't ask me...)

On the back of the 5,000 forint bill there is the building of the Academy of Sciences and Letters, established by Count Széchenyi, who is on the front of the banknote. As a comic biweekly found out after the note was issued, the etching was made after a contemporary photo: the designer has parked a selection of East European made cars at the building. Certainly not manufactured at the time of the count.

CHANGING MONEY
January 1997 was a historic date in the modernization of Hungary: changing forints to foreign currencies was totally liberalised. There happened a veritable revolution in changing money for tourists. There are hundreds of services that change your money, also the ATMs. Despite that you will no doubt be solicited to change money in the street at a slightly better rate, there are a large number of con-men walking the streets: some pass on forged notes but most simply work a switch whereby the tourist finds himself with a heap of toilet paper bundled up in genuine notes at either end of the roll.

THE SINGLE MOST IMPORTANT BOOKSHOP

is certainly Írók Könyvesboltja ("Writers' Bookshop", VI. Andrássy út 45, at Liszt Ferenc tér) in a former, famous café, called "Japan", for its once fine Oriental décor, which is still to be spotted behind the awful, nondescript panelling cum fluorescent tube interior, from the mid-sixties. You can sit and have tea, watch the crowd leafing through the incredibly high number of new publications and literary reviews from all over Hungary and from the Hungarian speaking regions of the nearby countries. Hungarian literature is the shop's forte, and there is a book première almost every afternoon at 4 p.m. Also look for the innovative window displays of new titles. The shop, after a lengthy process was sold in the end to its enthusiastic staff, who needed to borrow a huge amount of money for the purchase, of course.

THE SINGLE MOST IMPORTANT ANTIQUARIAN BOOKSELLER

is obviously Mr and Mrs Borda, in their home. They used to work for a state-owned chain, then opened a small, elegant shop in a remarkably civilized part of New Leopold Town. But they found the rent too high, and had to deal with too many customers just looking for some detective novel "they just had to have", they retreated to their home. They have published about a dozen carefully compiled lists. (One of the first item in the most recent one was the bus card of Endre Ady, the great poetic genius from the 1910s.) It's a very serious operation, open only on Tuesday and Thursday afternoon, 4 to 8, otherwise by special commission. (VII. Madách Imre tér 5. T: 142-2086.)

LISZT MUSIC ACADEMY is the most important venue of

the prodigously lively classical music scene. (VI. Liszt Ferenc tér 8, at Király utca.) It's in a landmark art nouveau block with a big concert hall, worth visiting even on the occasion of a minor musical event. The smaller room opens from the first floor, where there is a huge painting: "The Spring of Arts". Musical graffiti in the Gents' room, downstairs: "Viva Brüggen!". Béla Bartók and Zoltán Kodály used to teach upstairs. State Opera House (VI. Andrássy út 22) is a jewel, completed in 1884, lovingly restored for its centenary. It houses 1200 people. There is an other, much bigger, much less fancy opera venue, called the Erkel Színház (VIII. Köztársaság tér), where the productions that attract really large crowds are performed.

LETTERS, STAMPS Everyone thinks that bigger post offices

are quicker because they have more staff — they do, but they are also busier and queues are long. Try the smaller post offices. Since our walks begin at Vörösmarty tér, note the position in a side-street at the northern end of the square: POST OFFICE No. 51 Dorottya utca 9. (T: 118-6441.)

The only post office round the clock is Post Office No. 62 at Western Railway Station (VI. Teréz körút 51 - 53.)

You will notice that some addresses are given beginning with their district number, in Roman, and some with a four-digit postcode in Arabic. For speedier delivery of letters, the postcode should be used. The correct way of addressing an envelope in Hungary is:

> KOVÁCS JÁNOS
>
> BUDAPEST
> King Kong utca 6.
> 1052

The logic of the postcode is that 1 indicates Budapest, the next two digits the Budapest district, and the final digit the sorting-office's division of the district. The same address would be found under. "V. King Kong utca 6." in an address list.

ART MOVIES AND THE RECENT MULTIPLEX CRAZE

Hungarian films so popular with serious movie-goers back in the 70s and 80s all over the world are hardly produced any more. Budapest cinemas are now swamped by new commercial American movies, plus a couple of Greenaway and Luc Besson films. "You can't substitute a real producer with committees" — remark serious analysts. And the mild totalitarian state gushed money like water on the film industry, and it had its special expectation. While only some 2 per cent of the moviegoers in Hungary is interested in the local crop.

As many as 3 new multiplex cinemas opened last Autumn — the number of seats almost doubled. And the prodigious art movie supply is still here. Almost like in New York and Paris.

THE SINGLE MOST IMPORTANT FOREIGN LANGUAGE BOOKSHOP

is the one with the deceiving name: "Bestsellers", operated by an immigrant from Britain, Tony Lang, who had some Hungarian blood, but no prior command of the Hungarian language. He moved to Hungary to buy a shop — it happened to be a food shop, with permission to sell "other goods". For a year there were some bottles and some Heinz sauces to demonstrate that it was a food shop after all. It sells all kinds of fiction, non-fiction and reference books. Also newspapers and magazines and fine stationery. A centre for the expatriate community. Open until 6 p.m. — on Saturday, too.

KATONA JÓZSEF THEATRE

is one of Europe's best theatre companies, member of the 8-theatre European Theatre (British members: National Theatre and the Royal Shakespeare Company.) Veterans of over a hundred performances abroad. They have a large repertory, including Platonov by Chekhov, Taming of the Shrew and A Midsummer Night's Dream by Shakespeare. Their latest hit is The Broken Jug by Kleist. They play in a small house, and in an even smaller studio nerby, called "Kamra" or Larder, established in 1982, by innovative (though mainstream) actors and directors ostracized from the National Theatre. There are only about 250 seats, so it's not easy to get in.

Budapest eggheads tend to know someone in the company. Worth the effort! (V. Petőfi Sándor utca 6.)

EGGHEAD EXPAT PAPERS Any of the two competing
English-speaking weeklies, the slightly older *Budapest Week,* (more and more losing its original alternative flavour) and *Budapest Sun,* that was originally launched by an American professional couple. They both have excellent movie and TV listings for English speakers. None of the two papers have real insiders' information about politics and life and are easy to attract into biassed opinions. The staff of both papers changes all too often. They don't have long enough memories, if you know what I mean.

There is also the *Budapest Business Journal,* which is serious stuff, even with an excellent Parliament Diary, written by a serious political analyst who heads the local branch of a British firm.

PAPERS BUDAPEST EGGHEAD EXPATS READ
They tend to read the *Budapest Week,* out of tradition, but often point out its weaknesses. They are all said to subscribe to *The Hungarian Quarterly,* a prestige review, notable for its translations of modern short stories and poetry and with a lively review section, country and its history. A most readable publication written in impeccable English, by senior Hungarian opinion-makers.

Also, expatriate eggheads are beginning to appreciate the *Budapest Review of Books,* another quarterly, with a very funny column at the end called the BRB Guide to Budapest, about life in Budapest intellectual salons and comments on the cultural scene. Some of the occasional readers are on the brink of subscribing to it. Or both. Most of them go through them in libraries. (See under "Reading", p. 216.)

THE BIG FLEAMARKET is located at the entrance of Motorway 5, (XIX. Nagykőrösi út 156.) It's a huge antique store crossed with a junk store, plus shops for all kinds of recent goods. It's a social safari to go there and see what is being sold, especially by the day-vendors. Closed on Sunday, and Monday is not a good day. Greatest conoisseurs go there at seven on Saturday. Since variety in both old and new stuff has returned to inner city Budapest — and prices reached almost Vienna level out here — the market has lost some of its allure. But not all of it. (Males have the privilege of musing over the self-reflective newspaper-clippings in the Gents' loo.)

THE SINGLE MOST IMPORTANT ESOTERIC CLASSICAL RECORD SHOP is Concerto. The attention of
some Budapest eggheads was drawn to the shop by the British Gramophone magazine. The owner (now moved to Toronto) made a small fortune by importing a carefully selected list of LPs from the then Soviet Union, then selling them to Western eggheads as rarities. To those who still stick to the analogous routine, and consider LPs far superior to CDs. The shop is in a curious block called "Block 15" — where the Budapest City Hall launched its aborted rehabilitation campaign. They could not lure similar-

ly chic businesses here. The street name means "Drum street". No tourist ever sets foot there, though not far from the city centre. (VII. Dob utca 33. T: 121-6432)

STAIRS

STAIRS The most famous, the best known stairs in Budapest, the most appropriate to meet wife, girlfriend or girl friend is of course that of the National Museum, in Museum Gardens (off Kálvin tér). That is where people think Sándor Petőfi, the youthful leader of the 1848 Revolution recited his freshly written poem, the "National Song" on the afternoon of March 15. (Research proved he did not. Not here, not him.)

Another one, ideal for first or second date, first kiss in daylight, is on the Pest riverbank, off the embankment, halfway between Chain bridge and Elizabeth bridge, somewhat nearer the latter. The more passionate the relationship is, the nearer the water you have to sit, in order not to be disturbed by the others.

The trendiest stairs these days are indoors: still, not in a staircase, but in the foyer of the French Institute. If you have a look at it on the occasion of a vernissage, you will see how well it serves its purpose: to see better and be seen better. The two reasons one goes to a vernissage for.

The naffest and by far the most ridiculous stairs are to be seen at the corner of XIII. Váci út and Dózsa György út, at the base of the "skyscraper" of the Municipal Waterworks. About twenty meter wide, long patch af stairs. They were never used for a moment. There are dozens of pre-cast concrete flowerbeds placed across the stairs, very near the bottom... The world's ugliest and least used stairs.

TWELVE PLACES TO MEET A BUDAPEST FRIEND

7 a.m. Burger King(!), the second floor, by the rail, with a view of the Grand Boulevard. Recent, post-modern glitz. (VI. Oktogon tér 3.)

9 a.m. Café Gerbaud, in the middle, flat-ceilinged room, under the oil painting "The Altar Boy and the Apprentice Confectioner". It opens at 9, so you manage to be there, before the other tourists, whom Budapest eggheads avoid. (V. Vörösmarty tér 7.)

11 a.m. The big oak table in the main hall of the Museum of Ethnography, the former Supreme Court. (V. Kossuth Lajos tér 12. Closed on Monday.)

1 p.m. The top of the stairs of the National Museum — the left side. A landmark building from 1847, the setting for the start of the 1848 Revolution. (VIII. Múzeum körút 14-16.)

3 p.m. CD Bar, a small shop where you can listen to some Purcell overtures through headphones, sip a coffee, and not admit you are just waiting. (VI. Székely Mihály utca 10.)

5 p.m. The gallery of Café New York — but don't expect to be served there. The birthplace of modern Hungarian literature. (VII. Erzsébet körút 9-11.)

7 p.m. In front of the fancy modern clock, in the courtyard of the Hotel Taverna (V. Váci utca 20.)

9 p.m. The Korona Passage in the Korona Hotel, at the very back, under the mural depicting the siege of Buda in 1686. (V. Kecskeméti utca 14. The left wing.)

11 p.m. Café Művész, the inner room. Traditional splendour, elderly clientele — but not that hour. (VI. Andrássy út 29.)

1 a.m. Paris, Texas, trendy new café (IX. Ráday utca 36.)

3 a.m. Picasso Point, the hottest student café in town. Under the rocking horse attached to the ceiling, upside down. (VI. Hajós utca 31.)

5 a.m. Copy General. After the owners of Talk Talk Café were forced to discontinue round the clock operation, there is no other public indoor place, than this very very smoothly run shop, where you are likely to bump into architecture students who desperately try to meet their last deadline, and some eccentric composers with fresh music pieces to be given to the string quartet the coming morning. If your friend happens to be late (which is highly uncivilized at that time of the day), and you want to pretend some activity, please don't copy this book, but something else… You should rather buy another copy for your friend…

STARING AT OTHERS
AND GETTING AWAY WITH IT Coming up and down
on the escalator of any of the underground stations. Especially at Kossuth Lajos tér (lower middle class), at Lehel tér (working class) and at Blaha Lujza tér (perfect mix). Or riding Bus 15 from terminus to terminus at sunset. Since people switch on their lights, but do not draw their curtains right away. Not nice, not even in Hungary. A sort of "applied people-watching" — a scholarly study.

HUNGARIAN PAPERS
HUNGARIAN EGGHEADS READ They tend to read
Magyar Hírlap (a Swiss-owned, formerly liberal daily, they switched to it from *Magyar Nemzet*, the one they had read for thirty years), *Heti Világgazdaság* (the 15-year-old Economist-like weekly, not printed on green paper any more), *Élet és Irodalom*, a literary weekly (or they have just cancelled it), *Hócipő* (a hilariously funny biweekly — ask a Budapest friend about the meaning of the name), but they also keep an eye on the formerly Communist, now (German-owned) independent *Népszabadság*, the daily with by far the biggest circulation. (Some years ago Péter Esterházy, the influential writer wrote about this paper: "Now it is only the name of it that I hate". *Népszabadság* used this quotation the next week to advertise itself.)

THE PRESIDENT OF THE REPUBLIC Bare-headed,
grey-haired, rotund, with an eternal knowing smile, his face is to be seen in the media. Árpád Göncz speaks fantastic English with an unmistakable Hungarian accent (in prison, after 1956, where he learned his English, there were books, but no tapes). Unlike eggheads, he is never hot-headed, and can talk to kings, peasants and billionaires alike. Will pay attention even to you if bumped into at a reception. His book of short stories "Homecoming" is soon to be published by Corvina, my publisher.

CHOOSING YOUR PLACE TO STAY

Budapest is no Mecca for hotels, though the situation has improved a lot. Staying at a hotel in Budapest is obviously a situation I have never been to — I have only a limited pool of independent information to rely on. What comes next is not a comprehensive list. That is available at every tour operator all over the world.

As unfortunately most serious travellers come only for a few days to Budapest, location is crucial. So my tips tend to have a bias towards reasonably good locations.

For Affluent Newly-weds Who Want to Rejuvenate themselves After Eventful Nights

RAMADA GRAND HOTEL *XIII. Margitsziget. T: 311-1000. F: 153-2753.* 246 rooms. A hundred years old establishment on a large island, ideal for jogging and long walks. You need a car to comfortably get to town in five minutes. Say hi to me if you pass me and my pal, who comfortably trot on the path in the Pest side. Around 9, on Sundays. The Mayor of Budapest, Gábor Demszky always overtakes us. (No bodyguards.)

For a Conference-hopper who Wants to Avoid Fellow Conference-hoppers

ALBA *I. Apor Péter utca 3. T: 175-9244. F: 175-9899.* On the corner of Hunyadi János út. A 95-room hotel in Buda, at the foot of the Castle Hill. No panorama, as it overlooks a side street of Main Street (Fő utca), which is parallel with the river. Very near Castle District. Very good access to main sites. A fine Greek restaurant in the same, tiny street.

LIGET *VI. Dózsa György út 106. T: 269-5300. F: 269-5329.* 139 rooms. A singularly pleasant, though not very silent site, opposite the side of the Museum of Fine Arts and the Zoo, that is to say, the City Park (Városliget). Nice post-modern building with a sauna and gym. The somewhat too obtrusive copper statue at the corner is often ridiculed, and called "Ophelia Going Mad" by some locals.

VICTORIA *I. Bem rakpart 11. T: 201-8644. F: 201-5816.* 27 rooms. Right on the Buda riverbank, overlooking the old Chain Bridge. For years the owner was in a fierce legal battle with the City Hall: the proprietor added one more floor, hoping that in these turbulent times (when democracy knocked on our doors) it would go unnoticed. It didn't. The extra floor is still there. Try to book a room on the top floor, that particular one.

For a Tennis-freak Junior Manager of a Multinational Company

FLAMENCO *XI. Tas vezér utca 7. T: 161-2250. F: 165-8007.* 348 rooms. A lesser known hotel, close to the centre of South Buda, with quiet grounds and an artificial lake. Large indoors tennis facility, 200 metres from the hotel.

Hotel for a Man to Impress Highschool Sweetheart, After 50 Years

HILTON *I. Hess András tér 1-3. T: 214-3000. F: 156-0285*. 323 rooms. Superb location on Castle Hill, overlooking the Danube. Remains of a 13th-century convent are built into this fine building. (See "First Walk" for details.)

KEMPINSKI HOTEL CORVINUS BUDAPEST *V. Erzsébet tér 7-8. T: 266-1000. F: 266-2000*. 367 rooms. This is a full block post-modern tour de force by contemporary Hungarian architect József Finta and associates. With three elegant façades and one plain one — the latter is said to be a sort of a revenge by insiders. It faces the metropolitan police headquarters. They allegedly demanded that no windows should face that direction. You should check the result. By the way, the police building was traded for a new police buliding, also designed by Mr Finta. It is called "Cops' Palace" (corner of XIII. Róbert Károly körút and Teve utca, near the Pest end of Árpád bridge.)

"I Hate Big Hotels"

ART INN-SIDE *V. Királyi Pál utca 12. T: 266-2166. F: 266-2170*. 32 rooms. Many Budapest people haven't heard about the place — a block of flats, which used to be an important student movement stronghold and student hostel briefly after World War II. Very conveniently located in a quieter part of the inner city, a 100 metres from the underground, 200 from the busy centre. A nice memorial tablet inside.

"I love the Opera and Classical Music"

K + K HOTEL OPERA *VI. Révay utca 24. T: 269-0222. F: 269-0230*. 115 rooms. An obvious, purposefully built hotel for music lovers, with immaculate service. With function rooms. It is parallel with grand Andrássy út. Literally 50 metres from the Opera House, with phenomenal public transport connections. Ask for the room where Peter Greenaway and wife stayed.

"I Want Fin-de-siècle Splendour and Want to Have a Pool Indoors"

GELLÉRT *XI. Szent Gellért tér 1. T:185-2200. F: 166-6631*. 233 rooms. Traditional grand hotel with windows looking on the most beautiful of the bridges, Gellérthegy and its own large swimming pool. (See more of it during "Walk Three".)

"I don't Want to See the Marriott from the Outside"

BUDAPEST MARRIOTT *V. Apáczai Csere János utca 4. T: 266-7000. F: 266-5000*. With 362 rooms, apartments. All rooms overlooking the Danube. As the building is really prominent, the only solution to the problem is staying there, and enjoying the panorama. Budapest people refer to it as "The Inter", as it used to belong to the Intercontinental chain. (Now it is the fate of former Forum Hotel, also on the riverfront, so beware of misunderstanding...) President Carter stayed here during his two Budapest visits. He insisted me to follow him to the Presidential Suite, and gave me an autographed edition of his book — in turn of my showing him around. I thought I would never see him again. Since I saw him again twice. Once next morning, while jogging on the riverfront (he did the same), and once again when he came to Hungary in one of his building campaigns. Never say never (more)!

"I like Traditional Splendour, but I don't Mind Minor Glitches in Decoration and Service if I Can Pay Accordingly"

ASTORIA *V. Kossuth Lajos utca 19-21. T:117-3411. F: 118-6798.* 130 rooms. Landmark in centre — the cross-road here is named after it — and recently redecorated retaining its old-fashioned style. The first democratic government was formed here — the one that declared secession from Austria, in October 1918. You can visit the room, but can't stay in it.

NEMZETI *VIII. József körút 4. T: 269-9310. F: 114-0019.* Traditional splendour of the Grand Boulevard days, when cars didn't yet spoil this cross-roads, when the National Theatre, pulled down in 1964, spilled its fashionable crowd to the restaurant of this hotel. 76 rooms, a suite and a conference room. Built over an underground station: Blaha Lujza tér (Line 2).

"I Love the Urban Jungle"

SAS BÉKE RADISSON *VI. Teréz körút 43. T: 132-3300. F: 153-3380.* 246 rooms. Recently modernized hotel on the city's main thoroughfare. Well served by public transport. Right on Grand Boulevard. Some 15 years ago they deservedly razed 90 per cent of the hotel, kept only the façade and some interior embellishments, including the oversize wall paintings in the "Shakespeare Restaurant". The "Café" on the first floor is posh but has nice sweets and good espresso; don't expect quick or even immediate service.

"I Want to Stay in a Historical Part, but Don't Want to Pay for it"

KULTURINNOV *I. Szentháromság tér 6. T: 155-0122. F: 175-1886.* 16 rooms. One of the most improbable small hotels in the world. In the grand building of the pre-war Ministry of Finances, now the possession of the Foundation for Hungarian Culture, that was established to facilitate connections with over the border ethnic Hungarians. Modest, dormitory-type rooms, for a reasonable price, 200 metres from Matthias Church (150 out of which you have to take in the endless corridors of the building, somewhere grand, somewhere shabby). The fancy name used to belong to a state-owned company for training executives for cultural institutions and businesses.

"I Want a Small, Old-fashioned, Family-run, Five Star Hotel"

I'm afraid it is the wrong place to come. That genre does not exist in Budapest or Hungary, unfortunately.

Swapping Flat with My Hungarian Peers

WHAT AD TO PUBLISH AND WHERE Any of the two English-speaking weeklies, either the *Budapest Week*, or the *Budapest Sun*. You can rely on one of the agencies advertising themselves there — competition is fierce and it makes them do a fairly good job. You can also try to write a letter to the Internet paper called "Internetto": a Letter to the Editor, *http://www.internetto.hu*.

Twelve Acceptable Second Choices if You Desperately Want to Come

ATRIUM HYATT *V. Roosevelt tér 2. T: 138-3000. F: 266-9101.* With 355 rooms, 28 apartments. Town centre, on the river, the usual quality, if you can afford. Replicas of Hungarian Classic painting hang along the first floor — you can order an official replica of any of the paintings in the National Gallery. They have it painted for you, and issue a certificate as well. Oh yes, and there is the aeroplane, too. (See "Walk One".)

DUNAPART *I. Szilágyi Dezső tér. T: 155-9244. F:155-3770.* 32 rooms. Anchored at the Buda embankment, the converted steamer is an interesting addition to the Budapest hotel scene. Obviously, it has differing prices depending on what your room faces: Houses of Parliament or the noisy embankment full of traffic. Also a restaurant, with reasonably good food, run by efficient, very attractive Chinese waiters.

GRAND HOTEL HUNGÁRIA *VII. Rákóczi út 90. T: 322-9050. F: 268-1999.* 511 rooms. Ten minutes walk from inner city. Some rooms looking onto Keleti (Eastern) Railway Station. Entirely rebuilt in 1985. Largest hotel in the country. Excellent food in "Fiaker Söröző", or beer hall, which is actually a quite good restaurant, with oversize, tasty portions. (You can actually see a "fiaker", a two-horse-drawn coach at the entrance.) Real Budapest patriots know the difference between the "fiah-ker" and the "khonf-lish". The difference is an extra horse to the advantage of the former, and the extra prestige to go with it. The difference between the Trabant and the Volkswagen Golf, in fin-de-siècle terms. By the way, kids love the giant paper aeroplane out of ceramics in the foyer.

HELIA THERMAL *XIII. Kárpát utca 62-64. T: 270-3277. F: 270-2262.* 262 rooms. Just opposite the middle of Margaret Island, in the immediate vicinity of a pre-fab housing estate. Thus, half the rooms have superb, the other half less than perfect views. Don't forget to inquire when reserving a room. Water from the springs of the island. Swimming-pool of course. Not very far from a station of Metro 3.

MERCURE BUDA *I. Krisztina körút 41-43. T: 156-6333. F: 155- 6964.* 396 rooms. Just between the Southern Railway Station and beautiful Blood Field, or Vérmező, the name of which commemorates the execution of the Hungarian Jacobines in 1795. Also, from this side, a nice panorama of Castle Hill. Again, not very pleasant to look at, but very nice to look out of.

MERCURE KORONA *V. Kecskeméti utca 14. T: 117-4111. F: 118-3867.* An unmistakable, much discussed building on a key dowtown site, on busy, noisy Kálvin tér (special, treble windowpanes). (See "Walk Three".) 433 rooms, plus small conference facilities on two sides of a street, with a "Bridge of Sighs" between the two parts. Excellent access to all the sights, three minute walk from the river. Pleasant atrium enclosing the reception desk. With some historical paintings bought by the hotel, by maverick, visionsary painter Győző Somogyi, who lives north of Lake Balaton, in a village called Salföld, a frequent destination of egghead pilgrimage.

NOVOTEL BUDAPEST CENTRUM *XII. Alkotás utca 63-67. T: 186-9588. F: 166-5636.* 324 rooms. On the road leading to Erzsébet híd, surrounded by hills, completed at the beginning of the eighties. Beside it stands the Budapest Convention Centre, also a concert venue. Not a very good location, unless you like your conference here.

ORION *I. Döbrentei utca 13. T: 156-8583. F: 175-5418.* 30 rooms. A small place near the Buda end of Elizabeth bridge. It used to be the very first private hotel after the small business boom of the early 80s. It was built according to the rules. When it was ready, the authorities realized that it was bigger than they anticipated. Lowered the acceptable maximum number of rooms — the proprietor had to sell the place to some state business… A good location if you want to take long walks on nearby hills.

PANORAMA *XII. Rege utca 21. T: 175-0522, F: 175-9727.* On top of Szabadság hegy, with a large park, and newly built bungalows. Try to be booked in the main building, for the sake of better panorama. And try to use the old cog-wheel railway (fogaskerekű vasút). The hotel is just by the terminus. By the way, it used to be called Red Star Hotel for forty years. Would you think so?

TAVERNA *V. Váci utca 20. T: 138-4999. F: 118-7188.* 224 rooms. Impossible to be more central and in Pest's main shopping street. Discussed in the "First Walk" in connection with its post-modern style. As a minority opinion, I admit, that I like the concrete connecting element at the top. It was so refreshing after so many decades ruled by the rectangle. Especially in Budapest. (I still like it, together with the statues on the pillars.)

THERMAL HOTEL AQUINCUM *III. Árpád fejedelem útja 94. T: 250-3360. F: 250-4672.* It is on the Buda riverfront, near the Buda end of the northernmost bridge over the river. Aquincum was a Roman settlement. To the left of the main entrance there is a large tablet from a Roman find. Some interesting piece of architecture nearby, including a Synagogue in neo-Classical style (a rarity in Hungary, now used as a television studio), and a 900-year-old Catholic Church, and a branch of the Municipal Gallery, in a pretty 18th-century house. One of the best, non-naff Hungarian restaurants is in walking distance. (See "Kéhli" in the Chapter "Eating Well".)

THERMAL MARGITSZIGET *XIII. Margitsziget. T: 311-1000. F: 269-4589.* 206 rooms. On the island in the Danube, the hotel offers a wide range of services. Much less elegant than the Grand Hotel. But the air is the same. If you have kids, you can rent one of the two rival cart services: the "bringóhintó" or the "sétacikli".

THREE OFFICES

American Express V. Deák Ferenc utca 10. T: 268-8680. F: 267-2028. Open October to May: 9 a.m. to 5.30 p.m. Monday to Friday, 9 a.m. to 2 p.m., from June to September 9 a.m. to 6.30 p.m., 9 a.m. to 2 p.m. on Saturday. Proverbially quick and efficient service: the average number of rings from the outside calls are rumoured to be registered by the computers at each telephone and staff is awarded accordingly. Hotel reservation for a 10 dollars fee.

IBUSZ V. Apáczai Csere János utca 1. Open 24 hours a day. That oldest of the travel companies in Hungary books rooms for about 80 per cent of the hotels, and rents out rooms of all kinds, sells plane tickets, also changes money.

Tourinform V. Sütő utca 2. T: 117-9800. They don't reserve hotels, but give ideas in that respect, too. It has free hotel brochures. Open every single day of the year, from 8 a.m. to 8 p.m.

BUDAPEST BESTS : : BUDAPEST BESTS : : BUDAPEST BESTS

Ferenc Bodor, gallery director, columnist, a fine judge of pubs

My favourite outings in the city. The strangest and most engaging panorama of the town is to be had by taking the Cogwheel Railway up to the Széchenyi Hill stop and by walking from there along Melinda út to the former Majestic Hotel. From behind the building the panorama of an unknown metropolis lies before us. And we can marvel at those buildings constructed between the wars, in the functionalist vein, now little run-down and used for housing.

The discreet pleasures of the proletariat. From the Pest abuttment of Margit bridge we cross by ferry to the Kék Duna landing stage in Római part, watching the city shrink to the size of a picture postcard. Going across the bulky iron bridge — classified as a monument — keeping an eye on the city to the right, we reach Népsziget ("the people's island") which, in the people's language is also known as Mosquito Island. From one of the few restaurants with gardens comes the sound of the dance area. In another garden it's time to indulge in eating fish from the bottle. At the city end of the island a concrete bridge leads us to the metro station. An outing only recommended for those who enjoy the simple, proletarian pleasures of Summer.

A stroll through Socialist Realist Past. "Socreal" architecture is, in our days, ripe.

The finest example of a housing estate in the style is that in the XIVth district, between Nagy Lajos király útja and Kerepesi út. The reliefs over the entry doors and the whispering trees give it the appearance of a film set. The strange, enclosed spaces, the passages and deserted playgrounds are lit by ancient striplight advertisments. Coming out towards Fehér út metró station, brings us to the "Mimóza Eszpresszó", where the lonely piano player caters for those who want to dance. Recommended for lovers of *couleur locale* at weekends.

(Ferenc Bodor died in 1994 — he could not live up to see signs of positive changes in his beloved city, most of which — no doubt — he would praise.)

FINDING YOUR WAY

The greatest help for visitors to Budapest is a friendly office just half a minute's walk from the junction of the three underground lines, the

Right in the heart of the city, at Sütő utca 2, the office is open from 8 a.m. to 8 p.m. seven days a week. (There is a second now, off Vörösmarty tér, in 2. Dorottya utca.)

You can get virtually all information here in German, English, Russian and French, sometimes even in Italian. The office has the most up-to-date information on transport, accommodation, activities, sights, on everything a tourist might be interested in, and it's all on their computer. They will help you to get accomodation only in certain special cases but they will always help you with the necessary addresses and telephone numbers. They keep a range of travel brochures here as well. There are about twenty people on its changeable, but remarkably experienced staff, who are willing to pass on their own knowledge of the city. They will also do some detective work to find out where some special goods can be bought. I spent a whole morning in this office checking on various data and was struck by their enthusiasm. In need you can always rely on them. In the heroic times they were rumoured to have sewn a button back on a student traveller — which they can't do as a rule.

TOUCHSCREEN INFORMATION You'll find eight
touchscreen information sets all over town — two at Ferihegy Airport, one in Southern Railway Station, one in Astoria underground station, one in the Central Market Hall, one in the Royal Castle, at the Hungarian Culture Foundation, and two at the Tourinform offices. The number of the machines is promised to treble soon, and the awesome variety of information available in Hungarian will soon be available in English and German as well. (Now only part of it is.)

Apart from the usual kind of information, the system provides sophisticated orientation help — it helps with routes by mass transit, or by car. The owner and the initiator of the project, a new organization, Tourism Office, Budapest is eager to hear your comments about the system, so be so kind as to send them your comments, flattering or devastating: H-1364 Postafiók 215. Or *info@budtour.hu*.

THE BUDAPEST CARD is another new institution, intro-
duced in March 1997, a sort of three-day general, non-transferable pass to free mass transit and free entry to 55 museums, and substantial discount to sightseeing, baths, restaurants and a plethora of other things. Everything that makes Budapest special. The date of purchase is stamped when the card is issued, and you have to sign it the way you do a credit card, which the

whole object resembles to. It can make your life comfortable, puts many things at your fingertip. The price for 1997 is 2900 forints for adults and 2000 forints for kids. You can buy it everywhere, from travel agencies, through ticket offices of Budapest Transit Authority to museums and other places.

MAPS
In hotels and travel agencies you are given a miniature one-page map — a highly insufficient one. The ideal solution depends on your aims and status.

The Best Map for the One-weekend Conference Tourist
Who Wants to Get Away for a Short While

BUDAPEST: THE INNER PART *(Budapest belső területe)* Under the not very attractive, green and red cover there is a very practical, easy-to-use map. The back shows the inner city areas in such detail that even the numbers of the buildings are indicated at corners of the streets. (Scale: 1:7500!) There is a street index including the streets of the maps on both sides.

The Best Map for a Couple that Stays in Downtown
but Wants to Discover the City for Themselves on Foot

BUDAPEST WALK The usual, beautifully printed map which you can unfold at home and leaf through in the street. It shows clearly the structure of the city. The inset map shows such a small area that it is almost useless. Full street index. Attracts muggers.

Map for a Young Couple from the Ukraine
on Honeymoon, Who Stay with Relatives in the Outskirts

THE MAP OF BUDAPEST A map showing the whole city, the districts of the city are in different colours — wich is sometimes of help even to a foreign visitor. All tram and bus routes are indicated. Full index. Includes a very well designed inset map of the centre.

Map for a Serious Lonely Traveller Who Swapped
His Torino Flat for an Elegant Home Near City Park

EURO CITY BUDAPEST A red, spiral-bound booklet, very clearly and cleverly designed, somewhat expensive, though. It must have been designed far from Budapest — it covers a very large area of Pest, but very little of Buda. Full, easy-to-read index.

Map for the Business Traveller Who Wants to
Visit Premises for His/Her Central European Headquarters

THE ATLAS OF BUDAPEST A large-format, spiral-bound book, covering 28 settlements around the city. The scale is 1:20000, (Sections 8-81, and 1:10000 in the inner city parts). With street numbers and one-way indication. There is a haystack of soulless information, not much to use for, at the back of the book. Also easy to use, quite large print, full index.

Map for an Architecture Freak Who Wants to Visit
Every Single Address in the "For Serious Addicts" Part of This Book

CARTOGRAPHIA'S BUDAPEST *(in a transparent plastic folder)* Basically a brand new, locally edited version of the Walk map, simply printed as a traditional flat map (i.e. you cannot leaf through it). Separate section details metro system. Full index on the back. Landmark buildings in primitive but useful 3-D drawings.

MAP SHOPS

TÉRKÉPBOLT VI. Bajcsy-Zsilinszky út 37. T: 112-6001. Off Arany János utca Underground, Blue Line 3. A small shop — don't expect a London or New York style vast shop, where you can buy the surface of the globe in small sections, even if it is a totally sea-covered part. But have a look at the awkwardly coloured wall maps for schools.

TÉRKÉPKIRÁLY XIV. Bosnyák tér 5. Same building as the company headquarters. At the terminus of Bus 7. T: 221-9707. F: 163-3402. Here there is the total selection of all the Budapest maps. If you are there, have a quick look of the double map: the replica of an 1896 map of Budapest, and the remake of the same area, same colouring, same size. You should be sorry that you don't speak Hungarian: the otherwordly, greatgrandma flavour of the words is as appealing as the charming typography and design. The two come in one plastic folder. Can be a nice present for a Hungarian, who has made your Budapest stay nicer than you expected.

THE BASIC SETUP OF THE CITY Now let's lay out a

map in front of us and try to keep the structure of the city in mind. It is very rare that a city has two parts that are so different from one another. The hilly part in the west is Buda; across the river, twice in size and totally flat, is Pest.

In the Middle Ages the two were independent, in fact it was just over 125 years ago that they joined with Óbuda to form the modern city. In the 15th century, when Buda was first in its heyday, it was considerably larger and more important than Pest. The number of its inhabitants is estimated to have been about 24,000, whereas Pest had only 4,000. (After the Turks were driven out, towards the end of the 17th century, Buda had about 600 and Pest about 300 inhabitants.)

THE DANUBE, which is strictly speaking the main thoroughfare,

divides the capital in two as it flows southwards. At the northern limit of the city the river is almost a kilometre wide, a little further down it encircles two islands. Downriver from Margit (Margaret) Island the Danube narrows considerably. It is at its narrowest at the foot of Gellért Hill, only 230 metres wide. Its average water-level is 96 metres above sea level. The hills of Buda are between 150 and 500 metres in height and, with the exception of Gellért Hill, rise gently. The higher peaks form a semicircle some 8 or so kilometres from the city centre. Even Pest is not as flat as it seems to be, since it rises steadily and the X. district, Kőbánya, is at the same height as Castle Hill. All this explains why we get such a magnificent view of Pest from the vantage points in Buda. Since the rise on the Pest side also forms a semicircle, with some poetic exaggeration, Budapest could compete with Naples or Rio de Janeiro in this respect. It is also rare that a large city provides the characteristic landscapes of the whole country. To the west, beyond Buda, there are the hills and valleys typical of Transdanubia, whereas to the East, not so far from Pest, behind some small hills the Great Hungarian Plains stretches out perfectly flat. True, to the north there are mountains, though with the highest peak at 1,015 metres, they are not very high.

A lot more will be said about the history of the seven bridges over the Danube, and we will also have a close look at them during our walks. Just now, let's find them on the map. In this book they will always be referred to by their Hungarian names. (Remember that "híd" is the Hungarian for "bridge".) There is an island between two of the bridges. The bridge south of the island forms an obtuse angle in the middle. This is Margit híd. Let's take this as our starting point.

BRIDGES AND BOULEVARDS
The historic centre of Buda can still be seen today on Castle Hill, from that of Pest hardly anything has survived. The historic city centre of Pest used to be situated between Lánchíd and Szabadság híd; that is, between the first and the third bridges south of Margit híd. This is what we call the city centre or

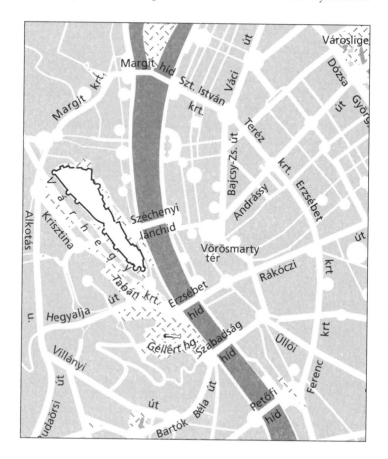

downtown even today; officially it is the southern part of the V. district. The edge of this district is flanked by the Kiskörút (literally the "small boulevard"), which consists of József Attila utca, Károly körút, Múzeum körút and Vámház körút.

The main street in the city is Váci utca. Halfway along this street there is the Pest end of Erzsébet híd, the first of the two modern bridges in the city. On the Buda side, the road from the bridge turns sharply to the right and starts climbing steeply. It leads straight onto the motorway to Vienna and to Lake Balaton.

From the Pest end of Margit híd runs a semicircular avenue, built after the Parisian pattern. This is called the Nagykörút (literally the "great boulevard") and reaches the Danube at both ends, joining Margit híd in the north and Petőfi híd in the south. "Grand Boulevard" is actually a nickname — no part of it is actually called like that. It is the overall name of Szent István körút, Teréz körút, Erzsébet körút, József körút and Ferenc körút.

The semicircle continues on the Buda side, although not quite as regularly as in Pest. Thus the circle is completed by Irinyi József utca, Karinthy Frigyes út, Villányi út and Margit körút, and there we are again at Margit híd (most of this can be travelled on by Tram 4/6).

It is more or less true to say that Budapest was built within this circle by the turn of the century, with some additional building along main roads running out of town such as Andrássy út, which ends in Városliget in the east. The bridge north of Margit híd, Árpád híd, is the beginning of an outer semicircular ring. Its parts are Róbert Károly körút, Hungária körút and Könyves Kálmán körút. The latter has just reached the Danube again in the south, when Lágymányosi híd, with its special, oversize mirrors (to evenly light the road) was built, right beside the present rail bridge, Déli Vasúti Híd. Pest had spread more or less this far by the beginning of World War II. Beyond the outer semicircular roads are connected by five major roads that carry traffic from the city towards the suburbs: Váci út, Andrássy út, Rákóczi út which continues in Kerepesi út, Üllői út and Soroksári út. Underground lines run all along, but the last.

Budapest, with an area of 525 square kilometres, is the home of somewhat less than 2 million people, one in every five citizens of this country.

VANTAGE POINTS
The most famous vantage points, Castle Hill and Gellért Hill, are included in our first and third walks. Some more places worth visiting are:

THE LOOK-OUT TOWER ON JÁNOS-HEGY The tower is situated at the highest point over the city, on top of the 529 metre high János-hegy or John Hill. Four platforms, one above the other, encircle the wall of the tower. On an average day visitors can see places 75 kilometres away from here in all directions, but on especially clear days some have even seen the High Tatra Mountains, 215 kilometres away. The best way to get there is by Bus 190 and the Chairlift.

THE TERRACE OF THE RESTAURANT *BELLEVUE*, **MARRIOTT HOTEL** *(on the bank of the Danube)* The restaurant is on the 10th floor of the hotel. Only for patrons of the restaurant, as Americans say.

THE LOOK-OUT TOWER ON JÓZSEF-HEGY *(II. Józsefhegyi út)* This small look-out tower, built in brown stone, is neither very well known, nor in very good shape. There is a full view of the city with all the bridges, the Danube Bend and all the Buda hills. The easiest way to get there is by Bus 91 and 191. I hope the neo-nazi graffiti will have gone by the time you get there.

MARGIT HÍD — THE "ELBOW" At the "elbow" of the bridge, opposite the island, as close to the river as possible. This is a breathtaking, unusual view, a kind of third panorama of the river. A famous playwright and theatre director proposed to build the new National Theatre here. Was not taken seriously, mainly because of the costs. (And other problems.)

MARTINOVICS-HEGY *(at the top of XII. Gaál József út)* From this 259 metre hill there is an unusual view of the city, especially of Castle Hill. In fact the top of the hill is a nature reserve almost directly above the busy Moszkva tér. It is also a favourite rendezvous for dog owners and their dogs. Dusk, when streetlamps are being lit, is an especially pleasant time to walk up here. 15 minutes from Moszkva tér on foot.

ÁRPÁD TOWER Best to get there by Bus 11 and then walk up Látó hegyi út from the terminus. A charming spot, unknown to tourists or travellers. The tower itself echoes rural folk architecture from Transdanubia.

THE DOME OF BUDAPEST CATHEDRAL (THE "BASILICA") *(V. Szent István tér)* Opened relatively recently, the lower observation desk around the dome is still not known to Budapest people. It takes 303 steps (no lift). Some steps after 200 the scene changes: out of a specially built tube you

---

BUDAPEST BESTS : : BUDAPEST BESTS : : BUDAPEST BESTS
Péter Molnár Gál (MGP), wit, theatre critic; the wickedest pen

There is a small restaurant in the old Józsefváros, the **Gólya** (in Bókay János utca). Its regulars include the local shopkeepers and tradesmen, folk musicians and the occasional off-duty whore. Outside in the courtyard in Summer a curtain of trained vines almost reaches your soup plate. Inside it's all wood-panelling, the old white of the hall cupboard has been given a fashionable brown coat. The menu card has four or five simple dishes, always a delight. Your conversation scintillates at the Gólya's tables. (Provided I cut the band's amplifier lead with a pair of pliers.)

Wherever you eat well, eat plenty. For the next time you get there you won't find again what you so enjoyed before.

There is still a **tobacconist's** at number 2. Nádor utca. A white-haired, smiling, elderly lady stands behind the counter. I'm always in a good mood for a few hours after dropping in there.

In Budapest you can't dunk your bread in the same sauce twice. The city is going through a time of transition. As it has been doing for five hundred years.

Don't eat! Smoke! It makes you slim.

get to the inside of the dome, in a wrought iron construction. Then you get to the space between the inside and the outside of the dome — quite a thrilling experience. The panorama outside keeps you amazed for at least 15 minutes. Take your time, and try to discover the hidden sights, that are always kept as secrets for ordinary mortals. Don't forget about the Drop on top of the Nationale Nederlanden building, and other delicacies. (More about the church: see "Walk Two".)

TAXI As in everything in Budapest, there are far-reaching changes on the taxi-front as well. As opposed to the grim situation of some years back, nowadays you can get a taxi at any time and in almost every part of the city within minutes and there are also a number of taxi companies waiting for your telephone call.

There is a chaos on the taxi-front in Budapest. Obviously, never mind how serious an offence you commit, you cannot really be stripped off your permit.

You can be charged anything, but you should be informed about the price. There are about five kinds of rates, according to the time of the day and the zone — even I don't understand it. City Hall wanted to regulate this jungle, by maximizing the prices, but the Constitutional Court overruled the decision. Every six months there emerge new ideas, then nothing happens.

In the streets you hail a taxi. It is for hire only if the "TAXI" sign is lit up on top of the car. By phone, you have to give the address, then your full name and telephone number. Almost all the taxi companies take orders in English.

Try to avoid the "hyenas" queueing at hotels and at the railway stations. The worst are those working at the airport. Insist on the meter being turned on — and on paying in forints. At the airport the situation is so bad, you are better off taking the Airport Shuttle. At hotels insist on the receptionist ordering a taxi for you. If not, you can be sure of going on a zigzag route, of being overcharged and fooled.

I maybe biassed, and not very often resort to taxis, but there are four companies I can't really be fooled by, so I can pass this information on to you, order these taxis yourself by phone, or insist on the receptionist in your hotel to order a taxi from any of the four companies. You can usually ask for a non-smoking car, I mean a car the owner of which doesn't smoke and does not let passengers smoke.

Budataxi: 120-0200
Citytaxi: 211-1111
Főtaxi: 222-2222
Yellow Pages Taxi: 155-5000

Taxi drivers in Budapest are generally outgoing and talkative people and actually do circulate the latest news and know about everything. It is worth asking them if they can speak any foreign languages. And remember to check whether the meter in on. You are not supposed to pay if it isn't. However, an English-speaking driver is still a rarity in Budapest, and probably ends up at a VIP service.

Most locals remember the telephone number of the first and at one time the only (state) taxi company; however most of their best drivers, who used to know the city inside out, have gone private. (Look for the taxi driver's badge of honour on the dashboard: a plaque given for 1/4, 1/2 and 1 million accident-free kilometres.) One of the oldest of taxi driver jokes: A driver drives straight through all the red lights without hesitation. When he arrives at a crossing where the traffic lights are green, he stops immediately. "Can't we go now?" asks the customer, who is shaken up from the ride. "No way", the driver says. "This is when the taxis are coming from the right."

METRO (Underground) Most people travel by underground with a monthy pass. Those who do not have this (or a day ticket) have to buy a tram ticket in the ticket office of the station. You have to say: "Kérek egy villamosjegyet." *(Kheh-rekh edj vil-lah-mawsh-yed-yet.)* You have to put your tram ticket into the slot of one of the orange ticket-punchers, which will cut off a corner and time-stamp your ticket. You can use this ticket for an hour on one line only; you can interrupt your journey if you wish.

The first underground line, coded yellow, runs between Vörösmarty tér in the city centre (all our walks start from this square) and the terminus at Mexikói út. The journey takes just over 10 minutes. The entrances to most stations and the notices on the walls are copies of the originals; it was only in the 1970s the old trains were unfortunately replaced by more modern cars.

The second line, coded red, takes passengers from a large housing estate in the east of Pest to the centre of Buda to Moszkva tér and to the Déli (Southern) Railway Station. The line crosses under the river, between the Parliament and Lánchíd. The journey takes about 20 minutes. In the rush hour, trains run at 2 minute 7 second intervals. In all stations, there is a rubber strip on the edge of the platform. You may not step on this until the train has stopped in the station. If you do stray onto it, a voice will, with increasing hysteria, start coming over the loudspeakers: "A biztonsági sávot kérem elhagyni". *('Leave the Security Strip, Will You?!')* Naturally, most foreign visitors do not understand the warning, which will be repeated until a Hungarian passenger taps the visitor on the shoulder, showing him to step back.

The third line, coded blue, is the newest. It takes 28 minutes to take passengers from an industrial district in the south-east through the downtown area to the northern part of the city. In the rush hour the trains on this line are at an interval of two minutes 20 seconds.

The three lines have a busy junction at Deák tér. Tickets are available at every station, until about 8 p.m. at the regular "pénztár". After that time you can get one in the section called "forgalmi ügyelet". There you can have a look at the black and white monitors the network is followed on.

Underground trains run between 4.30 a.m. to 11.10 p.m.

The night Bus 78 serves most of the route of the second underground line, while the night Bus 182 follows the toute of the third line.

BUSES Most people in Budapest travel by bus, some 40% of all passengers. There are more than 200 bus routes in the capital. All the buses which run on these routes are Hungarian made with automatic gears. They

are manufactured at Ikarus, once the fifth largest bus factory in the world, a stumbling industrial giant, now on the way to be reorganized and gathering momentum. Perhaps half of them are articulated buses - a landmark of Budapest not less than the double-deckers of London. On busy routes, buses whose number is in red, are the fast buses; the route is the same as that of the buses whose number is in black but they stop at far fewer stops. Boarding these buses should be given careful consideration. Bus numbers in red which are also followed by a red letter E (e.g. 73E) are express non-stop service. These buses stop only at the two termini. Most bus stops indicate the stops on a route on a board.

After boarding the bus, passengers must look for a punch-machine to validate their tickets. You put your ticket into the slot of the machine upside down and pull the rim of the slot firmly towards you. The machine punches the ticket or, at least, indents it and such tickets are accepted by the Inspectors, who either wear a uniform when getting on the bus or disguise themselves as housewives carrying large shopping bags. In either case an inspector states: "Kérem a jegyeket ellenőrzésre" *(Keh-rrem ah yedj-e-ket e-len-owr-zesh-re)*, i. e. "Show me your tickets for checking". Inspectors are often tolerant of confused foreigners. City buses are traditionally blue; now all colour, since advertisements have appeared on them. You can board the bus through any door. The bus stops only if there is someone waiting to get on or to get off. If you wish to get off, you signal to the driver by pushing the button above any of the doors. People do not queue at bus stops: you board the door nearest you when you can.

TRAMS There have been trams in Budapest for more than a century, the tracks laid by competing compaines, all of which had their trams in their own livery. Until only twenty years ago there were still various types of trams and people had various sentiments towards certain types. Some trams had an open platform and more adventurous passengers, or those who could not find any room inside the tram, stayed outside. Most Budapest children naturally preferred the platform, which provided the sense of being masters of a ship as the tram swayed along.

Nowadays all the trams are yellow and all have doors that close automatically. A few years ago many tram routes were replaced by buses but this trend has now stopped and a new tram line was even laid (Tram number 1 on the Outer Boulevard). Tram tickets have to be validated in exactly the same way as bus tickets. If the tram is packed, you pass your ticket over to someone beside the punch and they will punch it for you.

Trams start running early in the morning, some as early as 3 a.m. Information on the first and the last trams on a route can be read at every stop. (Utolsó kocsi indul = The last one leaves.)

A Word of Warning: You cannot buy tickets on trams or buses. You have to buy them in underground stations or at newsagents.

TROLLEY-BUSES There have been trolley-buses in Budapest since 1949 and there are 13 routes at present. Their numbers allegedly start from 70 only because it was on Stalin's 70th birthday that the first line started operating. You can travel on trolley-buses with tram tickets. The cur-

rent-collectors of trolley-buses frequently come loose, providing a favourite piece of street-theatre when the driver jumps out of her seat, assembles a long pole, catches the loose current-collector with it and puts it back onto the overhad wire. (Trolley-buses and trams are usually driven by women.)

Every bus, tram and trolley stop has a sign which shows when the last vehicle starts from the terminus on that route, usually between 11 and 12 p.m. You can find information on all-night trams and buses which run even after midnight. For a visitor the best value is, no doubt, the Budapest Card, or a day ticket.

OTHER TRANSPORT

THE COG-WHEEL RAILWAY (Fogaskerekű) began running in 1874 and has since been electrified. It climbs up into the Buda hills, starting from Városmajor near Moszkva tér and reaching Széchenyi-hegy station in 16 minutes. The distance between the two termini is 3,7 kilometres and the difference in height is 327 metres. The trains run from 4.25 a.m. to midnight and bus tickets must be used.

CHILDREN'S RAILWAY starts from where the cog-wheel train line ends up on the hill. The trains run on an 11 kilometre narrow-guage track and provide an enchanting trip through the woods. What is special about it is that the line is run by children, naturally with adult helpers in the appropriate positions.

THE CHAIRLIFT runs 8 metres above the hillside from a valley called Zugliget up to the highest peak in the city, the look-out tower on János-hegy. There is a 262 metre difference in height between the two termini and it takes 12 minutes to make the journey. It is in operation between 9.30 a.m. and 4 p.m., in Summer between 9 a.m. and 5 p.m. There is no service on the weekday following holidays and Sundays.

THE CABLE CAR (Sikló) train was reopened in 1986, entirely reconstructed after damage suffered during the war. It takes visitors from the Buda end of Lánchíd up to Castle Hill in 1 minute. It carries prams and wheelchairs as well. Tickets on the spot.

DRIVING
I wouldn't recommend it to anyone who doesn't know the town very well. Not even the occasional emigré who comes back for a visit. A couple of factors make it hell to drive in Budapest.

Cars are more than seven years old on the average. Pollution is somewhat less than before, more and more cars run with catalysator, still, the air can be heavy. Cars still double, even treble-park.

There has been a small revolution in Budapest recently: a parking enforcement revolution. Hundreds of meters were installed, with notices in three languages.

The former regime was strong in politics, but — perhaps it's not common knowledge — was weak in everyday life, unable to enforce its petty rules (traffic, parking, housing, building, etc. regulations).

Vans still load in daylight, at high noon, causing bottlenecks at every corners. Also cars go wrong, even my one-year-old wonderful company car, a very dark blue Opel Astra, with 16 valves (registration plate: FFH 619. If you dent it, just leave your check under the wipers).

Traffic manners are non-existent. The bigger car you have, the more aggressive you are.

Women drivers are considered easy game. If you want to see Budapest driving at its best (worst), try the Pest side of the Lánchíd (Chain Bridge). There is only one lane of the three around the square (the middle one) that entitles cars to get onto the bridge. Stand at the corner with a gas mask and watch the Ayrton Senna manoevres to get into that lane; within five minutes you are guaranteed a fine display of mutual recrimination when fender meets offender.

So take a taxi. Or take a tram. But above all: walk.

AT THE WEEKEND Budapest empties every Friday evening
for the weekend between Spring and Autumn. Families rush off to "Balcsi" — Lake Balaton — or to their "plots". Their summer places are somewhere along the 180 kilometres of the shore of the lake. The more desirable places are on the hills of the Northern shore of the lake, which shelves more steeply on this side. Family "plots" are usually somewhere around Budapest and are, quite simply, a small piece of land with a small house built of stone or wood usually with a lovingly cared-for lawn and vegetable garden. For many years, the very high number of "summer houses" has been due to the narrowness of the housing market; people simply have not been able to afford to buy their own home in the greenbelt or on the fringe of Budapest but have wanted to have a sense of space, a garden of their own. Indicatively, the first motorway built here links Budapest not with Austria or Yugoslavia, but with Lake Balaton. During the Sunday evening jam the number of lanes could be doubled without having any noticeable effect. At the weekends then, the tempo of Budapest becomes more relaxing. Buses and trams run less often, far fewer cars take to the streets. Shops are open between 9 a.m. 1 p.m. on Saturdays, food shops generally until 2 and the larger stores until 3.

A FOOD MARKET ON SUNDAY XIII. Lehel út, corner of Váci út, at the Lehel tér stop on the Blue (No. 3.) Metro. Not packed. A spectacle in itself. From 7 to 11 a.m.

NIGHT PHARMACIES Pharmacies close at 8 p.m. at latest
but those below provide a night service. When you ring the bell, the duty pharmacist gets up, opens a small window and dispenses the required medicine. All pharmacies display the address of the nearest night pharmacies in the window. ("A legközelebbi éjszakai ügyeletet tartó gyógyszertár".) The list here, therefore, is not complete. You have to pay a 100 forints surcharge, if not in emergency.

II. Frankel Leó út 22. T: 115-8290

VI. Teréz körút 41. *(On the corner of Szondi utca)* T: 111-4439

VII. Rákóczi út 86. *(At Baross tér)* T: 122-9613

XI. Kosztolányi Dezső tér 11. T: 166-6494

XII. Alkotás utca 1/B. *(At Déli Railway Station)* T: 155-4691

XIV. Bosnyák utca 1/A T: 183-0391

As in so many other places in this book, your attention is drawn to the number 117-9800, the **Tourinform** number, which is in operation between 8 a.m. and 8 p.m. They will be able to understand the problem you are trying to communicate and will be able to give you accurate advice on where you can turn to for help.

AMBULANCE: 104 If for any reason you cannot get through to this number, ring 111-1666. They can usually handle calls made in English and German. However they recommend that you get someone on the spot to report the incident and its location in Hungarian and only as a last resort try to make the call yourself. To use this and any other emergency number, you still have to insert a coin into a call-phone. This will be returned to you after the call.

FIRE BRIGADE: 105 The alternative number if 105 is unobtainable is 121-6216. Calls can be dealt with in Russian, speakers of other languages should contact the police. (See below.) Under Hungarian law, even fires that have been extinguished have to be reported. Otherwise you can't claim on your insurance policies. Call-boxes return your coin after an 105 call.

POLICE: 107 If you cannot get through, call 118-0800 or 111-8668. These numbers are for emergencies only, not for enquiries or for routine police business. Calls can be handled in English, French, German, Polish, Russian and Spanish. For calls in other languages an interpreter can be obtained. For other police affairs, see General Information for a list of the Budapest District Police Stations.

"I DON'T FEEL WELL!"

Many of the embassies hold a list of doctors and dentists speaking the language of their nationals. And there are some ads of English-speaking doctors in the English-speaking weeklies. If you are in real trouble, in panic, you can try the Medical School clinics, the following ones

I. SZÁMÚ BELGYÓGYÁSZATI KLINIKA (Internist Unit)
VIII. Korányi Sándor utca 2/a. T: 133-0360.

II. SZÁMÚ BELGYÓGYÁSZATI KLINIKA (Internist Unit)
VIII. Szentkirályi utca 46. T: 113-8688.

III. SZÁMÚ BELGYÓGYÁSZATI KLINIKA (Internist Unit)
XII. Eötvös út 12. T: 175-4533.

I. SZÁMÚ SEBÉSZETI KLINIKA (Surgical Unit)
VIII. Üllői út 78. T: 113-5216.

I. SZÁMÚ GYERMEKGYÓGYÁSZATI KLINIKA (Pediatrics Unit)
VIII.Bókay János u. 53. T: 134-3186.

II. SZÁMÚ GYERMEKGYÓGYÁSZATI KLINIKA (Pediatrics Unit)
IX.Tűzoltó utca 7-9. T: 133-1380.

FOGPÓTLÁSTANI KLINIKA (Dental Unit)
VIII. Mikszáth Kálmán tér 5. T: 113-1639.

NŐGYÓGYÁSZATI KLINIKA (Gynecology Unit)
VIII. Baross utca 27. T: 133-1130.

PHARMACIES
The Hungarian word for a pharmacy *(patika)*, "gyógyszertár", has little resemblance to its name in other European languages. The loanword from Latin is "patika". They are listed under this latter heading. In town there are some fine old pharmacies wich are highly regarded; simply looking into them seems to have a curative effect. In most chemists, the pharmacists are able to speak English and German. By an old custom, a jug of water and glasses are laid out on a table in the pharmacy so that medicines can be taken on spot.

Some Pretty Pharmacies

PÁZMÁNY PÉTER PATIKA V. Egyetem tér 5. T: 117-5306.
Open 8 a.m. to 5 p.m., closed Saturday and Sunday.

KÍGYÓ PATIKA V. Kossuth Lajos utca 2/a. T: 118-5679.
Under the arcade. Open: 8 a.m. to 5 p.m., Saturday closing at 2 p.m., closed Sunday. Advice given in English and German.

OPERA PATIKA VI. Andrássy út 26. T: 153-1753.
Open: 8 a.m. to 8 p.m., closed Saturdays and Sundays.

BUDAPEST BESTS : : BUDAPEST BESTS : : BUDAPEST BESTS

Richard Baltimore III, former Deputy Chief of Mission, US Embassy

Budapest, if you want to get to know this town well, plan on hoofing it. While downtown, look up, you may discover a seldom noticed recessed statue, elegant turret or an original turn of the century roof design. Meandering into apartment courtyards may reveal anything from an elaborate iron gate to an antique elevator.

Architectural eclecticism at its best: the upper portion of the former stock exchange, now Hungarian TV headquarters, on Szabadság tér which has been described as "Angkor Vat meets the Greek Temple". **Best soup in town:** venison with tarragon at Kispipa restaurant, in Akácfa utca. Finest turkey dishes: Szindbád restaurant, in Markó utca. **Most unusual brew:** "fig coffee" at Museum restaurant, at the National Museum. **Choice local throat drop:** "Negro, a torok kéményseprője": the chimney sweeper of the throat. **Waiters with the best memory:** Hotel Forum Grill where following a forty months absence my favourite dish was served as casually as if I had been away for a weekend. **A hidden first class restaurant in Óbuda:** Garvics at Ürömi köz 2. **Most misleadingly labeled statue:** Roul Wallenberg in Buda, commissioned by then US ambassador Nicholas Salgo. Plaque gives credit to local city council.

Hungarians are a very friendly people, dogs or small children often help break the ice quickly. Athough I have travelled in 78 countries, this is the only city in which a kind smiling restaurant hatcheck *néni* ("aunt") retured my overcoat and commented nonchalantly that she decided to sew its loose button while I was eating. On an entirely subjective basis, here are a few of my personal choices.

THAT AWFUL HUNGARIAN LANGUAGE

Enzensberger, the globetrotting German poet once complained that Hungary is the only country with Latin script he ever visited, where he can't make out even a pharmacy sign. He's right: pharmacy is "gyógy-szertár" in Hungarian, this monster of a word was coined, together with hundreds of other new words, to save the country from becoming a German-speaking one for good. This happened in the first two decades of the 19th century — and miraculously, Hungary did not become another Ireland: a small country with a very old, lively art and literature, without its own language. By the way, the official language of Hungary until 1844 wan not German, but Latin. (The still widespread Latin literacy of the educated classes lingered on for another hundred years, until the otherwise beautiful Russian language was forced on Hungarian schools.)

One can learn how to read Hungarian in half an hour (its spelling is logical), but a lifetime is too short to understand it, not to mention speaking it — it is not even an Indo-European tongue: it belongs to the Finno–Ugric family of languages. Finnish is a distant relative: totally uncomprehensible for us.

If you have a look at a Hungarian-speaking book, you will see a lot of diacritical marks: two of which, "ő" and "ű" is missing even from the IBM standard character set, making Hungarian computer buffs' life a hell. On the average, every sixth Hungarian letter is accented in some way or other — though only the vowels. There are long and short vowels, consequently, it is still possible to write "metric poetry" (e.g. hexameters) in Hungarian, while in English, or Modern Greek, for instance, it is not.

The only good news is for the very obstinate: there is no gender for nouns, and word order is quite free — as experts say: it is "fluid"; different positions of a word carry a slight difference in meaning. This freedom, needless to say, is due to the unusually rich morphology of the language. If you take a closer look at any Hungarian book you will see very long words, most of them divided at the end of lines.

Though there are only three tenses, present, past and future, Hungarian conjugation is incredibly tricky: there are two separate sets in each of the three tenses: the "transitive set" and the "intransitive set". So when I want to say "I read a lot" or "I am reading", I use one set, and the other when I read something in particular. And what is so weird for learners of it with English background: the imperative is the most complicated business to put together... For most foreigners Hungarian is intriguing, if not barbaric in sound. Eva Hoffmann, an American author talks about the "utterly perplexing sounds of Hungarian language, with its Bartókian syncopations and sensuousness. Even when they speak English, Hungarians manage to transport some of the off-rhythms and softness of their own language into that flatter tongue, English, and give it strange, lunar resonances." Do we?

Believe me, Hungarian is not an ugly language. Here is the list a Hungarian poet made of what he thought are the most beautiful words in our language: láng (flame), gyöngy (pearl), anya (mother), ősz (autumn), szűz (maiden), kard (sword), csók (kiss), vér (blood), szív (heart), sír (grave). In a language where words tend to be three-syllable long...

TWELVE MOST IMPORTANT HUNGARIAN WORDS AND PHRASES

Yes (Igen), **No** (Nem), **Thanks** (Köszönöm), **Hungarian** (Magyar), **Nice** *(in most sentences:)* (Szép), **Can I Have a Glass of Water?** (Kérek egy pohár vizet), **Red Wine** (Vörösbor), **White Wine** (Fehérbor), **Naff** (Ciki).

TWELVE COMMONPLACE SENTENCES YOU CAN MAKE US HAPPY WITH

Maga sokkal jobban tud angolul, mint én magyarul...
(Your English is far better than my Hungarian.)
Nagyon szép ország Magyarország.
(Hungary is a very pretty country.)
Budapest rengeteget fejlődött, mióta itt jártam.
(Budapest has developed a lot since I was here.)
A magyar boroknak alig van párja a világon.
(Hungarian wines have hardly any rivals anywhere in the world.)
A magyar nők nagyon csinosak.
(Hungarian women are very pretty.)
Mindenki tudja, hogy a magyar diákok szokták megnyerni a matematikai olimpiát.
(As I hear most years Hungarian students win the Olympics in matematics.)
A mai napig jól emlékszem arra, amikor az Önök aranycsapata 6:3-ra legyőzte az angolokat a Wembley stadionban...
(I clearly remember when your Golden Team defeated the British 6 to 3 in Wembley. — Only for people over 50, since it happened in 1953...)
Szépek a magyar bankjegyek!
(How nice the Hungarian banknotes are! — A downright lie.)
Szeretnék Szentendrére elmenni, megnézni a világhírű Kovács Margit Múzeumot.
(I want to get to Szentendre, to visit the "world famous" museum devoted to the art of the late Margit Kovács, the ceramist. — Practically unknown abroad.)
Szerintem Önöket már az isten sem mentheti meg attól, hogy 2000 körül bekerüljenek a NATO-ba és az Európai Unióba.
(I think you can take it for granted to be accepted in NATO and the European Union around 2000. — An idiomatic phrase, literally "now not even God can save you from beeing accepted...")
Tényleg nagyon igazságtalan volt az 1920-as Trianoni Békeszerződés, de ha bent lesznek az Unióban, egész Európa az Önöké lesz, az összes tengerekkel...
(The Versailles Peace Treaty was really very very unjust, but now that you soon get into the Union, you'll have all Europe, with all its seas...)

THE SHORTLIST

The Good, The Ugly and The Naff

THE GOOD

The Most Important Accessory to Tour Budapest with: A pair of binoculars. (Cheap and reasonably good Russian ones in the fleamarkets.) You should examine the façades and spires.

Best Place to Sip a Coffee and Feel the Tremor of the Underground Under Ground: Café Gerbaud, lefternmost tables.

Best Place to Feel You Are Just a Piece of Dust, Doomed to Failure: The Hungarian Historical Paintings Show on the second floor of the National Gallery, Royal Castle.

Probably the Nicest Small Museum, if You Want to Meet Your Girlfriend in Secret: _Ráth György Museum_ in a beautiful, art nouveau villa in VI. Gorkij fasor 12. More guards than visitors.

Waitress with the Nicest, but not Sexy Smile: In _Kanári Salad Bar_, XIII. Pannónia utca 3.

Best Traditional Glove Shop: _Ékes_, V. Régiposta utca 16.

Nicest Pharmacy: _Pázmány Péter Patika_, V. Egyetem tér 5.

Most Artistic Burger King Shop All Over World: Best Obvious View of Budapest: VI. Oktogon tér. Fancy interior, looks like a "grand café" in Amsterdam. With a big mural by László Lakner.

Best Antique Shop for Art Nouveau: V. Kamermayer Károly tér 3.

Best Place to View St Stephen's Church ("The Basilica") from: The terrace of a small, shabby café that changes owners and names so often: VI. Bajcsy-Zsilinszky Endre út 19.

Nicest Art Nouveau Bank Hall: _Post Office Savings' Bank_, V. Hold utca and Perczel Mór utca.

Biggest Pancake: _Korona Passage_, a New York style public space in the left side of Hotel Korona. Self-service.

Grandest Public Bath: _Gellért Bath_, XI. Kelenhegyi út 4.

Cosiest Map Shop: In the Arcade called _Párisi Udvar_, V. Ferenciek tere 5.

Fanciest Cinema from the 30s: _Atrium_, Margit körút 55.

Biggest Public Building: Obviously the _Houses of Parliament_, built 1887-1904. It's 268 metres long, built on a 2 meter thick concrete foundation. Far too big for the square, for the purpose, for the country.

Narrowest Block: _I. No.26. Döbrentei utca_, corner of Döbrentei tér. There seems to be no gate at all. (It's on the other side).

Longest and Most Mysterious Chain of Arcades: In _VI. Terézváros_, between No. 16 Dob utca and No. 11 Király utca.

Biggest Architectural Hoax: _Vajdahunyad Castle_ in Városliget, originally built out of cheap materials, for the Millenary Exhibition (1896), to represent the various styles in Hungarian Architecture. Later built to last for good.

Ice Rink in the Most Romantic Setting: _The lake_ in front of the above castle, in Winter.

Loveliest Great Flood Memorial Tablet from 1838: _corner of V. Királyi Pál and V. Szerb utca._ The area flooded in 1838 is shown in red marble in a map. The water level is also shown, like on many blocks.

Most Moving Monument: The *Raoul Wallenberg Monument*, II. Szilágyi Erzsébet fasor and Küküllő utca.

Fanciest Gilded, Old Style Cinema: Probably the *Uránia*, VII. Rákóczi út 21.

"Green Tram" Rebuilt: *VII. Rózsák tere*. This is the torso of an ambitious programme of the early 80s: to rebuild all the remaining ones. There must be some problem with the profitability of running these places...

Prettiest Art Nouveau Façade: Former Parisiana Cabaret, now *Új Szinház* (New Theatre), VI. Paulay Ede utca 35.

Best Swimming Pool: *Komjádi Béla Sportuszoda*, II. Árpád fejedelem utca 8. Not always accessible for ordinary mortals, i.e. non Olympic-level swimmers.

Most Traditional Shirtmaker: *Fleischer*, VI. Nagymező utca and Paulay Ede utca.

Best Non-naff Hungarian Style Restaurant: *Kéhli Vendéglő:* III. Mókus utca 22. (Open only in the evening.)

Most Accessible Upper Middle Class Home from the 1880s: *The Post Office Museum*, VI. Andrássy út 3., first floor. (Second for Americans.)

Best Button Shop: *Dénes Vándorfy*, V. Váci utca 75. (Only women's ones).

Best Place to Watch Second Hand Furniture and Not to Buy Anything: *Tűzoltó utca Furniture Store*, IX. Tűzoltó utca 14.

Newspaper with the Fanciest Name: Either *Hócipő* or *Magyar Narancs*, ask about them from a Hungarian friend or a receptionist. (Sorry, it's a short list.)

The Ten Greenest Spot in Pest in May: The *southern Slope of Gellért Hill*, the *top of XII. Martinovics-hegy*, *V. Szabadság tér* (at the weekend), *XIII. Margitsziget* (between Grand Hotel asnd the Rose Garden), *IX. Népliget*, *XIV. Városliget* (except for the weekend), *The Botanical Gardens:* (VIII. Illés utca 25.), *I. Vérmező* (or "blood field", thus called because of the executions of 1795, held here), *"May 9th Park"*, on an island, north of Margaret island, *XII. Városmajor*, from where cog-wheel railway sets out, towards even greener spots in outer Buda.

Most Mysterious, Oversize Stone Lady: in the yard of the former Two Lions Inn, in *IX. Kálvin tér 9*. Originally in the middle of the square; that much survived WW2. The whole statue recarved and reerected. V. Erzsébet tér. It's called the Danubius Fountain.

Nicest Modern Statue in the Castle: *The Knight and His Page*, on the wall overlooking Buda, at the bus parking lot, between Szent György tér and Dísz tér (Károly Antal, 1983). This is the enlarged "copy" of one of the mid-15th-century statues that were excavated nearby in 1974. It gives the experience of seeng a new, perfect statue, not just the fragments.

Funniest Classroom Slogan: *"Double Bookkeeping is one of the most glorious inventions of humankind and it should be encouraged to be used in each and every household."* (Johann Wolfgang Goethe.) VII. Wesselényi utca 57, first floor, visible from the street.

Shabbiest Old Shop: corner of V. Hold utca and Aulich utca, an *optician* who shares the space with a watchmaker. You can have some black and white shots printed here + a rarity in town.

THE UGLY

Biggest Bookshop in Town: *Fókusz könyváruház*, VII. Rákóczi út 14.

The Only Bookshop Open Until 11 p.m. Every Day: *Láng Téka*, XIII. Pozsonyi út 9. Open so late because it shares the space with a video rental outlet.

Biggest Residential Block: *III. Szőlő utca,* at the Buda end of Árpád bridge. A ludicruous, kilometre-long, ten-story, pre-fab block.

Most Expensive, Most Extensive Scaffolding in Town: All over the *Institute of Sociology,* in VIII. Pollack Mihály tér, the former Festetich Palace. It's worth visiting: grand scale, oversize floor tiles inside, more or less preserved.

Most Unfinished Planned Avenue: *VII. Madách Imre út* — ends after 200 metres.

The Street Most Crowded with Fake Fin-de-siècle Lamps: *V. Váci utca.*

Aristocratic Palace in the Most Pitiful State: V. Reáltanoda utca 12. The former *Blaskovich Palace,* where "Kincsem", the Miraculous Mare (1874-1887) used to live in the yard. She won all her 54 races. Have a look at the second floor.

Most Traditional Surviving Street Toilet ("Green Tram"): *VI. Nagymező utca,* at the corner of Paulay Ede utca. You should wear a gas mask on entering the premises.

Top Twelve Restaurants Taxi Drivers Take the Unsuspected Moneyed Tourist, Where No Gourmet Ever Goes: *Császárkert, Kárpátia, Mátyás Pince, Margitkert, Ménes Csárda, Monarchia, Paradiso, Nautilus, Vasmacska, Új Sipos, Régi Postakocsi,* and ... (You can fill in here the names of most of the Castle District restaurants.)

Most Intrusive Recent Public Building in Buda: *the extension of MTI,* Hungarian News Agency, the aerial part of it even disrupts the Royal Palace silhouette from Pest.

THE NAFF

Cheapest Kitch *"Antique"* Shop: VII. Hernád utca 7.

Most Traditional Looking, though Somewhat Posh Café in Buda: *Angelika,* I. Batthyány tér.

Most Elegant Gate Leading Nowhere: Opposite the back of the National Museum Garden, VIII. Puskin utca 8. You can't enter it, for two different reasons.

Best Steak in Naff Environment: *Fehér Bölény* (White Buffalo) restaurant, V. Bank utca 5.

Least Naff Danube Cruise: *Legenda Ship* at ten. With really nice student hostesses, who manage to behave with the kindness of a far-away relative.

The Twelve Naffest Things you can Do in or After Budapest:
- to use a taxi from Ferihegy Airport to downtown Budapest,
- to go to a restaurant and accept a table near the gipsy band, because you can't get away,
- drop a piece of extra red pepper into your fish soup,
- to drink a lethal concoction for apéritif called "Puszta coctail",
- to ask a friend to tell the story of the National Theatre building,
- to go anywhere on bike except for Saturday and Sunday mornings, until 9.30 a.m.,
- to change money in Váci utca, and risk being outwitted by street moneychangers, when the margin is so little,
- to attend a so called Gulyás Party, a 30-year-old, continuous, naff mass event, a raid against the purse of lower middle class packaged tourists,
- to drive to downtown,

— to pop in any restaurant, without consulting a local friend,
— to quarrel with a policeman, one that doesn't wear a glass,
— **not** to buy "Paul Street Boys" by Ferenc Molnár in English
   and read it back home on the train or the plane,
— **not** to came back.

Naffest New Style Pastry Shop: *Perity Mestercukrászat,* VI. Andrássy út 37. Mirrors, white coloumns, Christ on the Cross, four TV sets with MTV on, plus a lot of gold and a standard telephone set.

Textile Shop with the Largest Number of Hungarian Coat of Arms Communist Style: *Merino Textile Shop,* V. Petőfi Sándor utca 20. Elderly people still call it "The Brammer", with reference to the last pre-war owner. Watch out for the coat of arms on the ceiling, just at the columns.

Best Obvious Tricky Snapshot in Town: *Several bridges together,* from Castle Hill, from the front of the Royal Palace.

Second Best Obvious Tricky Snapshot in Town: *The Statue of St Gellért,* taken from the Pest side, through Elizabeth bridge.

The Naffest Lampshade Specialist: in *V. Molnár utca* at the corner of Irányi utca.

The Ghastliest Public Building: The *60s office block* in Vörösmarty tér, a blatant contrast to everything that is precious in the very centre of the city.

The Copy of Palazzo Strozzi of Florence: on the Grand Boulevard, *off Oktogon square:* VI. Teréz körút 15. On the ground floor: one of the three "central wedding halls".

The Dumbest Thing to Have Changed in Budapest: the kind of *Yellow Shade* of trams.

A CLOSING REMARK TO THE SHORTLIST

As it is obvious from the proportions, written by a wicked pessimist Budapest person, Good Things in Budapest easily outweigh the Bad, the Ugly and the Naff things. So: it is worth coming here. Even regularly coming back.

BUDAPEST BESTS : : BUDAPEST BESTS : : BUDAPEST BESTS

Mihály Ráday, television anchorman, coucilman, crusader

"At Least Adopt a Horse!" — that was our publicity slogan in 1995. We tried to raise funds to give a facelift to the **Városligeti körhinta** with a nicely printed 4-page colour brochure. We managed to find some old pictures, so re-designing was well under way — that of the dome, which was pulled down after World War II, that of the almost entirely stripped façade, and we also planned to reproduce the carved gates which were replaced by hideous ones made out of aluminum: an act worthy of a prison sentence.

It was the then British ambassador who gave the campaign its first momentum. He told me one day: "My mission in Hungary will be over in six months. Before I leave I would gladly contribute 500-600 pounds to the restoration of something of value in Budapest. If you have an idea, don't hesitate to tell me." Not much later I called him once and asked if we could meet in the Amusement Park. And we could. His Excellency, Ambassador of Great Britain and Northern Ireland in Hungary, got on the "körhinta". We had a great ride. I also told him that the old name of our Amusement Park used to be English Park until the Communist coup d'état in the late 1940s. Then I declared my claim. With the help of his one million forints we could start planning and the real work.

It was him who taught me the charming British word "merry-go-round". He called it that way, not "carousel", as Americans. Hungarian anglophiles prefer the latter, since that was the title given to the American musical version of the celebrated play by Ferenc Molnár, originally entitled "Liliom", a sentimental comedy on the love of a merry-go-round operator and a servant girl. Thanks to Sir John Birch and all the other generous donators, today the old **körhinta** is ready from the outside and just as beautiful as it was when it opened in 1906.

Have you already inspected the comely frescos of the **körhinta**? Have you noticed the hand-carved and hand-painted torch-bearing angels, the chariots, the ships, the fine "magic steeds"? Have you noticed that every single horse has its own, distinctive face and features and their genuine- leather saddles were made by the craftsmen of the turn of the century? You haven't? It's long overdue.

Otherwise, if asked, what to see in Budapest, I tend to suggest two things. Two things not available to the west of us. Turkish baths and Hungarian Art Nouveau. So: visit Király Bath, Rác Fürdő or Rudas, then off you should go to Pest, where you can admire how the yellow ceramic bees of Ödön Lechner, architect on the walls of the former Post Office Savingsbank (today National Bank) building, heading for their hives. ("Walk Two" in this book, I presume.)

By the way. You haven't been thinking of adopting a horse, have you? One, at least... *(Drop me a letter, addressed to City Hall Budapest, if yes!)*

A CITY INHERITED

THE WALKS

The following five walks try to show visitors
all the improtant sights of the city. My intention is to orient
the visitors during the walks and to provide an image
in depth of the city.

FOR SHORT-STAY VISITORS: THE FIRST WALK The magnificent view from the top of Gellért Hill and walk around Parliament building is worth adding to this route. The route itself can hardly be made quicker by car: most of it takes us into pedestrian precincts.

FOR THREE OR FOUR DAYS: THE FIRST FOUR WALKS These routes include all the important sights. Completing them all, you will have a clear idea of the structure of the city. It is possible to follow part of the routes by car to save time.

AN INTRODUCTION TO EVERYDAY LIFE: THE FIFTH WALK There are few tourist attractions included in the fifth walk. It helps the visitor to glimpse the life of the districts along Grand Boulevard. This walk is, in a way, halfway between the first four walks and the chapter "For Serious Addicts". It makes no sense to follow this route by car.

THE BEGINNING AND THE END: VÖRÖSMARTY TÉR It was not difficult to choose Vörösmarty tér as the starting and finishing point of all our walks. It is right in the heart of the city, near the river, close to the big hotels and to the junction of the three underground lines. The middle of the square has a statue, erected by donations, to the memory of Mihály Vörösmarty (1800-1855), a major figure of romantic poetry. Carved from Carrara marble, it has to be covered in ugly canvas (recently transparent plastic) from late Autumn until early Spring to protect it from cracking. In Winter the middle of the square looks as if Christo the land artist had been there.

The poet himself is the centre of the composition, the figures around him are reciting his famous patriotic poem, whose opening line is carved into the pedestal of the statue. (*"Be faithful to your land forever, O Hungarians."*) Below this line the black, round spot contains the most precious of all the donations. A beggar offered the lucky coin he inherited from his mother towards the erecting of the statue. Now you have to peer to find it among all the graffiti.

The dominant building of the square today is, unfortunately, a hideous modern office building.

There used to be a German theatre on the site, housing 3,500 people, and later a department store. A photograph of these buildings can be seen on the thick poster-pillar behind the statue (the building with the pediment is the theatre, the department store was the building called Haas Palace). The present "Palace of Musical Art" was finished in 1971 and reflects the bleak modernism of the 1960s, a sort of parodistic extension to Vigadó Concert Hall, a sort of Budapest Barbican Building. The building has a highly indecent nickname, that does not translate into English. In the middle part of the complex there is the rehearsal hall of the State Symphony Orchestra. Now they have to pay rent to the building originally erected for them — the complex now belongs to a foundation that supports informal education in the country.

The big window, displaying posters for various concerts, that looks onto the square belongs to the ticket office, which can be accessed through the main entrance to the building. It sells tickets for musical events. At least twice a year a long queue of patiently waiting people is formed outside the front door. This is when the office starts selling tickets for various subscription concerts in Spring or Autumn.

To the right of the ticket office there is a gallery which handles contemporary Hungarian paintings; this is the **Csontváry Terem**, specializing in the more traditional trends.

The shop beside it is a busy record shop, once the biggest in the city, called the "Hungaroton Szalon". On the left is the classical music department, on the right everything else. The Hungarian classical music catalogue is also available here. It is worth having a look at this Hungarian label — the company was recently privatized and bought by a consortium of Hungarian business people, who pledged to revive it.

Opposite this modern building there is an Edwardian one. Its ground floor is occupied by the **Luxus** department store, for decades the only place to buy clothes of "import quality". Now it is just a string of smaller boutiques. The décor is unbelievably naff and ridiculous, using brass in every conceivable inch, and even more.

However, the greatest attraction of the square is the confectioner's **Gerbaud**, which has been in this building since 1870. Apart from a terrace, the café has three separate shops. The one on the left (entrance from Dorottya utca) is a separate café which is not always open, and can be rented for special functions. The main shop opens from the square itself and is always full of tourists. The one to the right of the building lacks the original splendour nowadays: it is a mere retail shop of Gerbeaud delicacies — you can't sit down any more.

It is worthwhile walking through all the rooms as the 19th-century decoration and furniture is quite remarkable and very varied.

The confectioner's occupies the ground floor of two neighbouring buildings, which is why the rooms are so different. In the vaulted, right part, if you can find a table near the corner window, you can feel and hear the trains of the old underground line thundering underneath. In one of the high rooms, with a richly decorated flat ceiling, there is the portrait of Émile Gerbaud, the Swiss confectioner who bought the shop in 1884. He started selling his cakes at reduced prices; until that time only the very well-to-do could afford cakes here. He was the one to invent **konyakos meggy**, this Hungarian bonbon speciality which is dark chocolate with a sour cherry inside, matured in cognac. The story goes that he himself smashed the punch cakes whose colour was not what he had prescribed. The service in

Gerbaud is still very polite, although a little impersonal and strikingly slow. The waitresses are too busy and they have no time to chat about the guests in the code-language their old-time counterparts did. The choice, however, is first class, unlike the layout of the menu. Apart from Hungarian specialities, all the classics of Viennese confectionery are available.

Kis Gerbaud, the little shop in the right wing of the building, used to be a world apart: an eminent meeting place for the "Gerbaud-ladies", i.e. old ladies who used to live better lives, wearing a lot of jewellery and waiting for their friends with a cup of coffee with whipped cream on the table. This place has been converted into a cake-shop. You can't sit down any more. You can't even drink a cup of coffee. It is difficult for me to recognize the place where my ersatz-grandma aunt, Mrs Rudolf Bozóki, née Irén Engländer (1904–1976) dragged me to, almost every first Tuesdays of the month, to boast with my reasonably good grades to her fellow Gerbaud-lady friends, and stuffing me invariably with a cake called "corner block" (sarokház), a chocolate cake with a lot of whipped cream. The ladies had strong perfumes, relatives in the States and Britain, and bad news about every conceivable subject. And they had a terrific time, in the centre of this Central European city, one that had seen good days.

Some say that nearer and nearer the Millennium, the good days are on the horizon again. Let's check it out together.

WALK ONE

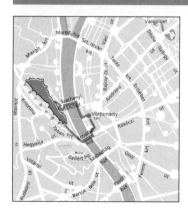

The Castle Area and

Váci utca takes us across the river to Buda, looks at some houses from the Middle Ages and at a very old church, which King Matthias would not recognize, even though he was married there twice. We shall visit the Royal Castle, which, finally, has a proper dome. We cross back to Pest by a modern bridge and plunge in the busy life of the city centre. We shall even visit a charming flowershop.

Time: 7-8 hours. It's so long that every now and then I mention places to sit down for a coffee or a meal. It's just the name — you have to find the address and comments at the back of the book.

THE PROMENADE (DUNAKORZÓ) When viewed from the river in the second half of the last century, neo-Classical Pest was hidden behind large hotels. Here, on the river bank stood the Carlton, the Bristol, the Hungaria and the Ritz; they were of the same height as the only building remaining from that period, the one on the corner of Vigadó tér. (Only one of these hotels survived the war, but was later pulled down.) The space in front of these hotels, the Korzó, became popular for promenading when tram tracks were laid along the old walk.

This row of hotels contained no less than nine cafés, all overlooking the river, all of whose terraces merged into one another. People from everywhere in Budapest, of all walks of life used to stroll here from Spring to Autumn. This was a tradition that had survived from the time when Pest was a small town, when there was always a place to go to meet friends and to socialize. Pest once had three such promenades but this was the most important and the busiest — having no less than four rows of benches. (The other two were Váci utca and Bástyasétány, which will be visited later during this walk.) Dunakorzó relaxed the stricter rules: near strangers walked together or even talked to each other. There is a story of a famous bohemian writer who was once accompanied by a young man on the Promenade. They strolled along together chatting. Suddenly the writer was greeted by a passerby. The young man asked who it was. "How on earth should I know?" replied the writer. "I do not even know who you are!"

Evenings were especially beautiful here with the cafés illuminated. There was music in all of them: the best Gipsy and jazz bands played here. At a safe distance from the bright terraces, sat people who used to come here all the way in from the suburbs to listen to the music but who could not afford to sit in a café.

Now that a new row of hotels has been built, the promenade is beginning to come to life again after its apparent death. Although it is mainly tourists who stroll here, slowly the locals seem to be returning as well, especially the older generation. At night, however, sleaze dominates at the lower (Erzsébet-híd) end, with all three sexes offering themselves for sale.

Copies have been made of the old-time "Buchwald-chairs", although now you do not have to pay 20 fillérs to the "Buchwald-ladys" with the big leather bag when you want to sit down. Hopefully, the money will be found to keep the chairs free of rust somehow.

THE CUTEST OF THE CUTE LITTLE PRINCESSES The little bronze statue perching on the railing (by László Marton, 1990) has sit there for only a couple of years, though some tourists might think it a hundred years older. The statue made most sculptors furious. A lot of artists and critics have found it downright kitch. Tourists, including Prince Charles, loved it. The latter did so much that he acquired a copy, and invited the artist to London, where a show was devoted to his work. (See his Liszt-statue during "Walk Five", p. 146.)

HOTEL FORUM, HOTEL HYATT 1E, 1F *At the Pest end of Lánchíd.* Both hotels were built in the early 1980s, almost at the same time, bringing the Danube bank back to life. They are far too big, they have spoiled the inherent scale of the riverbank. They do not fit here. The austere post-

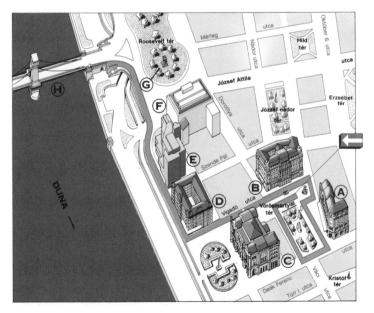

1 A Luxus Department Store, **B** Gerbaud confectioner's, **C** Vigadó Concert Hall, **D** Thonet House, **E** Hotel Forum, **F** Hotel Hyatt, **G** Statue of Ferenc Deák, **H** Lánchíd — Chain Bridge.

modernism that the Prince of Wales preaches, would have fitted much better here. They do not even match the Marriott Hotel south of them. It was built 15 years earlier — a long time, especially for Budapest hotel architecture. Not that they were unsuccessful buildings as such. I do not hold the common Budapest opinion that the Forum, which has 408 rooms, looks like a tape recorder standing on its side; it reflects the afternoon sun in too many angles for that (József Finta, 1981). In the Forum Hotel the salads of the Grill Bar and, especially, the cakes of the Viennese Patisserie on the first floor have gained the highest reputation. (And there is a large artwork on one of the walls, one that defies definition: a colour wooden relief that passes into a statue in some points... With characters recognizable to Hungarians.)

The Hyatt, or more correctly, the Atrium Hyatt Hotel has 356 rooms. The hive-like building reveals its true self from the inside. All its rooms open onto a circular gallery around a central courtyard, hence the name Atrium (Lajos Zalaváry, 1982). Over the atrium hangs a replica of the first Hungarian-built airplane. The café underneath is one of the most pleasant, coolest spots in Budapest.

At the entrance of the Forum Hotel is a statue of József Eötvös, a 19th-century writer and politician. The inscription says: "Erected by the Nation" and the small tablet was added by Hungarian secondary school pupils and teachers on the occasion of his 100th birthday.

There was a pontoon bridge over the Danube between Springtime and Autumn from the Middle Ages onwards. In Winter the river froze up and even carts could pass across the thick ice. Of course, there were times when a large number of citizens got stuck in Buda when the thaw set in. In the winter of 1800 the entire magistracy of Pest went over to Buda for the wedding of the Austrian governor and were not able to return to their own city for weeks.

It was impossible to build a bridge of wood and stone over a river of this width. In 1820, a young captain of hussars, Count István Széchenyi, had to wait at the bank of the river for a week while travelling to the funeral of his father. He decided to found a society for building a bridge. He brought over from England an architect, William Clark, and a masterbuilder, Adam Clark, who in spite of their names, were not related to each other. Even the iron was imported from England. After protracted and fiery debates, Parliament passed the law that even the aristocracy should pay the toll on the bridge. Some members of the Upper House declared that they would rather make a two-day detour to the south and cross the river by ferry, so intent were they on maintaining the noblemen's exemption from tax.

LÁNCHÍD **1H–2A** Linking Roosevelt tér (Pest) and Clark Ádám tér (Buda). The bridge was built between 1842–49. The span between the pillars is 202 metres. The weight of the original structure was 2,000 tons. It was not quite finished when Austrian troops withdrawing to Buda towards the end of the Hungarian War of Independence tried to demolish it. The charges, however, had not been laid properly and no damage was done to the bridge; however, the colonel who gave the order to set off the explosive charges was blown to pieces.

"When the bridge was ready, its English creator was so proud of it that he declared he would drown himself if anyone could find any faults in his mas-

2 **A** Lánchíd — Chain Bridge, **B** I. Fő utca, **C** A café in the remaining part of a block destroyed during the war, **D** Hunyadi János út 1., **E** The entrance of the Tunnel, **F** The lower end of the Cable Car, **G** The upper end of the Cable Car, **H** Sándor Palace, **I** Várszínház — Castle Theatre, **J** Ruins of the former Ministry of Defence, **K** Statue of a Hussar, **L** Batthyány Palace.

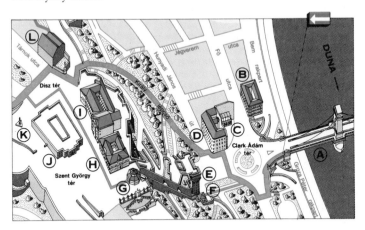

terpiece", begins an old anecdote. "So the people came and examined every lit-
*tle part of it, but in vain. They could not find anything wrong with the bridge.
Then one day an apprentice cobbler discovered that the lions at the end of the
bridge had no tongues. And Clark committed suicide..."*

*In fact the lions were made later than the bridge itself, and the sculptor gave his
word that the lions do have tongues; you can't see them unless you stand directly opposite them. In January 1945 German soldiers were, unfortunately, rather
better at preparing demolition charges for bridges. They also pushed the button
and dropped the central span into the Danube.*

THE TUNNEL *under Castle Hill was built in 1857; the contemporary Budapest
joke was that it was built to have a place where the bridge could be pushed into
when it rained.*

CABLE CAR (SIKLÓ) **2F–2G** The almost 100 metre long track, with a
slope of 4,8 in 10, was opened for passengers in 1870. The idea was to provide cheap transport for clerks working in the Castle District. It used to be
operated with a steam engine. Its successor, completed in 1986, is powered
by electricity, although it still uses a cable; with the down car counter-bal-
ancing the up car. It runs from 7.30 a.m. to 10 p.m. Closed every other
Monday. At the lower terminus there is a long queue during the daytime
even outside the tourist season, so if you get off the bus here, try the steps
of Király lépcső. Castle Hill rises only 50-60 metres above the riverbank,
so you can walk to the top in 5 to 10 minutes. If you make a little detour
to the left at the first point where paths cross, you can admire the fine proportions of Lánchíd from above the Tunnel and you can also see the cable
car from a little bridge over the tracks.

CASTLE HILL, this 1.5 kilometre long, flat rock, packed with houses, could be compared to a floating stone galley. At first sight the district may look poor and provincial compared to some old city areas which have remained substantially intact since the Middle Ages in Western Europe. Apart from some stately town houses, most of the buildings are simple plastered burgher's houses. The streets, all of which lead towards the old gates, follow the shape of the hill. It was after an unexpected, devastating Mongolian attack in the middle of the 13th century that the first citizens of Buda moved up the hill. Later the Royal Court was established on the hill, and with this began the quite lengthy golden age of the district. Buda became one of the most important cities in Europe in the 15th century. The number of its inhabitants is estimated to have been about 8,000. Buda was a melting pot of different nations: "Pontiffs of Italian culture live in the neighbourhood of noblemen used to the rough life of soldiers…Swiss civil ambassadors open their doors to Turkish aristocrats", writes a historian. Buda started to decline under Turkish rule (1541–1686) but the siege and bombardment of 75 days before its liberation in 1686 left it in ruins. Austrian authorities counted 300 inhabitants in the city. Reconstruction began, retaining the outlines of the old streets but building only two-storey houses instead of the three-storey houses of before. A Baroque city came into being, hiding the old ruins behind its thick walls. The Castle became a disctrict of government. It was besieged again in 1849, followed by another reconstruction; later the ministries moved here. Again, after a long period of peace, it was battered into ruin in January 1945, before the eyes of the anguished civilian population. A completely surrounded German force held out here for almost a month. This was the 31st (!) siege of the city.

The last reconstruction lasted for a long time — too long for the ministries, which moved out allowing museums to take their place. Most of the houses of the district are still used as flats, some of them have just recently been modernized. Cars have recently been banned from the area and now it is only the people who live or work in the area and guests of the Hilton Hotel and taxis that are allowed to drive here. The Castle has become quiet again. According to an architect-writer, the spirit of the city retired here. There is a peacefulness up here that cannot be found anywhere else in Budapest. The Venice Charter, regulating the reconstruction of historic buildings says, "If a building has more architectural layers one over the other, the reconstruction of the remains of some earlier state can be permitted only on condition that by doing so only parts of lesser value should be demolished while the reconstructed part should be of a great historical, archaeological or aesthetic value…" The whole city of Buda is a good example for such reconstructions. While the rubble was being cleared away after the war, many remains dating from the Middle Ages came into light and these were not walled up afterwards. From what we have left it seems to be certain that the walls were painted in different colours everywhere, with black, white and green patterns. Even the doorways of the ruined houses held surprises. Dozens of niches were discovered among the ruins whose function is still not clear to archaeologists. Some think they were resting places for nightwatchmen, others say they were used as stalls by broadcloth traders. In total, 63 such niches can now be seen in the Castle area. Apart from some other Hungarian towns, they cannot be found anywhere else in Europe. The oldest ones from the 13th century are rounded off a simple round arch, later they were more and more richly decorated. It might have been a kind of competition between the old residents of Buda to have the most beautiful niche.

The great attraction of the Castle District lies so much in the unity of the place and in discovering it alone that I was very reluctant to choose a route with the most interesting sights. The tablets on the walls of the buildings give information about them as to the century they were built in (SZ.= "century", after Roman numerals), or any previous buildings on the site (HELYÉN = "on the site of").

The wall of the Castle is well preserved almost everywhere. Except for some short sections, you can walk around on the wall. Let's start our walk here and see the part overlooking Buda. If we walk from the gate called Fehérvári kapu to the round bastion nicknamed the "Sour Soup Bastion" (Savanyúleves Rondella) we are walking where once the promenade of the Buda side was. Nowadays it is fairly quiet.

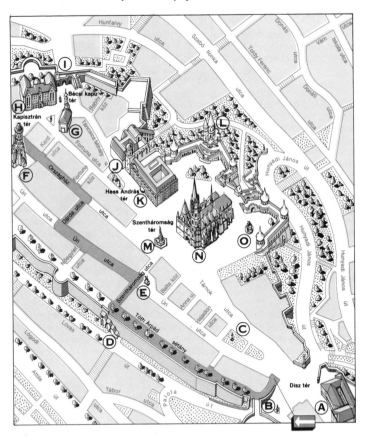

3 **A** Várszínház — The Castle Theatre, **B** Statue of a Hussar, **C** Memorial to the soldiers of 1848, **D** Way up to Castle Hill, **E** Statue of András Hadik, general of the Hussars, **F** Maria Magdalena Tower, **G** Lutheran Church, **H** National Archives, **I** Vienna Gate, **J** Statue of Pope Innocent XI, **K** Hilton Hotel, **L** Fishermen's Bastion, **M** Holy Trinity Column, **N** Matthias Church, **O** Statue of St Stephen, First King of Hungary.

THE STATUE OF ANDRÁS HADIK **3E** "The most hussar of the Hussars": that was the nickname of this daredevil general of humble origin (1710–1790), the commander of Buda Castle, a favourite of the Empress Maria Theresa. In the pediment there is a glass case with the names of the heroes of the Imperial and Royal 3rd Hussar Regiment. The statue (by György Vastagh Jr.) was unveiled in 1937. Experts say that it is a perfect image of the ideal, effortless, elegant cooperation between horse and rider. If you go very close, you can see that the testicles of the horse are shiny yellow. Generations of students of engineering have come and touched the parts on the morning of difficult exams. It allegedly brings luck.

A rest: Café Miro — Úri utca 30.

ÚRI UTCA **31.** A three-storey building, its façade is almost completely Gothic. In its present form it was possibly built in the second half of the 15th century, under the reign of King Matthias, using an even older house. The façade, which had been rebuilt several times, collapsed during World War II, and some medieval remains became visible. This building is the only proof that there used to be three-storey houses in Buda. There was enough of the wallpainting left to resconstruct the original. The function of the five windows in the arched protrusion is unknown. There are niches in the doorway, the staircase was restored in Baroque.

ORSZÁGHÁZ UTCA **18–20–22.** These three houses, built in the 14th and in the 15th century, can show most of what the Castle District might originally have looked like in the Middle Ages, and explain why it used to be called Olasz utca (Italian Street). On the gate of the house in the middle the initials stand for the name of Johann Nickl, the butcher who had the house rebuilt in 1771. The present tenant does not want to lean out of the windows, as was customary in the Middle Ages when the doorbell rang, so he put a rearview mirror on his window and keeps his house locked.

MARIA MAGDALENA TOWER (MÁRIA MAGDOLNA TORONY) **3F**
On the corner of Országház utca and Kapisztrán tér. This 13th-century Franciscan church was the church of worshippers whose mother tongue was Hungarian in the Middle Ages. Under Turkish rule this was the only church which was allowed to remain as a Christian church, all others being converted into Moslem mosques. The chancel was used by Catholics whereas the nave was Protestant; in the end, it too was converted into a mosque.

Both chancel and nave were destroyed in World War II and have not been rebuilt except for one stone window, as a memento.

"THE FLYING NUN" *On the corner of Országház utca and Petermann bíró utca.* Quite a few street names have become protected by the city. Recognized artists were commissioned to make allegorical figures to illustrate them. This one was by Miklós Melocco in 1977.

According to the memorial plate next to the figure the convent of the Order of the Poor Clares was nearby (Országház utca 28.) in which later the Parliament held sessions. The building is now used by the Academy of Sciences. Some further protected street signs are at Dísz tér 8. and at Fortuna utca 4.

4 **A** Maria Magdalena Tower, **B** Military History Museum, **C** National Archives, **D** Vienna Gate, **E** Lutheran Church.

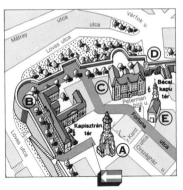

MILITARY HISTORY MUSEUM (HADTÖRTÉNETI MÚZEUM) **4B**

I. Tóth Árpád sétány 40. It was built as an army barracks in the 1830s, with remarkable twin windows. On both sides of the gate some cannonballs can be seen in the wall; these have not been removed, out of respect for the Hungarian army which liberated the Castle in the spring of 1849. On the round bastion, cannons from the Turkish era are exhibited, some of which have richly ornamented handles with imitations of a bird's head.

I have only daughters, who never drag me there. This museum was undergoing some deep leadership crises in the early 90s. The professional military historian director was breefly substituted with a politician, who fell out of office. Recently there was a brand new exhibition opened for the 1100 years commemoration, and there are regular concerts as well. A nice place for Sunday fathers with more than one sons.

TOMB OF A TURKISH GOVERNOR Near the left wing of the museum there is a small tomb with the following inscription in Hungarian and in Turkish: IT WAS NEAR THIS SITE THAT THE LAST GOVERNOR OF THE 143-YEAR-LONG TURKISH RULE IN BUDA FELL IN A BATTLE, AT THE AGE OF 70. HE WAS A HEROIC ENEMY. LET HIM REST IN PEACE.

Let's walk back into the centre of the Castle District past a modern building which is in ideal harmony with its surroundings (designed by Csaba Virág, 1979). The giant switches of the sectionalizing centre of the National Electric Supply Board needed the hard rock of the hill — that's why it had to be located here. The next building, the National Archives, does not give rise to such a question. The only question here is why it should be so big (designed by Samu Pecz, 1913–20). Quite a few medieval houses had to be demolished to clear the site.

A rest: Café Pierrot — Fortuna utca 14.

VIENNA GATE (BÉCSI KAPU) 4D Bécsi kapu tér was called the "Saturday Market" in the Middle Ages. This was the market at which non-Jewish merchants bought and sold. This is the northern gate of the Castle District on which all the four streets that run the length of the hill converge. From this square it takes only a few minutes to walk to the busy centre of Buda, Moszkva tér. If a child answers his parent back, they usually scold him by saying "Your mouth is as big as the Vienna Gate".

You can walk up to the top of the gate. Enjoy the panorama of Buda and the view of the relatively new Lutheran church in the square, built at the end of the last century. Parliament can be seen from an unusual angle. To the right of the Gate, next to the bastion wall there is a small grove. This is called the Europe Grove because the mayors of cities all over in Europe brought and planted rare trees here in 1972. There are 16 types of trees planted here, among them a Turkish hazel, a Japanese cherry and a cherry laurel.

BÉCSI KAPU TÉR 7. The building, which is standing on the site of a medieval house, received its present form in 1807, when a priest and teacher who lived here had it rebuilt. He also commissioned the portraits of Virgil, Cicero, Socrates, Livy, Quintilian and Seneca. There are beautiful gratings on the windows and on the door of a staircase in the gateway. In the first half of this century this was the house of Baron Lajos Hatvany, an erudite patron of arts, who spent the major part of the profit of his sugar factory on art patronage. In 1935–36 Thomas Mann was his guest here no less than three times.

MUSEUM OF COMMERCE AND CATERING TRADE (KERESKEDELMI ÉS VENDÉGLÁTÓIPARI MÚZEUM) *I. Fortuna utca 4.* The present building was built on the foundations of three medieval houses at the very beginning of the 1700s. It later became a hotel and later still an office building.

---

director's choice • director's choice • director's choice

DR. BALÁZS DRAVECZKY, DIRECTOR, HISTORIAN OF CIVILIZATION (59)

1. A specimen of the once abundant, by now perished grape of Buda — in the courtyard of the Museum, the former Hostelry "Fortuna", on the right side of the entrance. 2. A faience lavatory-set (basin, carafe) from the Grand Hotel Hungaria, 1871. It's decorated with vistas of contemporary Budapest. (Gallery One, "Be our guest in Budapest".) 3. A bedroom from Hotel Gellért, 1918. (Gallery Three, exhibition "Be our guest in Budapest".) 4. Ceramics advertisement of "Mineral Water" from the Margaret Island. (Introduction to the exhibition "Hungarian Commerce in the first half of this century") 5. The title "imperial and royal court supplier" was awarded for the most prominent producers and traders in the Austro-Hungarian Monarchy and it was advertised proudly on signboards, like the one you can see (Gallery One, "Hungarian commerce in the first half of this century".) 6. A complete furniture of a provincial grocer, with the accessories. (Gallery Four, "Hungarian commerce in the first half of this century".)

On the left there are three rooms used by the Museum of Catering Trades. Among the treasures there is a 40-centimetre-long Easter rabbit-shaped mould, an icebox with marble inside its lid and the entire furniture and equipment of a small confectioner's in Buda. One of the old attendants still remembers the old shop. "There were not more then five tables in it. At Sunday noon we streamed out of the church and dropped in for cake. Two ladies served the customers. They made their cream cakes in front of our very eyes. All these are gone now", she says. I remarked that small confectioners' are now opening again one after the other but she demurred.

"I'm a merchant's daughter myself and my father always told us that you need a whole life to establish yourself. These new ones want to buy a house and a car within four or five years. It is not the same..."

The new permanent exhibition, opened in 1996, for the Millecentenary Commemoration, is called "Budapest, Waiting for Guests". Not just objects and text, but life recreated was attempted, with considerable success. A room in the luxury hotel Royal (now closed), a café with a billiard table that could be overturned to become a dinner table, and other interiors ar recreated. There were more than 400 cafés in Budapest in 1900. There were distinct categories: café spectacle, café bar, café concert, café dance, boulevard café and café restaurant. There is a legendary table there from Café New York, with cartoons by most eminent writers, Ferenc Molnár among them. A very nice place with a very nice exhibition, veritably emanating the smell and atmosphere of the good old days.

A rest: Litea — in the courtyard of Fortuna utca 4.

RED HEDGEHOG HOUSE (VÖRÖS SÜN-HÁZ) *Hess András tér 3.* This is one of the oldest buildings of the district, its history can be traced back as far as 1390. The red hedgehog above the gate presumably comes from the coat of arms of its noble owner. After the Turks were driven out, the house was converted into an inn, where even theatrical performances and balls were held.

HOTEL HILTON 5B *Hess András tér 4.* This, the most elegant hotel in Budapest, was completed in 1976 and was given a warm welcome by both architects and experts on historic buildings. (It was designed by Béla Pintér.) At the opening ceremony the President of the Hilton chain called this hotel the most beautiful pearl in the whole string. One side of the hotel is the wall of the old Jesuit cloister built in late Rococo style decorated with plaits. The Gothic remains of a Dominican church are enclosed by the modern hotel in such a way that it can be visited. There are open-air opera performances in the Dominican Courtyard in the Summer.

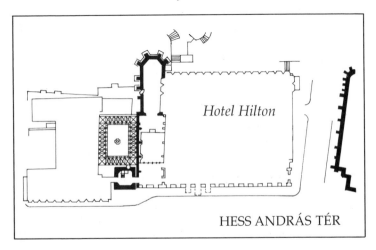

Hotel Hilton

HESS ANDRÁS TÉR

5 **A** Statue of Pope Innocent XI., **B** Hilton Hotel, **C** Fishermen's Bastion, **D** Statue of Stephen, First King of Hungary, **E** Matthias Church, **F** Holy Trinity Column, **G** Memorial to the Soldiers of 1848/49.

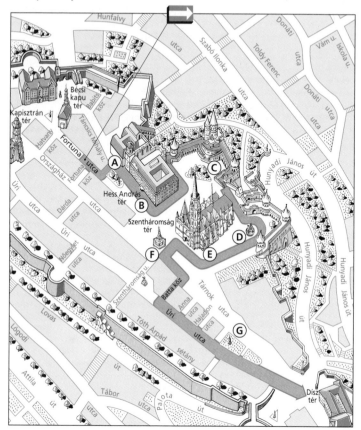

FISHERMEN'S BASTION (HALÁSZBÁSTYA) 5C A look-out terrace, totally unfit for defence purposes, with five round towers and a main tower with several floors. It was built between 1890 and 1905. In the Middle Ages the fishmarket was nearby and this part of the wall was traditionally defended by the Guild of Fishermen, hence the name. We have just seen its replica at the confectionery exhibition, only slightly more sugary than the original. While the tourists are at the dinner table, Halászbástya is visited by teenage couples intent on their first kiss when the musicians have left.

MATTHIAS CHURCH (MÁTYÁS-TEMPLOM) 5E *I. Szentháromság tér.* The real name of the church is the "Church of the Blessed Virgin in Buda", but it is universally known as the Mátyás (Matthias) Church. Its popular name derives from the fact that the legendary Hungarian king, Mátyás, held both of his weddings here. Originally it was the church of the

German burghers. The main eastern gate and the long apse are from the 13th century, the latter built after the French pattern and ends in the 7 sides of a regular polygon. The central part of the church was built around 1400. In Turkish times all the furnishings were removed, all the decorated walls whitewashed. Later it was converted into a Baroque church and by the middle of the last century it looked rather miserable. Between 1873 and 1896 Frigyes Schulek restored the church seeking all its original elements when pulling down the walls. His dream was a new building retaining the inherited elements. He added a row of chapels along the north wall. The 80-metre-high spire has a ground floor and first floor in rectangular form, above that there is an octagon. Up to the third floor Schulek kept the original tower intact but from there he finished it according to his own plan. It was also at the end of the last century that the walls were repainted on the basis of the fragments found at the time of the restoration.

There is a clash of opinion on the artistic value of the church. Some regard it as a masterpiece of European eclecticism, others claim that it is no more than overdecorated stage scenery. Both may be true. The building is evidence of all the knowledge the hardworking 19th century had on the Gothic period, but at the same time it is able to arouse emotions immediately, rather like the scenery in a film seen only momentarily. Anyway, the man in the street likes this church a lot.

HOLY TRINITY COLUMN (SZENTHÁROMSÁG SZOBOR) **5F** *In the middle of Szentháromság tér.* The square is at the highest point of Castle Hill. The 14-metre-tall monument was erected between 1710 and 1713 by the inhabitants of Buda to fend off another plague epidemic. There was no square in this place in the Middle Ages, only a street less than 10 metres wide.

THE OLD TOWN HALL OF BUDA — COLLEGIUM BUDAPEST
I. Szentháromság utca 2. The first session of the Council was held here in 1710. The statue on the corner of the building represents Pallas Athena, the guardian of towns; it has been there since the end of the 18th century and was made by an Italian sculptor. (This is a copy.) The various alterations on the building were carried out by half a dozen builders ranging from local masters to internationally known builders. The prison was in the yard, a place with such a low ceiling that even the shortest could not stand upright.

In 1873, the year of the union of Buda and Pest, the building lost its function. The building is much admired for the fine proportions of its windows and for its inner, forked staircase, treaded these days by foreign scholars. Collegium Budapest is an Institute for Advanced Studies, founded by and similar to Wissenschaftskolleg Berlin. The scholars come for six months or a year. They work here in the house, but live outside. Recently they acquired a site nearby, where they want to build an apartment house — worthy of the Collegium. Once I was invited to have lunch with the Dean. I expected a sort of High Table, but found myself in a noisy, lively cafeteria. In the heart of an institution that looks really like some of the smaller Oxford colleges.

I. Szentháromság utca 1-3. On the site of the buildings destroyed in the war some "neutral" buildings were built after the Italian pattern. Fortunately, before these could grow into an independent group, this trend was abandoned and today only "non-polluting-modern" buildings, which harmonize with their environment, are permitted. The planning rules are strict: in the case of this corner house, the bulk, the height and even the roof structure were strictly prescribed (György Jánossy, László Laczkovics, 1981). The traditional Hungarian aspect of towns favours vertical directions, lines running upwards. This explains why the architects omitted the third horizontal line under the roof. Thus the pillars in a way repeat the vertical directions of the church opposite, only on a smaller scale. The broken façade follows the medieval site.

(Further successful modern buildings in the Castle District: Úri utca 4., 10., 32.; Országház utca 6.; Fortuna utca 16.; Tóth Árpád sétány 30.)

Tárnok utca was the site of the weekly market of the German burghers on Wednesdays. Ordinary bread was sold from tables, black loaves from mats. Until the middle of the 15th century, bread was made without leaven. There was a wide choice of game and fruit. Only live fish were sold, on the second day their tails had to be cut off to show they were not quite fresh. Peaches and grapes could be sold only by special permission from the Council, as these could be used to make alcohol.

THE HOUSE OF A MEDIEVAL WARLORD

I. Úri utca 19. The house presumably belonged to an infamous Italian aristocrat of the 15th century. It is here that the only street-bridge has survived, although various documents mention quite a few such bridges. It was rebuilt in its present form in the 1830s. In Turkish times it was occupied by monks. In the courtyard a tomb and a sundial can be seen.

ENTRANCE TO THE CATACOMBS — WAXWORK EXHIBITION

I. Úri utca 9. There is an underground labyrinth, about 10 kilometres in length, under Castle Hill. The caves were joined to one another by the Turks for military purpose. Today a section of about 1.5 kilometres can be visited. It

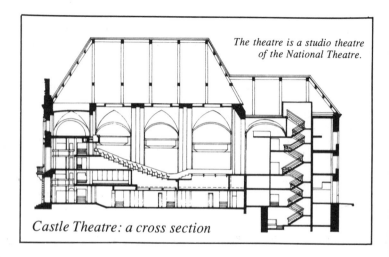

The theatre is a studio theatre of the National Theatre.

Castle Theatre: a cross section

has recently been occupied by a fancy waxwork exhibition — a memorial of Hungarian history which is both funny and serious. It is a completely private initiative which required a large bank loan; this is why entrance fees are considerably higher than in any museum subsidised by the state.

Guided tours in four languages start out every 10-20 minutes, visitors are not allowed in on their own because of the high risk of getting lost.

Water always drips in limestone caves and this one is no exception. After heavy rain the dripping resembles a shower in some places. The temperature is 14 Centigrade, the humidity is about 90, so making the figures of wax was out of the question. Instead of wax a plastic mixture was used, but even so the textile clothes become mouldy very easily. The show takes the visitor a long way back into the past of Hungary. It starts with the mythological beginnigs and finishes in the flourishing Renaissance court of King Matthias. Nothing of more recent but less glorious times is shown. Only a street sign on the wall reminds us of the time of World War II, when thousands of people lived through the siege down here, and some say that even the postman came down here to deliver their letters for a while. *(The Waxwork Exhibition is closed on Monday.)*

A rest: Korona Patisserie — Dísz tér 16.

THE LAST RUIN (AZ UTOLSÓ ROM) **6B** Once three-storey Ministry of Defence was reduced to a ruin at the end of WWII, during the siege of Budapest. Until quite recently, carpenters and electricians had workshops here, to serve the needs of the big museums in the Castle. Now public lavatories, tourist information centre will take their place. By 2000, some new blocks will be built, to close the square and make it similar to what it looked like before the war. The last blocks ever built in the area, I hope.

CASTLE THEATRE (VÁRSZÍNHÁZ) **6C** *I. Színház utca 1-3.* The building itself was completed in 1736, as the church of the Order of Our Lady of Mount Carmel in late Baroque style. In 1784 Joseph II dissolved this order, just as he did most other orders. The monastery was converted into a casino, the church gave place to a theatre. The latter was designed by Farkas Kempelen, the invertor of the famous chess automaton. The theatre had a wooden structure and housed 1,200 people for the performances which were in German. But it was also here that the first play in Hungarian was performed. The theatre was rebuilt several times but the wooden structure remained until, in 1924, a part of the gallery collapsed. The next performance was not until 1978, when the new theatre, of marble and concrete, but housing only 264 (!) people, was opened. Unfortunately, the dress circle and the foyer are not separated so even the slightest sounds can be heard from outside. And there are always some sounds from outside.

Today it is the studio theatre of the National. Success is an infrequent visitor here, I should say.

Beyond Várszínház, restoration work on the old-time Sándor Palace is already nearing completion. Before the war, this building used to be the office and residence of the Prime Minister. The latest news is that it is going to house the János Neumann Library Multimedia Research Centre.

6 **A** Batthyány Palace, **B** Ruins of the former Ministry of Defence, **C** Vár-színház — Castle Theatre, **D** Sándor Palace, former residence of the Prime Minister, **E** The upper end of the Cable Car, **F** Statue of the legendary Turul bird, **G** Modern History Museum (Royal Palace Wing A), **H** National Gallery (Royal Palace Wing B), **I** Matthias Fountain, **J** National Gallery (Royal Palace Wing C), **K** Statue of Eugene of Savoy, **L** National Gallery (Royal Palace Wing D), **M** Lions, **N** National Széchényi Library (Royal Palace Wing F), **O** Budapest History Museum (Royal Palace Wing E), **P** Gothic Great Hall, **Q** Palace Gardens, **R** "War Hammer" Tower, **S** Southern Round Bastion, **T** Tower of the "Gate of Sighs".

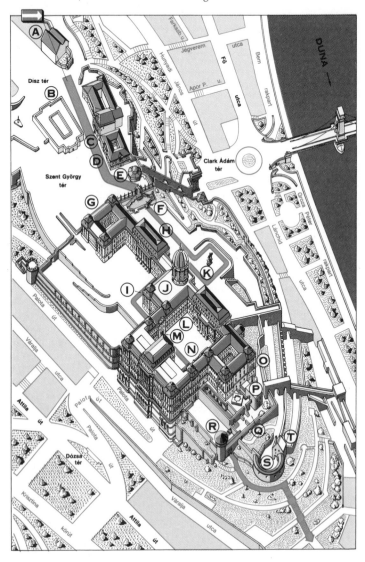

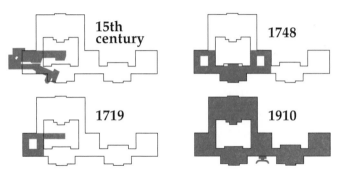

How the Royal Palace was built

ROYAL PALACE (KIRÁLYI PALOTA) 6G–6M

The history of the palace is very much like that of Mátyás-templom since this is also a mock-historic building with many original parts. However, it is even younger than the church: a Royal Palace whose royals have never been residents, only visiting guests.

The first Gothic Palace, which was built and added to for 300 years, was totally demolished. It was ruined by the Christian army which liberated Buda from the Turkish occupation in 1686. In 1715 work started on a completely new, much smaller Baroque palace. Its ground area was increased by 1779. After some minor reconstruction, the Palace was almost doubled in length at the end of the 19th century (now it is 304 metres long) and a huge wing was added at the back. All the halls on the ground floor could be opened into one another. The neo-Baroque palace, which also had some art-nouveau elements, had a false dome, with an attic underneath. Reconstruction finished in 1904 (by Miklós Ybl and Alajos Hauszmann). At the end of World War II, it was the last redoubt of the besieged German troops. The roof fell in all around and most of the furniture was destroyed. At the end of the 1940s, the experts on historic buildings decided that the palace should not be restored in its original form although it was still possible using the remains and some of the plans. They declared that they wanted to return to an earlier, 18th-century form of the palace, but at the same time they wanted to retain the dimensions of the 1904 version. So finally they built a Baroque façade which had never existed before and added a newly designed, though pleasing, real dome to the building. The idea behind all this was that architects of the time saw no value in eclectic architecture, even though this is now considered to be the most valuable feature in the buildings of Budapest.

The inhabitants of the city knew nothing of this dilemma, they were just happy to take possession of the Castle step by step again. Nowadays the building houses three large museums and the National Széchenyi Library.

CONTEMPORARY ART MUSEUM – LUDWIG COLLECTION (KORTÁRS MŰVÉSZETI MÚZEUM)

Royal Palace Wing A. When this *Wing A* of the Royal Palace reopened to the public, some 20 years ago, the sign over the entrance read: "Museum of the Working Class Movement" — not exactly stylish up here. However, its exhibitions always focused on the history of Hungarian civilization as a whole. And when the totalitarian regime started crumbling, the museologists were busy collecting the leaflets that called for demonstrations. When the small, primitive stencilling machine — earlier confiscated by the police — was solemnly given back to the samizdatniks, the museum wanted to buy it. It was not for sale. Later, the first freely elected Mayor, Gábor Demszky, himself of samizdat fame, donated it to the Museum as a present. Then the Museum's name was already "20th-Century History Museum of the National Museum". Then gradually they were swallowed by the National Museum and had to leave this building. In December 1996 they had to leave altogether.

The nucleus of the new art museum was a large deposit of Aachen-based billionaire industrialist and art patron Peter Ludwig. The Museum of Contemporary Art exhibits works after 1989, i.e. really recent art in the making. Director Katalin Néray and the Minister of Culture Bálint Magyar asked top Hungarian businesses to become co-funders of the Museum, and 13 of them did listen to. You can read their names on a tablet right by the entrance.

A very strong collection — occasionally entertaining and funny, even beautiful.

If only the awful red marble interior walls could be changed, originally designed for the Museum of Working Class Movement… If not, at least the totally functionless oversize stairs, big enough for Broadway musicals, could be dismantled… Anyway, there is the long-awaited museum. Let's rejoice.

Looking down from the western side of the Palace to the foot of the walls, you can see that archaeological excavations are still going on. It was, in a way, made possible by the devastation of the war and by the slow pace of reconstruction work afterwards. Although archaeologists have not found the very first 13th-century palace, some very remarkable finds have been made from the time of the Anjou dynasty (14th century). The stripes in the pavement of the courtyard mark the place of previous walls.

THE STATUE OF EUGENE OF SAVOY **6K** Opposite the front entrance overlooking the Danube is the bronze equestrian statue of the famous general (József Róna, 1900). It was he who led armies that liberated Hungary and began the expulsion of the Turks from Hungary. The commission for the statue was originally given by the town of Zenta, the scene of a decisive battle; the town however went bankrupt and could not pay the artist. Hauszmann, the architect who directed the final work on the enlargement of the palace, discovered the statue in the artist's studio. He persuaded the Prime Minister to raise funds and buy the statue with the help of the King-Emperor. Franz Joseph was willing to supply the money and, what is more, he ordered this statue should be erected in Buda instead of his own equestrian statue, as had previosly been planned. After the restoration of the Palace it was doubtful for a while if the statue of the "Austrian general" could be set up in Buda at all: it was rumoured that he could not abide Hungarians.

NATIONAL GALLERY (NEMZETI GALÉRIA) **6H–6J–6L** *Royal Palace Wings B–C–D*. The art of a small country is always a private affair and this is especially true of the art of the past. Still, those who spend half an hour *director's choice* • *director's choice* • *director's choice*

LORÁND BERECZKY, DIRECTOR GENERAL: 1. "Head of a King" from Kalocsa, circa 1200 (Ground Floor, in the Lapidarium, Wing D, left of the Main Entrance.) 2. Master MS: "Visitation", 1506. (Wing D, 1st Floor, opposite the stairs.) 3. Pál Szinyei Merse: "Picnic in May", 1873. (Wing B, 1st Floor, 19th-c. paintings.) 4. József Koszta: "The Three Magi". (Wing C, 2nd Floor, left of the staircase.) 5. Csontváry Kosztka, Mihály Tivadar: "Pilgrimage to the Cedars in Lebanon", 1902. (Wing C, 2nd Floor, left of the staircase.) 6. Gyula Derkovits: "Along the Railway", 1932. (Wing D, 3rd Floor, on the riverfront, in the middle.)

strolling around the exhibition of **Hungarian Painting in the 19th Century** will not regard it a waste of time. They should not bother about the names with strange spellings and historic figures unknown to them. The paintings in this exhibition, which takes up one floor of the gallery, breathe a definite awareness of life. There is a Hungarian word, *honfibú*, for this feeling but such a word seems to be missing from other languages. It can be best glossed as "patriotic sorrow". There is the grief of generations behind this word, the grief common to all for their ill-fated country. This short Hungarian word is one most frequently used in 19th-century patriotic poetry. Hungarian painting developed its unique character during the Romantic era. It is a deeply sentimental way of painting, even elements of horror are not foreign to it.

The painting of the late 19th century may seem familiar. Impressionism and other developments became popular in the rapidly developing Budapest, which, like Vienna, was a flourishing intellectual centre. Hungarian painting has one mysterious, lonely genius, three of whose major paintings can be seen on the staircase, on the landing between the second and the third floor in dim, protective light. Tivadar Csontváry Kosztka (1853–1919) first took a pencil in this hand when he was 27. Outside a village chemist's shop, where he was working, an oxcart stopped and he made a sketch of the dozing oxen on the back of a prescription form. It was then that he started to draw and paint. He sent his first drawings to a famous art teacher in Budapest, and later studied in Rome, Paris and in Munich. During these years he also opened his own chemist's shop to cover his expenses. He was already a well-known artist at the beginning of our century, although he was frequently attacked for his style. He had four exhibitions in his lifetime. After his death, his family had already agreed with some carriers to sell his large canvases for tarpaulin. When suddenly a 24-year-old architect turned up and invested all his inherited money in the paintings.

In 1949 the Hungarian Embassy in Paris exhibited some of his work. When Picasso saw the paintings he asked to be left alone in the room with the doors locked for an hour. At a later exhibition he told Chagall, "There you are, you old master, I bet even you could not paint something like this." Most of Csontváry's paintings can be seen in a museum in the city of Pécs, about 200 kilometres south-west of Budapest.

MATTHIAS WELL (MÁTYÁS-KÚT) 6l A bronze statue of King Matthias (Alajos Stróbl, 1904) as a huntsman, in the company of his shield-bearer, his chief huntsman and his Italian chronicler. On the right at the bottom, the beautiful Szép Ilonka ("Helen the Fair") can be seen, a girl of low birth who fell in love with the king while he was hunting, not knowing who he was. The nicest ears of any hunting dogs ever.

LIONS guard the entrance of Oroszlános udvar (The Lion Courtyard — designed by János Fadrusz, 1904). Two of them are trying to discourage visitors with their grim looks; the other two, inside the gate, roar angrily at those brave enough to enter. The huge door in the gateway between the lions leads to an elevator which will take you down to the bottom of the wing overlooking Buda, to the stop for Bus 16.

The entrances to the National Library, the Budapest History Museum and the National Gallery can be found in the courtyard, visitors can get to some of the exhibitions from here as well.

NATIONAL SZÉCHÉNYI LIBRARY (NEMZETI KÖNYVTÁR) *Royal Palace, Wing F.* The inside of the building was restored only in the 1970s. The building itself has two floors above the level of the courtyard, but the ground

The National Széchényi Library in Wing F of the Royal Palace, overlooking Buda.

The Main Reading Room

floor is really the fifth floor of the library. This is the so-called Ybl-wing (added in 1890–1902), which extends over the edge of Castle Hill.

The library has about 2 million books and even more manuscripts, musical scores and newspapers. Among these are the few codices which have not been dispersed from King Matthias's celebrated library. (These codices are called Corvinas, referring to the heraldic animal of the king: Corvus means "raven" in Latin.) There are 70,000 books shelved in the reading rooms. The Main Reading Room, which consists of several smaller rooms is not very elegant but very spacious, creating ideal working conditions with the view from the windows. It takes natural light from above. The books are taken to and fro by small carriages which run between the glass roof and the mock-celling. They are rather noisy if they happen to be working.

BUDAPEST HISTORY MUSEUM (BUDAPESTI TÖRTÉNETI MÚZEUM) **60**

Royal Palace, Wing E. A most carefully arranged intimate exhibition, the 2,000 years of Budapest can be seen here, presenting clear maps and the result of the 40 years of hard work to reconstruct the medieval Gothic palace.

Recently the "History of Budapest" Exhibition was extended to the present day, an exhibition that used all modern display techniques, and asking help from stage designers and other visual artists. It gives a very powerful context to history, not just the objects, significantly different in this respect from the grand exhibition of the National Museum.

After World War II excavations began around and under the ruined Baroque palace on an area of 30 acres. In the basement front hall of the History Museum there is a good plaster model of Castle Hill, shown as if the Palace had been removed from the top. On the surface there are several numbered ditches along which the excavations were led and, in the ditches, copies of what was found there. Above this model there is a graphic realisation, a white drawing on a black background of the Gothic Palace, as research believes it to have been. Its largest hall was 70x17 metres, where even tournaments took place.

Compared to this, the ten or so surviving rooms seem to be humble, nevertheless fascinating. These are the rooms which were restored from the wonderful palace, once famous all over Europe, praised in the writings of travellers and ambassadors. (In the second half of the 15th century, King Matthias had a larger income than either the English or the French kings.) Almost all of the restored rooms were outside the main building: a cellar, an ice-pit, a cistern, corridors. Only two major sights can be found here: the Gothic Hall, which presumably used to be part of the Queen's apartment, and the Crypt. It is in these parts that the "Gothic statues" are exhibited, which, after a very unquiet life, were found in 1974.

Sometime at the beginning of the 15th century, because of some hurriedly started construction work, about 50 stone statues were thrown out into a yard, which was later filled in. The statues probably portrayed the courtiers of the previous king, all dressed in clothes after the French fashion. (They were the playboys of the trecento, as the archaeologist who led the excavations called them.) So it is only these "dumped" statues that remain to us; most of those which were held

director's choice • director's choice • director's choice

DR SÁNDOR BODÓ, DIRECTOR GENERAL (53) 1. "Boot-shaped Bizarre", vessels of sacrifice ("áldozati edények") from the end of the Bronze Age. (2nd floor, in the staircase, Case V.) **2.** "The portrait of a man wearing capuccio" is an outstanding piece of the collection of stone statues once adorning the 15th-century palace. (Ground floor, Gothic Statue Find.) **3.** A painting depicting Buda and Pest, with vineyards on Gellért Hill (by János Szentgyörgyi, 1830, Modern History of Budapest, 1st floor, Room 3.) **4.** "King Porus is being Captured". A silver relief by József Szentpéteri, a piece shown at the 1851 London World Exposition. (1st Floor, the corridor across.) **5.** "An advertisement of the Telephone Courier", that predecessor of the radio, invented by Hungarian Tivadar Puskás. The ad encourages people to listen to "broadcasts" from the Opera House. (1st Floor, Room V.) **6.** "A View of the Bridges and the general panorama on the city". (The windows of the 1st Floor and 2nd Floor exhibition spaces.)

---

in high esteem did not survive Turkish rule. The secular statues are in the Gothic Hall (Room 11), the ones on a religious subject are exhibited in the Crypt (Room 16).

From Spring until Autumn visitors may go out to a small garden which is arranged in a medieval pattern and from there they may also climb the walls.

The Southern Courtyard of the Castle may be reached by going through the front hall of the History Museum. From there we leave the courtyard through Ferdinand Gate.

DEER HOUSE (SZARVAS-HÁZ) 7G *I. Szarvas tér 1.* This triangular café was built at the beginning of the 18th century in late-Rococo style. The signboard can be seen above the gate even today. It houses the Aranyszarvas Restaurant, famous for its game dishes. Until the 1930s the northern slope of Gellért Hill was packed with small, old houses with wine-cellars, later with pubs. This was Tabán, a popular place of entertainment, the "Grinzing of Budapest". All of these houses were demolished for hygienic reason, Szarvas-ház and the yellow building opposite have preserved the atmosphere of the old district.

THE STATUE OF QUEEN ELIZABETH, WHO ALLEGEDLY LOVED THE HUNGARIANS 7K The whole nation mourned the death of Elizabeth, wife of Franz Joseph, when she was assassinated in 1898. She was said to be a great friend of Hungarians and even spoke our language. This statue originally stood on the other side of the Danube. The people waited for forty years until it was set up again in 1986. Before the war there was another statue on this place; the statue of the ultra-right wing politician whose policies directly led Hungary to allying herself with Nazi Germany. This statue was blown up by communist resistance fighters at the time of the German invasion. A tablet in the ground near the statue of Queen Elizabeth commemorates this.

Elizabeth Bridge (Erzsébet híd) 7N-8A *Linking Március 15 tér (Pest) and Döbrentei tér (Buda).*

The predecessor of the present bridge was called so in honour of Queen Elizabeth. 53 (!) designs were entered for the competition, which was won by three German engineers. The plan, however, was rejected by the builders as it was a suspension-bridge and Hungarian industry could not produce cable of the required quality. Instead, a chain bridge was built between 1897 and 1903 using huge scaffolding all across the riverbed; but it followed the elegant arch of the prize-winning design. This bridge, reflecting the late eclectic centre of Pest was demolished by the Germans in January 1945. The damage was more serious than that to the other bridges and reconstruction would have cost too much. Its successor is a suspension bridge, designed by a Hungarian engineer, (Pál Sávoly, 1964). The two towers were built on the old piers and connected them with the suspension cables, each with 61 separate cables making up the bundle. The new bridge imitates the arch of the old one, which is perhaps why the people of Budapest like it so much. The opening of the bridge was on the afternoon of 21st November 1964 and turned

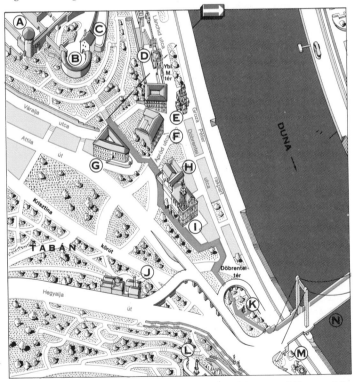

7 **A** "War Hammer" Tower, **B** Southern Round Bastion, **C** Tower of the "Gate of Gasps", **D** Entrance to Royal Gardens, **E** Casino and Restaurant, **F** Medical History Museum, **G** Deer House, **H** The house of Benedek Virág, an 18th century poet, **I** Tabán Parish Church, **J** Rácz Baths, **K** Statue of Queen Elizabeth, wife of Emperor Francis Jozeph I, **L** Statue of St Gellért, **M** Rudas Baths, **N** Elizabeth Bridge.

into an impromptu festival despite the drizzle. (Even my piano lesson was cancelled — I could go to see the new bridge, with my teacher.) The new Erzsébet híd has virtually become the symbol of the capital, the first modern yet beautiful attraction of the city. (See For "Serious Addicts" for some remarkable modern buildings.)

INNER CITY PARISH CHURCH (BELVÁROSI PLÉBÁNIATEMPLOM) 8B

V. Március 15. tér. Walking across the bridge from Buda, you would not imagine that there is a centaur-church behind the nondescript Baroque façade. From the waist down the church continues in a Gothic chanchel.

This is the building with the most eventful history on the Pest side. There are remains here even from the end of the 12th century, and each century has left its mark on the building (it was a mosque in the Turkish times); at the end of the last century, when the original Erzsébet híd was built, there were even plans to demolish it, as it was in the way of construction. Until the 1930s it was surrounded by small shops.

Váci utca stretches from Vörösmarty tér to Vámház körút, that is, as far as Szabadság híd, to the south. In the Middle Ages this was the length of Pest. The two parts of the street, to the north and to the south of Erzsébet híd, are very different from one another. The northern part is an overcrowded, commercial, naff, touristic pedestrian district, the southern part has just been converted into a no-traffic zone. According to a monograph on local history, the two parts of the street resemble each other just as little as a famous over-adorned prima donna and her sober, humble housewife sister. When the inhabitants of the city say "Váci utca", they only mean the "over-adorned" part and regard it as a legend. This place had developed into a most fashionable shopping street at the end of the 18th century and was becoming more handsome and richer until World War I. Ten of the present-day buildings witnessed the days when in the mornings the loud gossiping of maidservants, waiting for the horse-pulled rubbish-cart, woke up the tenants in the houses, and reliable "civil servants" in uniform caps, that is, porters, were waiting for orders, standing on the corner all day long. The shops often changed managers, as owners were continuously putting up leasing fees.

Today the same is done by the Municipal Council: the idea behind the ever increasing fees is that only quality shops should be found here. At the beginning of the 1970s, the steam-roller of modernization hit the street: all the shops were given uniform "modern" shopwindow frames, regardless of the style the building itself was built in.

Recent features of the street include the ethnic Hungarian pedlars from Transylvania, dubious money-changers and even the wandering Chinese who will write your name in ideograph — the latter has been a great hit with school kids.

The southern part of Váci utca has still not adjusted to the new situation. There is a sort of a Sleeping Beauty quality lingering on there. You can meet the occasional deputy mayor there, rushing to the Budapest City Council meeting (usually on the last Thursday of the month), the owner of the second hand bookshop, Mr Vincze, the visionary designer/businessman/gallerist, looking like a bespectacled Russian painter from the late twenties — and not in exile, and a very corpulent, bearded Serbian literary historian, being late from the Serbian Church sermon behind New City Hall (corner of Szerb utca and Veres Pálné utca).

1. *Romanesque Basilica
(13th century)*

2. *Gothic "hall church"
(15th century)*

3. *In Turkish times the chancel
served as a mosque (12th century)*

4. *Today — one-naved Baroque
church, since the early
18th century*

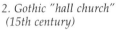

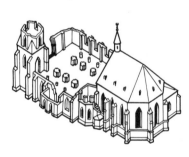

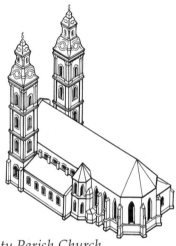

Phases of building the Inner City Parish Church

THE FORMER SECOND-HAND BOOKSHOP (A VOLT ANTIKVÁRIUM)

V. Váci utca 28. The plans for this building were made by the architect of
the Parliament in 1877. There has been a bookshop in here for about a
hundred years. György Lukács, the philosopher who lived nearby, went
into the shop every day in the last years of his life to see if they had anything interesting for him. He used to have a chat with the manageress who
wore spectacles and had curly hair that was just beginning to turn grey.
She has recently been forced to retire. My friends and I demonstrated
against this — in vain. Then the shop was sold on condition it would go
on operating as a bookshop. You can see the result.

8 A Elizabeth Bridge, **B** Inner City Parish Church, **C** Faculty of Arts, **D** Entrance to Haris köz, **E** Hotel Taverna, **F** Fontana Department Store, **G** Statue of Fisher Rézi, symbol of the fishermen's guild, **H** Statue of Mihály Vörösmarty, romantic poet, **I** Vigadó concert hall, **J** Hotel Intercontinental.

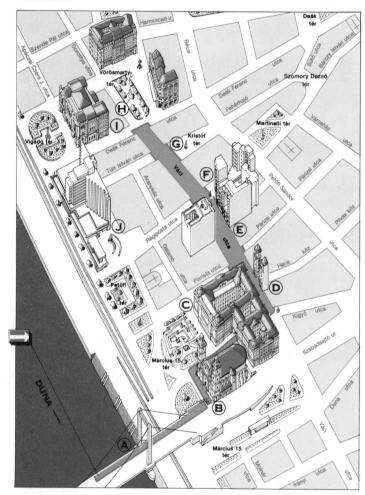

HARIS KÖZ 8D At the beginning of the century the owner of a piece of land in the neighbourhood of Váci utca had the idea of building a street on the site of his old bazaar. So as not to lose his ownership, he closed his street every year for one single day. The last such occasion was in 1949. In that very year the piece of land was nationalised, together with the street.

THE FORMER QUEUE AT THE ADIDAS SHOP *V. Váci utca 24.* Earlier if there was a queue in Budapest it was either bananas sold in wintertime or a famous novelist was autographing his/her new book. Adidas is an Austrian sportware brand, coined from the name of the owner, Herr Adi Dassler. The permanent interest used to be due to somewhat lower prices — the wholesale firm acts as a retailer here. But why not open another shop, and another and another — until there is no queue?

(I kept that sentence from the very first edition of 1989 — since then of course they opened another shop, interestingly enough, in Váci út, but the queue remained here for almost a year. Then it gradually disappeared. And now you can buy everything on earth in Budapest — it has become a consumer's paradise, with new shopping malls opening every other month. Even the Forint became convertible... An unbelievable thing. Since queues were obviously the consequence of the separate money, separate money was the consequence of the Wall. Can You follow me?)

HOTEL TAVERNA AND TRADE CENTER 8E *V. Váci utca 20. and 19.* It

took a long time for post-modernism in architecture to arrive in Hungary, although it fits into the eclectic townscape very well. On the small area where the hotel is situated the architect (József Finta, 1985) managed to find place for 224 rooms and catering for 600 guests. There is a café, a beer cellar, a confectioner's, a champagne bar, a sweetshop, a bowling club and a sauna. The façade gives the impression of permeable material. According to an architectural magazine "it is exterior and interior at the same time". Opposite the hotel the International Trade Centre (József Finta, Gyula Csizmár, 1985) was built on two neighbouring lots. The border was where the pillar of the façade can be seen. The passage is open to the public, from which you can look into the pleasant, intimate hall of the building. The figure on the pillar of the façade (Tibor Borbás) waves the flag of trade in his hands.

A rest: Café Zsolnay — Váci utca 20.

PHILANTHIA FLOWER SHOP *V. Váci utca 9.* The art nouveau decoration

of the shop, although it does not suit the classic façade of the building at all, has miraculously survived various hard times. Its name is the Greek for "the love for flowers".

Maybe one day the chandeliers will go. How could they do it with this interior?

THE SITE OF VÁC GATE *Next to the corner of Váci utca and Türr István*

utca. The white line on the paverment marks the site where the medieval city wall once stood with its northern gate, Váci kapu. According to contemporary sources, there used to be a "deadly hustle" around the gates. In 1789 it was quietly pulled down. (An event independent of the ones in France, of the same year.)

This has been a long walk. If you do not want to go back to Gerbaud again, you can sit in Anna presso (Váci utca 7.) or Muskátli (Váci utca 11/a.). The latter used to be the haunt of young artists who wanted to redeem the world at the very beginning of the 1960s, before the Hungarian beat-movement. They either do not come here any more or have become so conventional that you would not recognize them.

WALK TWO

The City and the Vízíváros Area takes us all around the city of Pest, passes at the back of the Parliament. As you can see the whole of the building only from a distance, we shall walk over to Buda, visit a Turkish bath and walk under the chestnut trees lining the river. We shall also look in through some gateways. Time: about 6 hours, refreshments included.

József Nádor tér used to be one of the most attractive squares of the City before the advent of the motor car. It takes its name from Archduke Joseph, the seventh son of Emperor Leopold, who was the governor or palatine (nádor in Hungarian) of Hungary from 1796 for over fifty years. His statue is in the middle of the square. The original plan was that he should face in the opposite direction but, because of the great construction work he originated, it was decided that he should look towards the City. After so much reconstruction some now think he should look the other way.

POSTABANK HEADQUARTERS *V. József nádor tér 1.* The Romantic-style building, originally a residential block (Hugó Máltás, 1859), was completely refurbished recently by the phenomenally successful Postabank Corporation, an Austrian-Hungarian joint venture. The eccentric founder /CEO/chairman of the board/newspaper tycoon/art patron Gábor Princz has his spacious study on the top floor, which was built as an addition in 1922. The carefully furnished room includes some valuable rare books, Hungarian and foreign, some excellent, three-dimensional artwork by László Fehér, the painter. To make up for the lack of a panorama on the Castle, there is a large photo of the view the inhabitant of the room would see — had the rest of the building been pulled down... There is a similar trick in the inner courtyard: a gigantic mural painting on the wall, a panorama on Váci utca, if the adjacent (Café Gerbeaud) building was not there.

Obviously, you can neither visit the CEO's room, nor the inner courtyard, but as there is no underground garage under the building, you might glimpse Mr Princz himself, somewhat stocky, black, curly-haired, in his early forties, entering or leaving his fortress. Wears a tie only if he absolutely has to. Otherwise in black, high-necked pullover. If he has to wear a tie, he often chooses blazing red ones. Or is it her celebrity primadonna wife who chooses the colours? They can often be spotted together at first nights, concerts and vernissages.

GROSS HOUSE *V. József nádor tér 7.* A typical neo-classical block of flats (János Hild, 1824). At the beginning of the last century it housed the famous Blumenstöckl pub where guests could choose from three set meals. The most expensive was 2 Forints, and for that price you could eat as much as you wanted to. (That was a different forint, of course. The present one was introduced in 1946.) Anyone who told a bad joke or argued loudly had to pay a fine into the Saracen-head money-box. Presently it is also used by Postabank. The bank exhibited some photos of lovely old relics along the arcade at the side of the building, documents that cant't reflect its own history, since Postabank was established in the late 80s.

CENTRAL EUROPEAN UNIVERSITY (KÖZÉP-EURÓPAI EGYETEM) 9H

V. Nádor utca 9. This Classicist chef d'oeuvre was completed by Mihály Pollack in 1826 for Count Antal Festetics. The street was called Tiger street at that time. Pollack (1773-1855) designed no less than 186 buildings, among them the National Museum. You can walk in through the circular hall unhindered, at least as far as the receptionist's counter. That is enough to see the secret of the inside: a recent extention that is much bigger than the original, still, invisible from the outside.

Budapest-born George Soros spent his adolescent years in hiding in his home town, helping his father saving Jewish lives. Later he emigrated, and was going to become a scholar and a philosopher, one of the pet students of Karl Popper. He was well over forty when he found his real vocation as alchemist: a prime mover of monetary long term markets. His passion for "opening up" Central European societies — i.e. democratizing them — became a passion for him in the early 80s. It was in the mid-eighties that he set up his Foundation in Budapest, first a joint one with the Academy of Sciences and Letters. This University is said to be the biggest single long-term charitable commitment of his, anywhere in the world. He hopes it to play a pivotal role of educating the future élites of East and Central Europe. Soros himself, now in his sixties (though looking considerably younger, speaking impeccable Hungarian) often comes to Senate meeting, which are held on the first floor, just obove the circular entrance hall, with the statues that represent the four seasons.

By the way the students do not live in the building, but 5 kilometres out of town, in Pest. Slowly CEU is conquering the whole block. Deep inside, the conversion of a big garage into a library is near completion. And the excellent bookshop is obviously open for you, even on Saturday afternoons, between 2 and 5, a highly unusual hour for an academic bookshop.

"PIRANESI HOUSE"
THE FAVOURITE BUILDING OF THE ILLUSTRATOR OF THIS BOOK

V. Zrínyi utca 14. The block was converted to its present form in 1879. Heavy, bombastic, still, somehow majestic. Does not care for light, rather blocks its way, rather attempts to impress the onlooker with a fireworks of forms and shapes, enough to fill two sketchbooks of any student of architecture. It inspired several of the artworks of András Felvidéki, the illustrator of this book. It reminds him of Piranesi. (The Museum of Fine Arts has hundreds of original prints by him.)

OKTÓBER 6. UTCA 3. 9I The house with the passage-way was built in 1844–45 and has recently been restored. Together with the two small spiral staircases hidden at the sides, it has four staircases. The statue in the garden honours Béla Czóbel, a great post-impressionist painter.

BUDAPEST CATHEDRAL: THE "BASILICA" 9J V. Szent István tér. The largest church in the city, holding 8,500 people. The dome is 96 metres high. The name may be misleading since, strictly speaking, basilica means a church of a totally different shape. (It has the rank of "basilica minor", hence the name.) It took so long to build it that it is remembered even in the saying "I'll settle up when the Basilica is finished."

Until quite recently no bishop resided here, but now, as the Archbishop of Esztergom was given the double assignment and was given the new name: Archbishop of Esztergom and Budapest, the church can be called a "Budapest Cathedral".

The work on the building started in 1851, when Pest was still a small town. The designer, József Hild, died soon afterwards, then Miklós Ybl, the architect who later designed the Opera House, directed the construction. On examining the works that far, he was astonished to find cracks in the walls. Ybl had a fence built around the half-ready church and set watchmen to guard it. Eight days later, in January 1868, the dome fell in. You can imagine the lack of traffic, since the disaster, which happened in broad daylight, had only one eye-witness: a baker's apprentice. In the newspapers, he gave an eloquent account of what he had seen: "I can see that small clumps of stone start rolling down from the tip of the dome. As they are falling slowly downwards, tumbling in the air, a kind of groanlike sigh permeates the air, and the whole dome is starting to tilt. First in absolute silence, then with a horrible roar." More than 300 windows were broken in the area. Inferior building materials were reported to have been used.

Then Ybl made new plans and work started again, almost from the beginnings. But he did not live to see the church finished, dying in 1891.

The Basilica was finished by József Kauser in 1906. Emperor Francis Joseph gave a speech at the opening ceremony and, it was rumoured, cast suspicious glances at the dome, which is 22 metres in diameter.

The general opinion is that the Basilica has insufficient light. Only mysterious patches and beams of light bring some life into the statues and ornaments at some lucky times of the day. Behind the main altar the statue of King St Stephen can be seen (Alajos Stróbl), who is the patron saint of the church. There is another statue of him above the main entrance. The mosaics were designed by Hungarian painters and made in Venice. The ground plan of the neo-Renaissance pattern forms a Greek cross.

The main façade is not on the busy Bajcsy-Zsilinszky út; it is on the opposite side. The Basilica is a rare example in city planning in the sense that during the time it was built the structure of the city around it changed. When the second plan was made there was already a need for a "second façade" and Ybl cleverly solved this problem. The walls outside the chancel are richly decorated with an elegant Ionic colonnade and with statues of the 12 apostles.

9 **A** Luxus Department, **B** Vigadó Concert Hall, **C** Gerbaud, **D** József nádor tér 7., **E** Statue of József nádor, Habsburg Regent, **F** József Attila utca 16., **G** Derra House, **H** CEU Building, **I** Október 6. utca 3., **J** St Stephen's Church, the "Basilica", **K** Bajcsy-Zsilinszky út 17., **L** Bajcsy-Zsilinszky út 19/a., **M** Bajcsy-Zsilinszky út 19/c., **N** Bajcsy-Zsilinszky út 34., **O** Hungarian National Bank, **P** Bank Centre.

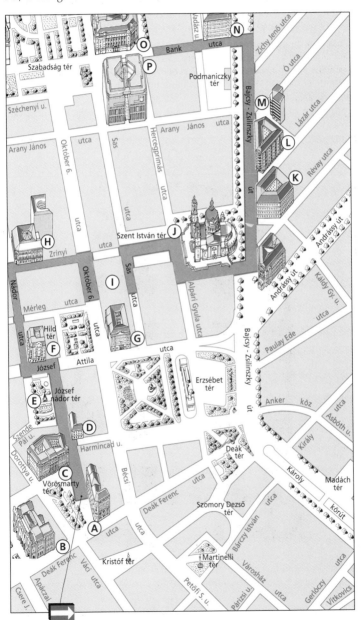

The Holy Right (Szent Jobb), the alleged right hand of (St) Stephen (1000–1038) is the most revered relic of the Hungarian Catholic Church. Though there is a gap in the story of the relic, between the death of the king and the first time the relic was claimed, it is relatively short. Historians don't say it's altogether impossible. It can be visited in a chapel to the left of the main altar. You drop a coin in the slot and the relic is lit up. If not right away, the guard knocks at the case, and behold, it does.

Under the church there is a large cellar, it was here that many of the important documents of the city and some valuable art treasures survived the last war. The windows of the church overlook Bajcsy-Zsilinszky út. In the second half of the 1960s some unknown student elements painted here with large letters: LENIN, MAO, CHE. Since they did not have paint sprays, they must have had to carry buckets of paint to the spot. You can

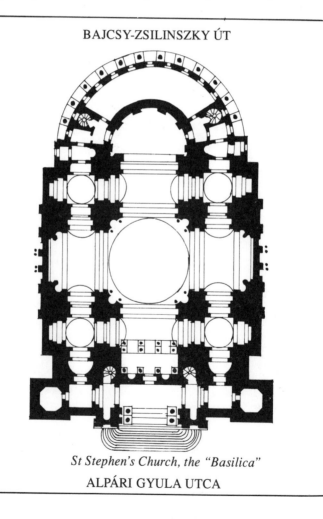

BAJCSY-ZSILINSZKY ÚT

St Stephen's Church, the "Basilica"

ALPÁRI GYULA UTCA

still see the fading graffiti on the wall. (After he read these lines, a friend of mine, a well-known scholar and critic called me and claimed responsibility.)

The chancel is worth looking at from the other side of the road as well, for example from the pastry shop. These few metres do make a difference. Or you can look at the Basilica again from an unusual angle, sitting on the terrace of the small café (corner of Lázár utca).

To know why it is an absolute must to go up to the dome and look out from the terrace, turn to page 29, "Finding Your Way / Vantage Points".

A rest: Café Kör — Sas utca 17.

A NICE BLOCK OF FLATS 9K–L–M *Bajcsy-Zsilinszky út 19/a, 19/b, 19/c.* In the 1930s modern architecture made a breakthrough in Hungary (for the second time) and much construction started everywhere in the city. The optimum use of space was combined with plans for healthy, cleverly arranged flats. This block is an example of how well this style could be fitted into the 50-100 years older surroundings (Jenő Schmitterer, 1940). All three gateways have their own surprises. The 19/a building has lead glass windows on the ground floor and interesting lamps on the capitals of the columns. The gateway of the 19/b block has pleasant proportions, and, what is more, on the ceiling behind the entrance the present tenants have managed to solve the problem of squaring the circle. The third block is in the best state at the moment. This one has the best preserved lighting, and even the mosaic glass has survived, reflecting the atmosphere of old times. All the tranquility and elegance of this style is summarized in the stone giant, resting on the edge of the roof of the 19/b block. It can only be seen from a distance so do not forget to look back.

Podmaniczky tér was once occupied by houses but cleared by the war. The square, housing a station on the Third (Blue) Metro Line, is becoming a new gate to the City. It was named after Baron Frigyes Podmaniczky, who was a leading figure in city planning in last century Budapest. The City Protection Association requested that the square be named in his honour.

THE MOST COMPLEX PUBLIC MONUMENT EVER — WITH A BENCH AND A CLOCK That of Baron Frigyes Podmaniczky in the middle of V. Podmaniczky tér. The legendary last century fighter for new urban projects holds a statue of Pallas Athena, which has become the symbol of preservationists. Traditionally she has a lance in her hand. Ask a Hungarian friend why, he/she thinks Athena hasn't got it with her in this statue. (In case he/she doesn't know: this is the subtitle of a television programme by maverick politician/cameraman/journalist/mediastar Mihály Ráday, President of Budapest City Preservation Society: "Our Grandchildren Will Not See It, OR THE LANCE IS SOMETIMES STOLEN FROM THE HAND OF PALLAS ATHENA, CITY DEFENDER". I told you it was complex... (Mihály Ráday's "Budapest Bests", see on page 44.)

HUNGARIAN NATIONAL BANK 10C *V. Szabadság tér 8-9.* The stately bulk of the National Bank shows an eclecticism already being made lighter by art nouveau (Ignác Alpár, 1901). Between the first-floor windows a fine relief shows people working; from peasants through mint workers to a tycoon just signing a bill. On the SW corner, toward the square you can see Hamlet, pondering about to be or not be, with the skull of poor Yorick. The inside of the building can no longer be visited.

BANK CENTER 10B *V. Bank utca/Sas utca/Arany János utca/Hercegprímás utca.* Architect József Finta, when showed me around said that this was the first time the developer let him choose the quality materials he wanted. He argued that the city should grow two or three floors in this part. The glass-walled higher levels obviously deceive the eyes. That is a bigger building than it looks. Half of it is occupied by the headquarters of National Savingsbank. You can walk through the building, with a detour through some fine shops, the Bang und Oluffsen designer hi-fi shop and a candy shop. In the lobby you can have a look at the nicest wheelchair lift in Central Europe. This would descend the handicapped to the cafeteria/restaurant to be built in the basement (still waiting for an investor).

A STATUE TO THINK ABOUT In front of Bank Center, towards the National Bank there is the nonfigurative statue of three independent pieces by Ádám Farkas, Professor at the Academy of Fine Arts. If you come from the direction of Hold utca, the statue obviously forms a lion. But only from this direction.

I asked the sculptor if it was intentional. He said, with a characteristic, cunning smile: "Yes and no." He is the President of the Japanese-Hungarian Artists' Club. Maybe he was elected because of his calm, cunning smile. Or has acuired it during his visits to Japan.

Szabadság tér (Liberty Square) is a hidden treasure of Budapest — it is not along any major streets or boulvards. You just bump into it, as if by chance. Until as recent as 1898, there was a huge military barracks here called "Neugebaude" or New Building. It was as big as the square Hold utca — Báthori utca — Nádor utca — Bank utca. The barracks was pulled down, and the square and the neighbourhood was built according to one idea, in a homogeneous way.

Out of the eclectic palaces one art nouveau block sticks out: the American Embassy. That's where Cardinal Mindszenty spent the years from 1956 to 1975. The archbishop was imprisoned in the fifties (needless to say, under false charges). In 1956 he was liberated, but when Budapest was invaded, he couldn't leave for the West. There is the statue of a stocky man in front of the building: that of the US General Harry Hill Bandholtz. As an officer of the entente peace-keeping force in 1919, he saved the treasures of the National Museum. He went to the building and "sealed" the doors — with the only (paper) seals he had at hand: censorship seals. These had the US coat of arms, so they kept Rumanian soldiers from looting the building.

POST-OFFICE SAVINGS BANK (POSTATAKARÉK) 10F *V. Hold utca 4.* "Hungarian style has not a past but it does have a future", said Ödön Lechner, one of the most influential architects of Hungarian art nouveau (1845–1914). When he finshed this building (1901) it got a warm welcome from his contemporaries, who saw the synthesis of a simple way of handling space and Hungarian folk ornamentation. The beautiful simplicity of the main walls give no indication how restlessly alive the building is inside and at the roof. You can walk into the main hall, where the cashiers work, in office hours, between 8 a.m. and 1 p.m. on weekdays. Torn banknotes are exchanged here for new ones. (By tradition you get back the same percentage of the value of the percentage of its undamaged surface.)

The greatest attraction of the building is undoubtedly its roof of green, yellow, blue and brown hexagonal tiles, hidden behind the yellow majolica waves, which crown the top of the main walls. The roof is full of flowers familiar from folk embroidery, angel-wings, Turkish turbans and scary dragon-tails. This, however, can only be suspected, even from further down in Nagy Sándor utca or opposite the market. A disciple of the architect asked Mr. Lechner: "But tell me, Master, who will enjoy those wonderful ornaments on the roof, if not visible from the pavement?" Lechner answered: "The birds will…"

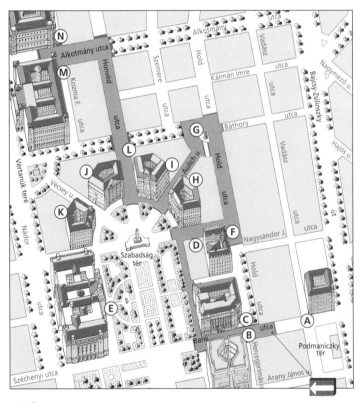

10 A Bajcsy-Zsilinszky út 34., B Bank Center, C Hungarian National Bank, D American Embassy, E Hungarian Television (former Stock Exchange), F Post Office Savings Bank, G Batthyány Eternal Flame, H–I–J–K Office Blocks, L Honvéd utca 3., M Ministry of Agriculture, N Ethnographical Museum.

At the time of the burial of the architect, all organized building workers stopped work for five minutes.

BATTHYÁNY ETERNAL FLAME (BATTHYÁNY ÖRÖKMÉCSES) **10G**

At the convergence of V. Báthory utca, Aulich utca and Hold utca. On 6th October 1849, shortly after the defeat of the Hungarian insurrenction against Habsburg rule, 13 Hungarian generals were executed in a country town and the Prime Minister of the Revolutionary Government, Count Lajos Batthyány himself, was shot on this site, which, as you were told above, happened to be the inside of a big army barracks. Batthyány is remembered by the permanent flame inside a red cup. (Móric Pogány, 1926.) Some years ago people living nearby were shocked to see that the flame had gone out and wrote indignant letters to a newspaper. The permanent flame has quietly been lit again.

In the dying years of the old régime, police broke up some demonstrations here using force.

AN ART NOUVEAU BLOCK OF FLATS **10I** *V. Honvéd utca 3.* There is a bus stop outside the building but nobody is tempted to look up while waiting for the bus, as the ground floor is so unattractive, totally spoilt by reconstruction. The building has four floors, the long open corridor on the "fifth floor" opens directly from the loft. Above that starts the two-storey-high, steep roof. From the other side of the street you can see all the majolica ornaments intact, only the plasterwork has been damaged. Here it is not enough to look into the gateway, you have to climb up at least as far as the first floor. Notice the tiles on the floor, the ear shaped painted windows, the doorframes and the brass peepholes in the doors (Emil Vidor, 1904).

The family of the one-time owner of the block still lives on the first floor, the "piano nobile". Though in 1949 no compensation was paid, the family has just been offered the possibility to buy the flat "back" from the state...

This part of the Fifth District, called Lipótváros (after Leopold, an Austrian Archduke) swarms with people during daytime; in the evenings it is completely dead. Its main street, the broad, elegant Alkotmány utca, does not really lead anywhere and so has little traffic. But this is the route taken by all important guests when visiting the Parliament.

THE STATUE OF IMRE NAGY *V. Vértanúk tere, corner of Nádor, Vécsey and Báthory utcas.* Imre Nagy (1896-1958) was a communist all his life, with an alleged dark career in the Soviet secret police in darkest 30s. During the dark 50s in Hungary, he was made Prime Minister in the very relative thaw in 1953. He was demoted in 1955, then during the 1956 revolution he was made Prime Minister again. But he was so used to greeting people as "comrades", that he used it when talking to the revolutionary demonstrators here in this square, who did not really like it...

He became a symbol of liberty, when forced to exile in Rumania, then tried in Hungary and executed in 1958. During his trial he could easily save his life, had he cooperated with the new regime — but he did not revise his opinion. He became a lover of liberty and independence in the first place, but still considered himself a Communist. He was buried in an unmarked

11 **A** Ministry of Agriculture, **B** Ethnographical Museum, **C** Statue of Lajos Kossuth, **D** Statue of Ferenc Rákóczi II, **E** Houses of Parliament, **F** Kossuth Lajos tér 13-15., **G** Statue of Mihály Károlyi, **H** Szalai Confectioner's, **I** A block inhabited by American diplomats, **J** Playground, **K** "White House".

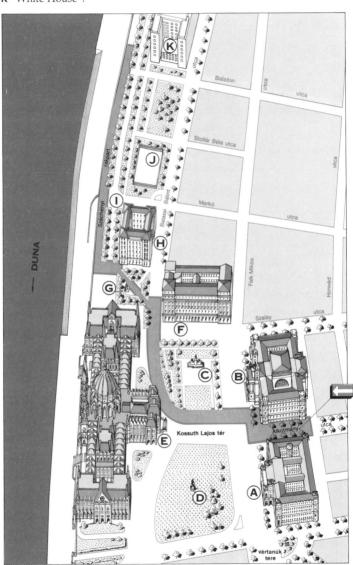

grave, and was found with the utmost difficulties. As a matter of fact, he was buried face down, a real disgrace. His name was simply unmentionable publicly between 1958 and 1988.

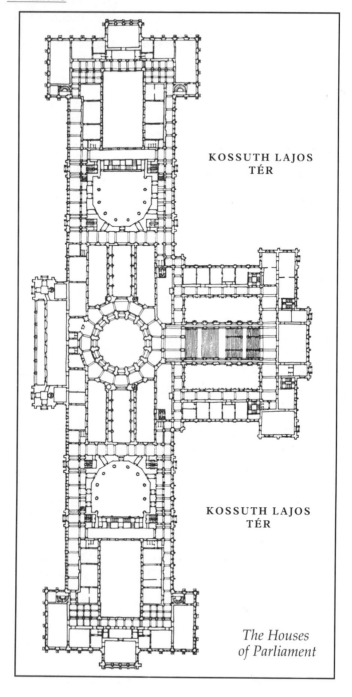

KOSSUTH LAJOS
TÉR

KOSSUTH LAJOS
TÉR

*The Houses
of Parliament*

His reburial on July 1989 marked the birth of new democracy. Tens of thousands came to Heroes' Square, where deconstructivist artists Gábor Bachman and László Rajk dressed up Műcsarnok Exhibition Hall in black draperies.

Imre Nagy is buried now in Parcel 301 of Rákoskeresztúr Cemetery, under the magnificent monument designed by György Jovánovics. (See "Twelve Impressions".)

This statue, erected on the centenary of the birth of Imre Nagy was given little praise, when unveiled. Critics found the symbolism — a bridge — cheap (it represents transition from totalitarian notions towards democratic ones), and everyone found the figure idealizing to the point of falsification. The martyr Prime Minister was a typical, stocky, overweight Hungarian peasant type, quite unlike this melancholic, café-type looking vaguely in the direction of the Houses of Parliament. (Tamás Varga, 1996.)

HOUSES OF PARLIAMENT (ORSZÁGHÁZ) 11E *V. Kossuth Lajos tér.*

"No more than a Turkish bath crossed with a Gothic chapel", ridiculed Gyula Illyés, a great 20th-century poet. Work on the Parliament started in 1885 and an average of a thousand people worked on it for 17 years. Its designer, Imre Steindl (1839–1902), was originally an apprentice stonecarver, then studied architecture in Vienna and Budapest. He was 44 when this work started.

When the building was nearing completion he was already so ill that he could direct the work only from a chair carried to the spot. He died just some weeks before the building was put into use. Parliament is 268 metres long and 118 metres wide. The spire is 96 metres above ground.

There are 691 rooms in the building, the length of all the stairs together is about 20 kilometres. It readily reveals its structure, especially if seen from the river. To the right and to the left of the central hall under the dome, the council chambers of what were formerly the Commons and the Upper House are situated. "I did not want to establish a new style with the new Parliament because I could not build such a monumental building, which should be in use for centuries, with ephemeral details. My desire was to combine this splendid medival style with national and personal features, humbly and carefully as is required by arts…", the architect said in his inaugural address at the Academy of Sciences. He must have meant Gothic when speaking of "style" even though the ground plan of the building shows Renaissance features and the way space is organized inside is very often Baroque in character. It is thus a summary of Hungarian eclecticism.

Kálmán Mikszáth the novelist (See "For Serious Addicts / Twelve streets and squares"), who went to the first session in the building as an MP, summarized his impressions by declaring "True, it's dazzling, still gaudy". The writer said this about the inside of the building, the outside was covered with white, Hungarian limestone. As it turned out, the stone was not hard enough. Renovations began as early as 1925 and have not been finished yet. There are guided tours of the Parliament for an entrance fee. Only for groups — whenever there is no plenary session. Visitors are allowed in through Gate XII, the first gate to the left from the Main Entrance with the Lions. You have to register in advance through the Office of Guides, T: 268-

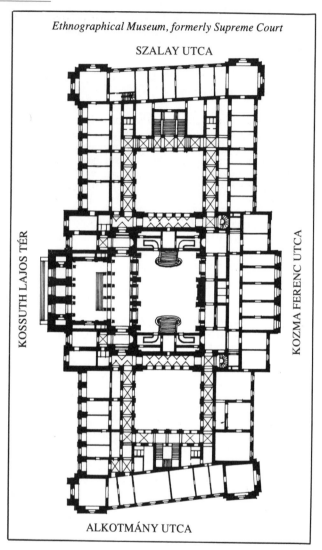

Ethnographical Museum, formerly Supreme Court

SZALAY UTCA

KOSSUTH LAJOS TÉR

KOZMA FERENC UTCA

ALKOTMÁNY UTCA

4000. Since that is a central, say: *"Keh-rem ahz eedegen-vehze-toeh-ket."* "Please, put me through to the guides."

Since the first edition of this book, much has happened to this building. The red star (not part of the original design) has been removed from the spire. But more importantly, since the last elections there is real work being done inside — Italian style politicking. As there is only one chamber (no upper house), one of the two large halls is rarely used. It is 5 per cent required to secure seats on the national list under our electoral system, so it is unlikely to have more than 7-8 parties in the House. (The system was copied from the German system, together with the institution of the "constructive no-confidence vote" that assures stable government.)

LIFE IN THE PARLIAMENT BUILDING Life is quite busy in the House and the whole building except for January, July and August. You can have an idea from having a look at Kossuth square: only MPs can park there. It is the workplace of not only of the 386 Representatives (half of them elected in constituences, half of them on party lists), but that of the President of the Republic (See "Crash Course", last entry, page 18., to the lefternmost part of the building, and the Prime Minister at the other end).

The tone of the skirmishes reminds one of the British Parliament. The Immediate Questions and Answers was introduced in 1994. And opposition leaders often disrupt the work of the House with their belligerent "before the agenda" speeches on Monday afternoons.

ETHNOGRAPHICAL MUSEUM (NÉPRAJZI MÚZEUM) **11B** *V. Kossuth Lajos tér 12.* Showing a strong resemblance to the Reichstag in Berlin, although much more elegant than its German counterpart, this neo-Renaissance palace was built to house the Supreme Court and the Chief Public Prosecutor's Office (Alajos Hauszmann, 1893–96). Building another dome opposite the Parliament seemed out of the question. From the Ticket

---

director's choice • director's choice • director's choice

DR. HOFER TAMÁS PhD, DIRECTOR GENERAL **(67)** 1. The main hall, the so-called "aula", from the side of the entrance. The fresco on the ceiling, entitled the "Apotheosis of Justitia" reminds us of the fact that this building was built as Palace of Justice (by Károly Lotz, 1896.) 2. The Gallery of Costumes. 25 kinds of Sunday dresses of "Historical (pre-1914) Hungary", among them Hungarian, Slovakian, Romanian, German, Rutenian, Croatian clothes. (Second floor, permanent exhibiton, Room 1.) 3. Two pottery brandy flasks, imitating a peasant couple. A potter's wedding-present for a friend. (Second floor, Room 10.) 4. The trousseau of the bride to be put on show in the courtyard, before the wedding, from 1898 (Kalotaszeg, Transylvania). Bed with home-woven sheets, clothes in painted boxes, embroidered shirts, lead glayed pottery wine jugs in baskets, a woman is on guard with a stick. 5. "Christmas table" (Sárköz, South Danube region). On Christmas night, everything on or under the table will be blessed. On the table, there is a "Christmas tablecloth", depicting a small church, and the birth scene, and the small figures representing animals: apple, garlic, and under the table: cereals, and corn. (First Floor, Room 14.) 6. The panorama on the Houses of Parliament from the balcony of the Main Hall. This balcony is unfortunately not open for the public, only when there is a function in the Main Hall. (This selection is from 1997, when the non-European collections of the museum was not on show. That's why no piece was included.)

Office you get into an astoundingly huge and richly decorated hall where it is well worth looking around and up. In the back there are some chairs around a big table where you can sit down. From here you can admire the ceiling of the first floor, the large painted windows and the splendour of the staircase. The fresco on the ceiling shows Justitia, the Goddess of Justice, sitting on her throne among the clouds. By her the groups represent various qualities; on the right Juctice and Peace, while on the left Sin and Revenge. Károly Lotz worked on this fresco for ten months.

The museum is a very pleasant place, and has recently attracted much attention with daring, unusual exhibitions, like the one that presented as higly self-ironic history of the country image propaganda of Hungary since 1896.

There are four statues in Kossuth Lajos tér, the Kossuth and the Rákóczi statues are in front of Parliament and those of Attila József and Mihály Károlyi near the river on the right and on the left of the Parliament. (See "Who was Who".)

An Elegant Block of Flats 11F *V. Kossuth Lajos tér 13-15.* This

was vacant land for a long time; the city authorities gave permission for a building with thousands of restrictions. All the measurements of the building, even the number of the windows, were prescribed to preserve the unity of the square. The building is a rare example of successful planning (Béla Málnai, 1929). The general conservatism of the 1920s changed the direction of the development of architecture: neo-Baroque became once again the most popular style.

The gateway is worth seeing even if this means climbing upstairs and looking down from above. The staircase is especially attractive from the bottom. The details of the doors to the flats are also quite remarkable. There used to be a row of cafés at the front of the building and all the flats used to have a dumb waiter.

Szalay Confectioner's 11H *V. Balassi Bálint utca 7.* Even during

the time of the catch-all nationalization after the last war there were some confectioner's in the city which remained in private hands. In time they earned a legendary reputation, even though all their proprietors did was to continue their trade like masters of the old school, wholeheartedly filling the pastry with custard and stirring the ice-cream. "He spares nothing from it", the older generation used to say. They used to know their customers personally and the staff did not change much either, most often family relatives took over in case of vacancies. The furniture also remained the same, all these shops look movingly obsolete in spite of some efforts to modernize them. You would not think that this strict, tall, bald man, Master Szalai, is a living legend. Perhaps the legend is not really about him though, but his cakes.

Until 1949 he had a bigger, more elegant shop nearby. (V. Szent István körút 7.)

A Playground 11J *Between Balassi Bálint utca and the river.* In the

grim 1950s there were only two things in a playground, swings and a sandpit. Swings were always painted red. Parents were always arguing with their kids to get them to fasten the safety chain and not to stand up on the swings. There were usually some see-saws as well, which gave a chance for social activities. You could "send your partner on a Summer holiday", (which meant that you kept him in the air for a long time) or let him go down fast and so "make him jump".

But the real socializing area was the sandpit. Unfortunately the old park-keeper would not allow us to bring water. "Watering again, are you!" he used to shout, waving his stick with the nail at one end for collecting dry leaves and litter. At that time there was much less for kids to do. And there was not even a single slide in town. Nowadays the best playground in town, according to my nine-year-old daughter, is in Margitsziget.

FALK MIKSA UTCA: ANTIQUE ROW It took about five years for the antique business to concentrate here most of the shops that is worth mentioning in Budapest these days. It is just a short section, between Szent István körút and Balaton utca. Ten years ago there was only one shop there, on the corner of the Grand Boulevard, then (and now) belonging to a chain of second hand shops and pawnshops, called BÁV, with a symbol of the Venus of Milo. Recently the old and declining shop was given a vulgar and tasteless facelift, since then no decent person sets foot there. The excessive use of brassrailing is an obsession with some nouveau rich owners of some middle size businesses. Maybe because it so much resembles gold?

NAGYHÁZI GALÉRIA *V. Balaton utca 8.* T: 131-9908, F: 156-9973. Open 10 a.m. to 6 p.m. Mon-Fri, 9 a.m. to 1 p.m. on Sat. The opposite end of the spectre: the biggest shop in Hungary, with possibly the highest standards and quality, priced accordingly. Furniture, paintings, chandeliers, and all kinds of peasant textiles: blankets, skirts, folk costumes, old and recent. They are friendly to obvious non-customers.

WHITE HOUSE 11K *V. Széchenyi rakpart 19.* For decades this building used to be the dreaded power centre from where the country was governed from. Dictator/reformer/father figure János Kádár ruled from here for 32 years. Characteristically, it was from the *Time Magazine* cover we could see the room he worked in for the first time in 30 years in 1986. There was a large oil painting over his desk: "Lenin, playing chess." (He really liked the game and was a brilliant tactician in inner-party power struggles.)

In an Orwellian way, there was the state coat of arms on this Party Headquarters, while a large red star on top of the Parliament — not vice versa.

"White House" houses the offices of MPs these days. Unlike in Washington DC, there is no special underground train to carry MPs to the Floor when there is an urgent vote.

You can't visit the White House, this pretty plain and rather bleak place. Even if you could, you wouldn't see the gigantic mural in the far end of the vast lobby, by a great Hungarian painter on the hard-working Hungarian society, since it is covered by the biggest curtain in Central Europe. (Once I peeped behind it — the mural is still there...) And there is a really big state coat of arms hanging in the middle, out of iron and coloured enamel.

Parties move around every four years, according to where the political merry-go-round stops on election day.

You cannot imagine how good the feeling was to take a right turn right away, after coming off the bridge from Buda — a privilege once reserved for higher party functionaries. This happened in 1989. Few people remember that happy moment any more.

MARGARET BRIDGE (MARGIT HÍD) 12C–13A *Linking Jászai Mari tér (Pest) and Germanus Gyula tér (Buda).* This was the second permanent bridge over the Danube, built between 1872 and 1876, designed by the Frenchman Ernest Gouin and built by a Parisian building firm. At the middle, the bridge turns at a 150' angle, partly so that all the piers should be at a right angle to the stream, partly so that the bridge should continue the line of the Nagykörút. The bridge has a branch that leads to Margitsziget (Margaret Island) starting out from the pier in the middle. This branch was included in the original plan but was only built in 1901. All that has remained of the original sturcture is this branch; for this reason we approach on the right side of the bridge so hat we can look under the arch.

MARGARET ISLAND (MARGITSZIGET) *Between Margit híd and Árpád híd.* The island, now one of Europe's finest parks, was formed in the Danube over the last million years. With a length of 2.5 kilometres and a width of 500 metres at the widest point, it can be strolled through in about 2 hours at a leisurely pace. However, it is well worth spending half a day here.

A bridge connected the island with the Buda bank even in Roman times. In the Middle Ages it was called the "Island of Rabbits" and was a Royal hunting reserve. The present name was given in honour of Princess Margit, daughter of King Béla IV; she lived in the nunnery on the island. During the Turkish occupation the whole island functioned as a harem.

There are more than 10 thousand trees on the island, most of them plane-trees, carefully planted by various Habsburg gardeners to counteract the ravage of floods. János Arany (1817–1882), one of the greatest poets of the last century, wrote his touching poems in old age, "Under the Oak Trees" here. In fact, although there are some oaks on the island as well, garden-ers say that the poet's favourite oaks were probably planetrees. Up to the end of World War II the island was the property of a private company and maintenance was financed from the entrance fees paid by the public. There are various amenities on the island: a swimming pool, a strand, a tennis stadium, an open-air cinema and an open-air theatre, a game reserve, a rose garden, a Japanese garden and a garden of statues.

On the northern end there is the famous old Grand Hotel, which is now the Ramada Grand Hotel. The terrace is a pleasant place to sit around and enjoy the shady trees, the tranquil and the elegant ambiance — every-thing which makes the island worth visiting.

Access: Bus 26 and 26A, terminus at Nyugati Railway Station in Marx tér. On Margit híd the trams, on Árpád híd the buses stop at the access road to the island. Cars are allowed access only from Árpád híd and only as far as the car parks around the hotel. On Saturdays from 10 a.m. to 6 p.m. "microbuses" take visitors on a sightseeing tour. (Only 1 May to 30 September.) Two enterprises

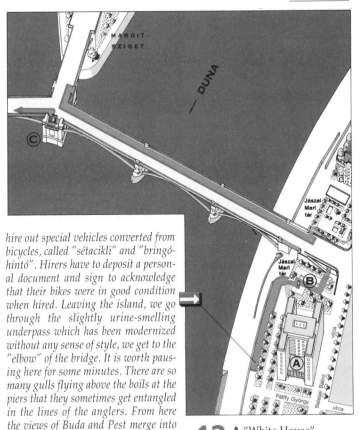

hire out special vehicles converted from bicycles, called "sétacikli" and "bringóhintó". Hirers have to deposit a personal document and sign to acknowledge that their bikes were in good condition when hired. Leaving the island, we go through the slightly urine-smelling underpass which has been modernized without any sense of style, we get to the "elbow" of the bridge. It is worth pausing here for some minutes. There are so many gulls flying above the boils at the piers that they sometimes get entangled in the lines of the anglers. From here the views of Buda and Pest merge into one another, with the Danube curving gently in the middle, embracing the City.

12 A "White House",
B Margaret Bridge.

On this bridge occured the greatest diaster in the history of the city. In November 1944, in the broad daylight of the afternoon rush hour, when hundreds of people were crossing the bridge on foot and by tram, the charges placed by the Germans on the section of the bridge between the island and Pest went off, presumably by accident. The number of casualties will never be known, but it ran into the hundreds.

THE PRZEMYSL MEMORIAL 13B *Left of the Buda side of Margit híd.* This, one of the most masculine lions in Budapest, symbolizes the Hungarian defenders of Przemysl, the fortress in Southern Poland. A Hungarian soldier modelled it in 1932. Memorials of the Hungarian victims of World War I have been set up at various places of the city, most of them erected from donations.

Margit híd continues to Margit körút (Margaret Boulevard). After about 200 metres the road takes a sharp turn to the left, still further it turns right and

13

A Margaret Bridge, **B** Przemysl Memorial, **C** Statue of General Bem, **D** Flórián Chapel, **E** Király Baths, **F** Military Tribunal, **G** "Point House".

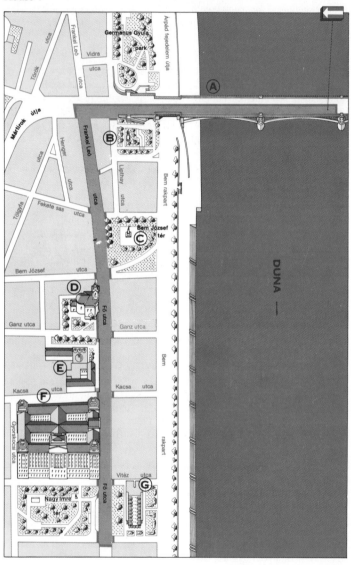

finally runs into busy Moszkva tér, the centre of Buda, which epitomises the traffic problems of the city. The winding Margit körút follows the line of a hill, Rózsadomb, on which first Summer houses and later elegant villas were built. In the 1960s and 70s hundreds of cube-like blocks were built next to the old, low buildings. The eastern slope of the hill is practically full. The other sides are also the scenes of busy construction work (Endrődi Sándor utca, Gárdonyi Géza utca, Törökvészi út). For Budapest residents, Rózsadomb is now a social category. If someone built a house or bought his own home in this expensive area, people just said that "they moved up to the hill". Rose Hill still remained the symbolic address associated with wealth, though it is common knowledge that real wealth has moved out to Adyliget and Budakeszi, the new suburbia.

A rest: Café Gusto — Frankel Leó utca 12.

To follow Walk Two, you should turn left to Frankel Leó utca, a street which could just as well be on the Pest side. You can see a notice in one of the ground-floor windows of No 9., which translates as TROTTING ALL YEAR ROUND, FLAT-RACING FROM SPRING TO AUTUMN. It is one of the two dozen betting offices in the city. The two types of racing have two separate race-courses and two separate sets of followers.

At No 1. there is a small shop of a skate-grinder. The old-fashioned notice in the window says: "Skates for grinding or assembling are welcome." Opposite on the ground floor of No 2. is the "Bambi" confectioner's just as it was in the trapezium-shaped cash desk and the figure of the (Disney) deer that inspired the name. The notice above the fridge containing soft drinks is seen in lots of other such places: DRUNK ELEMENTS WILL NOT BE SERVED. The other one above the cash desk reflects the spirit of the place better: ONLY FOOD SERVED TO THE TABLE MAY BE CONSUMED THERE. Which must mean that things sometimes happen differently here. Perhaps the old-age pensioners passing time at "Bambi" may be offering each other the home made cookies they have brought with them; I wonder.

STATUE OF JÓZEF BEM 13C *II. Bem József tér.* Of Polish nationality, Bem was one of the most successful generals on the Hungarian side during the 1848-49 Hungarian Revolution and War of Independence, and was especially revered by ordinary Hungarian soldiers. He was called "Father Bem" (Bem apó) by them. The statue (János Istók, 1934) depicts the small figure of the general, wounded, his arm in a sling, commanding his troops into attack at the bridge of Piski. The inscription says: ~The Battle of Piski~. And underneath: ~I Shall Recapture the Bridge Or Shall Die / Forward Hungarians / If We Do Not Have the Bridge, We Do Not Have the Country.

The bridge was recaptured. As the saying goes: "We won this battle as usual, it was only the war we lost."

After the crushing defeat of the revolution by the combined forces of the Tsar and Habsburgs, Bem escaped to Turkey. He adopted Islam, became governor of Aleppo under the name of Murad Pasha. The statue has always had an important role in anti-government demostrations, ever since it was erected.

FLÓRIÁN CHAPEL (FLÓRIÁN KÁPOLNA) 13D *II. Fő utca 90.* We are now entering Fő utca, which includes almost the entire history of the country. It was a baker who had the chapel built in the middle of the 18th century.

Before the quay was built there was flooding by the Danube several times. Then the area was filled up with earth. All the older buildings are considerably below street level because of this. The church was lifted by 140 centimetres in 1938. A modern painter, Jenő Medveczky painted the frescos in the same year. Now it is the parish church of the Greek Catholic community in Buda.

I saw a touching scene here, an old lady dusting the ceiling of the chapel with immense affection and thoroughness. She was using a long pole made up of serval shorter ones joined together.

KIRÁLY BATH (KIRÁLY FÜRDŐ) 13E *II. Fő utca 84.* The part built by the Turks, called the "Bath of the Cock Tower", was built around 1570 inside the Víziváros town wall, so that the garrison could enjoy the benefits of a bath even during a siege. It was a smaller copy of the famous baths in Buda. The neo–Classic wings were added between 1717–27. It took its present name (Király = King) not from some ruler but from the König family which owned the place for a time. The steam bath is a fine spectacle. After buying the ticket, go up in the spiral staircase and follow the sign GŐZFÜRDŐ (steam bath). In the dressing room the attendant hands over a cotton apron which you take with you into one of the free boxes. After undressing, you lock the door of the box with the key you find inside and tie it on a string on the apron. Memorize the number of your box and you can go straight into the bath. Taking a shower is compulsory, the sauna is not. You get to the actual Turkish bath, to a pool under an octagonal roof, which can be seen also from the outside, through a low door. There are mysterious beams of light of different colours coming through the hexagonal openings in the dome, illuminating the steam. Once you have been in and out of the steam of different temperatures and waters of 26-40 Centigrade enough times, the next stop is the towel room. You leave your apron at the entrance, take a towel and dry yourself. You dump the wet towel, take a dry one and go up to the first floor **Pihenő** to have a rest. There are notices here on the wall saying "Silence, please" and "Time of rest: 15 mins"; the latter is never taken seriously. From here you go back to your box, but you cannot open it with your key alone; like a safe it needs two keys to open and the attendant has the other one. It is customary to leave a tip for him.

The bath is open for men on Mondays, Wednesdays and Fridays, and for women on Tuesdays, Thursdays and Saturdays from 6.30 a.m. to 7 p.m. (on Saturdays to 12 p.m.). It is closed for maintenance on every first Thursday of the month. Apart from a steam bath, you can use the bath tubs, the sauna and several other facilities. On one of the corridors there is a red scale, the sort that used to be everywhere in the streets of Budapest. In the beginning you had to drop in 20 fillér, then two 20 fillér coins. Not long after that, the scales disappeared.

Fő utca is the main street of the district called Víziváros (literally "Watertown"). Looking up the streets to the right, for example, up Kacsa utca, you can enjoy a magnificent view of the slope of Castle Hill and you can get an idea of the poetic disorder of the district in the past. Imre Nagy tér, however, could well be a museum of modern architecture. In Fő utca 70-72 the severe block of the Military Court of Justice (13F) is situated, an excellent example of the primary aim of such buildings: to serve as a deterrent (1915). During the rebuilding of the façade it was perhaps felt that three revolving doors in the façade were too many and iron bars were placed on the ones at the sides; the one in the middle was replaced with a simple narrow door, which is not in the least in proportion with the large building. It truly seems impossible to slip out of this place unobserved.

The building opposite (Fő utca 69.) is a typical block of flats of the 1930s, while the red brick building opposite the side wall of the Court, on the other side of the square, was the first building in Budapest which was built during Winter — in 1941–42. After the last war, it was planned to build on the Danube bank, using tall buildings. All that was realized of the plan was the famous high-rise block, "pointhouse" (Fő utca 61., 1948) which is called that because all the flats open from one single staircase in the middle of the building. But the rumour went around that the origin of the name is that there was no point in building it, as it cost twice the price of a traditional block. (14A).

We have arrived at one of the finest spots of this walk, at Batthyány tér. Apart from its own buildings, its attraction lies in the fact that it is opposite the main façade of Parliament. (A quite unusual view of the Parliament can be enjoyed from the first floor of the Market Hall, from the windows of the stalls hidden on the left.) The quietly stretching huge building seems to be quite a long way away. You can imagine the power of the explosion when a German ammunition store went up here on 2nd January 1945, if all the windows of Parliament broke, even on the other side of the building.

The sleepy little square suddenly came to life in 1972, when this section of the Second (Red) Metro Line was opened. The terminus of the green suburban train (HÉV) is also here, under the square.

You can make a shortcut here to finish this walk; if you take the underground in the direction of Örs vezér tér, the second stop is Deák tér, which is just 3 minutes walk from Vörösmarty tér.

A WORLD FAMOUS LAVATORY (NYILVÁNOS VÉCÉ) *In the subway, Batthyány tér.* "A little money takes away every smell", to vary the Emperor Vespasian's famous dictum. This instruction, which was always a busy but scruffy place, was leased out to a private entrepreneur some years ago, who brought here the atmosphere of tropical countries, soft music and two chairs. The original owner in the mid-eighties was interviewed by journalists from almost every leading newspaper, as a symbol of New Hungary. Later on, he must have had a chain of video rental outlets, then he/she might have bought a business that was privatized. Who cares about a private toilet when 70 per cent of Hungarian economy was privatized?

Even during the heyday of the fame of this institution (Entrance: 5 forints then!) I remember a letter to the editor stating that there was somebody who almost got beaten up because he could not pay.

HIKISCH HOUSE *I. Batthyány tér 3.* The residence of an architect who lived at the end of the 18th century (the house was built in 1795). It is below the level of the square, as is every other old building here. There is a relief with four cherubs on the façade. They symbolize the four seasons.

THE FORMER "WHITE CROSS" INN *I. Batthyány tér 3.* The Ballroom used to be in the prominent middle part, which also saw theatrical performances. The ironwork on the balcony on the left is Baroque, on the right

14
A "Point House",
B St Elizabeth Parish
Church, **C** Statue of Ferenc
Kölcsey, romantic poet,
D Market hall, **E** Saint Anne Church,
F Calvinist Church.

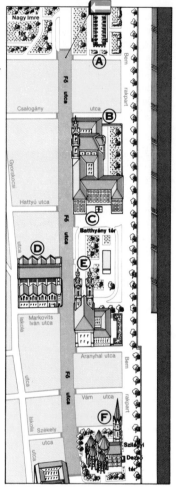

it is Rococo. Joseph II (1780–90), called the "King with a Hat" since he was never crowned, stayed here twice, to emphasize his puritanical character. You will be surprised at the large and wonderful courtyard hiding behind the gate. The Casanova Piano Bar entices those who like that kind of thing. They say Casanova himself put up at this inn.

To the left of the back gate of the building, there is the tradesmen's entrance of the Market Hall.

THE CHURCH OF SAINT ANNA

14E *I. Batthyány tér.* A building with fine proportions in every detail, to my mind, one of the finest. (Kristóf Hamon, Máté Nepauer, 1740–1762). Inside there is an Italianete eloganted, octagonal nave. One of the builders was Kristóf Hikisch, who used to live in this square, and whose house we have already seen. Since the church was built, it has been attacked by earthquakes, floods and wars.

On the ground floor of the vicarage one of the most pleasant cafés in Buda, the Angelika, opened at the beginning of the 1970s. Under the vaulted ceilling, the traditional middle-class of Buda make up most of the regulars, due to the slightly snobbish decoration and the pleasant staff. A place where ladies wear their hats as they take their coffee — and where the wayward boss takes the secretary.

If we walk further down Fő utca, we shall pass a neo-Gothic Calvinist church with an extremely complex ground plan on the left (Samu Pecz, 1896), then soon arrive at Corvin tér. It is surrounded by a concert hall (the so-called Vigadó of Buda), some charming Baroque blocks of flats (Corvin tér 2., 3., 4. and 5.), a church of medeieval origin, rebuilt in Romantic style, and the hillside. We turn left into Halász utca and leave the Víziváros district for the right. On the corner of Pala utca and Fő utca there is a late Baroque building wich used to belong to a Greek merchant.

From here you can see, and this is the only place you can see it well from, Roosevelt tér at the Pest end of Lánchíd. The square is enclosed by the Hungarian Academy of Sciences, the "Spinach-palace", Gresham Palace, the Ministry of Home Affairs and the Hyatt Hotel. Naturally the Roosevelt memorial tablet on the wall of a building in the square cannot be seen from here. The inscription on the tablet says: "FDR, 1887–1945, who, in the last war between the peoples of the world, fought for the freedom of the oppressed and for the victory of human rights. He helped democracy to win a final victory".

A rest: Café Angelika — Batthyány tér 7.

THE FRENCH INSTITUTE (INSTITUT FRANÇAIS, FRANCIA INTÉZET)

15E (*I. Fő utca 17. T: 202-1133, F: 202-1323*) When this chic institution moved to this prime location from its former, tucked away Theresa Town small palace, its weight quintupled in Budapest cultural life. (Apparently, its budget had too, as well...) Designed by George Maurois (1989), the building, opened in 1992, is an exemplary addition to the riverfront, the proportions of which successfully respects this never-before-seen-in-Budapest-style, highly original building that originally was going to house the French School, that's why it is cut into two, with separate entrances. (The Fő utca façade was designed for the school, and the rest for the Institute.) The silver cylinder flaunts the auditorium inside.

Apart from being a premier cultural location, host and co-host of everything from Baroque music festivals to jazzy events and philosophical talk-shows, I like going there for two things.

Number one is the panorama from the library — an entirely new one on Pest. You can enjoy it from 1 p.m. to 7 p.m. on weekdays except for Monday. There are wonderful lamps on the table. And yes, the books. It's a three-level space, with a lot of books off the shelf, displayed on the top of the rails. There are incredibly helpful and proud librarians (a lot of them, I gather). Proud of their library, the one they like to call "petit Beaubourg".

What seems to be even more promising, is the new community space, that will be open from now on from 9 a.m. to 9 p.m., or the end of the last programme of the day. They decided to call it "Café l'Orient Express", though the terminus of the famous train is Budapest, since it was re-started, and it does not go as far as the Orient.

The ladies who serve the ultra-strong espresso are nice and they whisper in French which is all too natural. The plexiglass dome of the café space gives you a different kind of panorama: different from the library's. It overlooks the courtyard of a typical Budapest block of flats. There are iron-railed gangways on every floor. So you can sip your coffee, read your paper and see the postman going around and distribute pension. And see the teenager coming home, bumping into Mrs. Kovács straight from the Batthyány tér market. This is a space that teaches you how to be inquisitive, without looking to be voyeuristic. No small feat.

Quite recently a monument was erected at the Institute, by Pierre Székely Péter (the artist insisted on carving his name in that double-decker way). The statue, that fits into the grid of the pavement in a nice way, is about flawless Hungarian-French friendship. On the western side there is a

French word: "affinité", on the southern surface, the Hungarian counter-part: "rokonszenv". On the northern surface it commemorates the wartime antifascist activities of the French embassy, and the inauguration of the new Institute by the Hungarian President.

CHAIN BRIDGE (LÁNCHÍD) 15J–16A

We have already crossed this bridge on the "First Walk". In its present form, this is the third bridge. During the renovation in 1987, sixty tons of paint was used and most of the 100,000 rivets were changed.

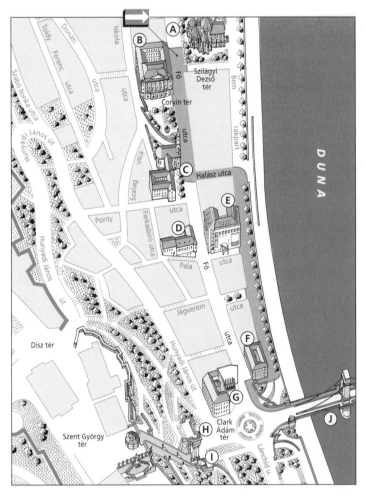

15 A Calvinist Church, **B** Buda Vigadó, **C** Church of the Capuchin, **D** Fő utca 20., **E** The French Institute, **F** Fő utca 1., **G** Café in the remaining part of block destroyed during the war, **H** The entrance to the Tunnel, **I** The lower end of the Cable Car, **J** Lánchíd — Chain Bridge.

16 A Lánchíd — Chain Bridge, **B** Hungarian Academy of Sciences, **C** Statue of István Széchenyi, **D** Gresham Palace, **E** CEU Building, **F** Statue of Ferenc Deák, **G** Hotel Hyatt, **H** Gerbaud, **I** Vigadó, **J** Luxus department store.

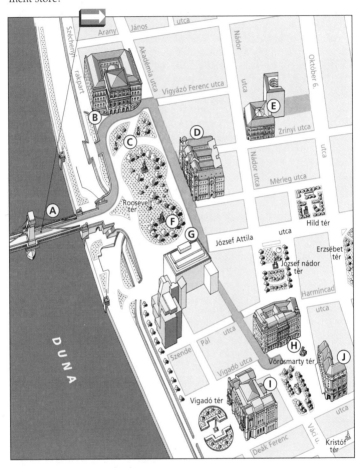

GRESHAM PALACE 16D *V. Roosevelt tér 5.* The plan approved in London for the centre of the English insurance company (Zsigmond Quittner, 1904–6) did not harmonize at all with the style of Lánchíd. In spite of the art nouveau style its proportions are surprisingly peaceful, and as one would expect, its surface is richly decorated. The banker who once founded the London Stock Exchange is in a gold setting so dominant that it can be seen even from the other end of the Tunnel. At sunset the portrait and the golden tiles of the façade, which are at other times of the day so pale, seem to glow. It makes a striking photograph if you can set up for it from the Buda side of the bridge. The figures above the windows of the first floor illustrate a working life and a carefree life, the latter undoubtedly being the result of buying a good insurance policy.

A rest: Mérleg étterem — Mérleg utca 6.

HUNGARIAN ACADEMY OF SCIENCES AND LETTERS (MAGYAR TUDOMÁNYOS AKADÉMIA) 16B *V. Roosevelt tér 9.* This institution,

together with so many others, was founded in the second quarter of the last century, in what is called the Reform Age. On the wall facing Akadémia utca the large relief immortalizes the moment when Count Széchenyi, in 1825, offered one year's income for the foundation of the Academy (Barnabás Holló, 1893). To the question of what he would live on, he answered: "My friends are going to support me..."

This was the first neo-Renaissance building in the city and was built between 1862 and 1864, to the plans of Friedrich Stüler, an architect from Berlin. On the second floor there are six allegorical statues on the façade, symbolizing the sciences which were studied in Hungary at the time. On the same level there are six statues of Galileo and Miklós Révai (a 18th-century Hungarian linguist), near the river Newton and Lomonosov, and towards Akadémia utca Descartes and Leibniz. Today the Academy has ten departments. By the charter of the Academy, the number of members who are younger than 75, can be a maximum of 200. Members get a monthly salary, receive all the journals of the Academy and have their taxi fares paid as well. This latter tradition developed from an earlier system, operational in the 50s, following the Soviet model, when there was a car park at the Academy, a sort of private taxi service. A recent innovation is the establishment of the Széchenyi Art Academy. The acceptance speeches are first class events here in this building. Last time Mr Zsámbéki, of Katona József Theatre talked about *The Broken Jug* by Kleist, not 30 minutes, as he should have, but a hundred. The large audience listened mesmerized, though.

The richly decorated interior of the building is unfortunately not open to visitors and the armed guard politely but firmly warns them off. The name of the institution stands modestly between the second and the third floors with golden letters. I remember that in my childhood there used to be a full stop at the end. Then this last-century full stop disappeared because according to the orthographical rules published by the Academy "there is no full stop after a title".

A rest: Restaurant Lou Lou — Vigyázó Ferenc utca 4.

The Academy used to dominate the square but lost its primacy at the beginning of this century when the headquarters of the two financial institutions were built. It fell back even further when the "Spinach-palace" was built, the office building so nicknamed because of its colour (Miklós Hofer, Tibor Hübner, 1979). Two foreign trading companies started the expensive construction (the weight is carried by steel balls), but ran out of finance. The building was finished by the state and finally three ministerial institutions moved in. There is also a canteen on the top floor for the staff.

Gresham Palace was built of durable material; its façade has resisted the ravages of time. The T-shaped passageway, however, has given up the struggle. The glass ceiling, which was once painted, was replaced by plain glass after the war. Only some fragments remained at the bottom. Relics of old decencies, as they say in Dublin.

Here we suddenly seem to arrive into a rundown district. From the passageway you can see the backdoor to the Gresham Casino, all sorts of office windows, where the lights are always on and an old-fashioned hairdresser's. Here is the entrance to an office whose plate has changed frequently. It has been a lonely hearts agency, an agency for the building industry and a shoeshop; a modest, hidden reminder of our age of entrepreneurs. There are offices, as here, in many residential blocks in the City area, often in the most inappropriate premises. Their staff, especially the women, do their very best to decorate these offices, keeping postcards sent to each other over the years on the wall or under the glass sheet on their desks.

The staircases have their own names (Gresham, Kossuth and Andrássy stairs). At some places here some of the old glass windows have been preserved. The walls of the inner courtyards are white or covered with light blue tiles.

Everyone agrees that the decline should be stopped some way or other. There seems to be no other way but to turn the block into a hotel. But the tenants — with the leadership of the grande dame of the Hungarian stage — protest. They want to stay.

By the way. The Roosevelt tablet disappeared during the recent renovation. A shame.

On the way back to Vörösmarty tér you can find some more information about the walk behind you, by browsing in the newly set up Info Touch system. Or stop for a moment in tiny Dorottya utca Gallery. Its big windows keep prospective visitors away. Everyone casts a hasty glance, feels that he/she has seen it all. No secrets, no longing to get in.

WALK THREE

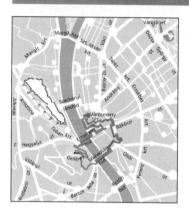

Gellérthegy and the Old City leads through the City area built at the end of the last century. We shall go over to Buda and climb a 141-metre-high hill, then come back across another bridge to Pest to have a look at some buildings which were built at the beginning of the last century. Perhaps we shall have some sausages on the way.
Time: about 6 hours.

VIGADÓ **17C** *V. Vigadó tér.* This single word is the full name of this romantic concert hall and ballroom. It means something like "merrymaking", a place for entertainments. When it was opened, a Hungarianized Italian word was planned for it, as were several other suggestions, ranging from "Gondilla" to "Búfúdda". It was intended as a concert hall and a ballroom and took seven years to build, beginning in 1859. It took so long partly because the builders needed several attempts to cope with the unusual task. The demanding designer, Frigyes Feszl, stuck to his guns and planned even the smallest sections. When the building was finished in 1865, it was received with unanimous obtuseness. Some found it to be too unusual, some others to be too Hungarian. Still others criticized the lack of uniformity and also said that the main façade was "bare" and the height of the main hall was monstrous (22 metres). An architect from abroad said, and perhaps not quite in mockery, that the building was "auskristallisiert Tschardasch".

In its present form, rebuilt after the war, it was re-opened in the Winter of 1980. Music lovers could hardly wait for the Large Hall accommodating 640 people. To make the once infamously bad acoustics better, pyramids were placed on it. The musicians were disappointed in spite of all that, but the audience was flattered by the amazing variety of colours. Restoration work has been done very carefully, for the colouring the original plans have been used and photographs have been consulted for other parts.

Unfortunately, the Large Hall and the equally luxurious staircase can only be seen when a concert is on and the foyer is open only after 12 p.m. when the ticket office opens. (The show-cases on each side of the main entrance were thought at first to be a bad practical joke, but later it turned out that they were meant to be set up there, so they stayed.) The Söröző Restaurant and the Gallery, which does not sell its paintings, are in a style different from the rest of the building. The Vigadó can be rented for balls or receptions.

The building is anything but uniform, the façades at the side are much simpler, and they cleverly hide the fact that the building is not straight but follows the line of the site which slightly breaks at an angle.

Vigadó tér used to be the busiest square in Pest. Before the permanent bridges were built, this was where the pontoon bridge was moored. Once Lánchíd was opened, calm fell on the square.

A rest: Amadeus — Apáczai Csere János utca 13.

THE MARRIOTT HOTEL 17D *V. Apáczai Csere János utca 4.* The hotel was opened in 1969 (designed by József Finta, László Kovácsy). All its 39 suites and 349 rooms overlook the Danube. About a hundred years after the scandal that broke out about the Vigadó, a new one started over this hotel. It is generally held that it is too high, its proportions are different from those of the city; what is more, it turns its back on the capital, looks like a fortress and at least the back, windowless side is, quite simply, ugly. As the comment goes, if you stay at the Marriott, you can't see it.

The lovers of the Duna-korzó would like to drive the noisy Tram 2 underground and have the promenade widened. As this plan would be expensive, there is no sign of it being adopted.

GREEK ORTHODOX CHURCH (ORTHODOX TEMPLOM) 17E
V. Petőfi tér 2. There used to be a large group of Greek merchants in Budapest who initiated much development. They commissioned an architect to build this baroque church (József Jung, 1791–94). Its southern spire was demolished in World War II. Nowadays services are usually conducted in Hungarian, always

17 **A** Luxus Department Store, **B** Gerbaud, **C** Vigadó, **D** The Marriott Hotel, **E** Orthodox Church, **F** Statue of Sándor Petőfi, **G** Contra Aquincum, **H** Péterffy Palace, **I** Faculty of Arts, Eötvös University, **J** Inner City Parish Church, **K** Klotild Palaces, **L** Paris Arcade — Párisi udvar.

accompanied by singing (at 6 p.m. on Saturdays; at 10 a.m. on Sundays and some other times as well on public holidays). The building is open to visitors from Spring to Autumn between 10 a.m. and 5 p.m.

STATUE OF SÁNDOR PETŐFI (PETŐFI-SZOBOR) 17F *V. Petőfi tér.*

The statue is a bit far from the taste of our times (Miklós Izsó, Adolf Huszár, 1882). It shows the poet at the age of 25, reciting his most famous patriotic poem, beginning "Talpra, magyar!" (Rise Hungarians!).

Petőfi (1823-49) started as a poor student and strolling player and soon became the most popular poet of his time, also praised by literary circles. A genius, he was a master of poetic form. He introduced the vernacular into Hungarian verse, acquiring inevitably the title of the Robert Burns of Hungary. His short life was the full life of a man whose love was returned, who had taken part in a victorious revolution and who had become a soldier to fight for his country. He was killed in one of the last battles of the Hungarian War of Independence. After his death the rumour that he was still alive circulated round the country for years and years. Most recently, the rumour was acted upon by a self-made millionaire, who sent a team to Siberia to dig up a grave. The corpse they happened to unearth later proved to be that of a young lady.

He is the first poet Hungarian children study in detail at school. Despite various attempts at translation, he is virtually unknown abroad.

Eighteen different streets and squares are named after Petőfi in the Budapest of today. (The size of the number is due to the creation of Greater Budapest in 1949, enclosing a number of suburbs within Budapest.) There are lots of the other things named after him: a museum, a bridge, an army camp, a radio channel, to mention just a few. His was the portrait on the 10 Forint banknote.

By the way, the self-made millionaire went since then bankrupt, not because he wanted to find the body of Sándor Petőfi, people say.

THE RUINS OF CONTRA AQUINCUM 17G *V. Március 15. tér.* An

open-air museum, showing the remains of the old Roman fortress. The eastern border of the Roman Empire was the line of the Danube, which means that only the Buda side was within the province of Pannonia.

From the end of the 3rd century an outpost was placed in this 84 x 86 metre fortress with walls of 3 metres. The name shows that it was situated opposite the nearby town of Aquincum. Documents mention that Emperor Julian and even Constantin the Great visited this place. There are other and more important Roman remains in a much better preserved environment in the Aquincum Museum, in the IIIrd district. From Springtime to Autumn Contra Aquincum is a popular place for the students of the Faculty of Arts, the building overlooking the square. They call the place the "contrete castrum", or at least they did in my time. Another place frequented by students is the steps by the river between Erzsébet híd and Lánchíd. The popularity is due to their being suntraps and ideal for sunbathing.

FACULTY OF ARTS 17I *V. Pesti Barnabás utca 1.* The university moved

into the building, wich was originally a Catholic monastery and school (Dezső Hültl, 1915-18), in the early fifties. The university is named after

Loránd Eötvös, the famous physicist. It also has a Faculty of Natural Sciences and a Faculty of Law. The real main entrance of the building is not in Pesti Barnabás utca, but through the famous "Gate B" in the narrow passageway between Váci utca and the Danube bank. This area is very busy during term time, from the beginning of February to the middle of May. The corridors on the ground floor and on the first floor are almost totally covered with posters advertising various meetings and amateur performances, university magazines and the university clubs. The most crowded place is the small, smoke-filled canteen on the first floor. It is raided by the students in the breaks during the lectures (usually between 9.30 and 10 or 11.30 and 12) for a cup of coffee or for the notes of a missed lecture. The current word is that the building will most probably be given back to the Pious Fathers, whose *gimnázium* it originally housed.

PÉTERFFY PALACE **17H** *V. Pesti Barnabás utca 2.* The building of the University dwarfs the little house, which looks even smaller as it is below street level. In old Pest which still had the city wall, all the houses had such measurements. (Probably designed by András Mayerhoffer, 1756.) The restaurant situated in the palace is actually much older than its name indicates; it is not 100 but at least 150 years old.

PÁRISI UDVAR **17L** *V. Ferenciek tere 5.* This block was built in 1909 (designed by Henrik Schmal) and the bank which commissioned it opened its offices on the ground floor. (Now used by IBUSZ Travel Agency.) The arcade has recently been enlarged by a new passageway which branches off and opens into Haris köz. The block is worth exploring. If you take the lift between the bookshop and the leatherware shop and go up to the top floor, you can walk over to the other staircase and down the stairs again. The lift used to be in the middle of the staircase. From the windows between the first and the second floor you can look down on the witty roof structure of the yard.

FRANCISCAN CHURCH **18A** *V. Ferenciek tere 2.* The church shows the influence of Italian Baroque and not that of the Austrian version, which resulted in yellow churches with the "radish helmet" towers. After the medieval Franciscan pattern, a separate tower was built near the church at the vestry. There was a Gothic church on the site in the 13th century. The present building was finished in 1758, in the honour of St Peter of Alcantara (1499–1562), who founded a branch of the Franciscan Order. His statue is in the niche in the middle, above the window of the choir. Above the front gate is the crest of the Order: two arms with stigmatic hands, of Jesus and of St Francis of Assisi. On the left-hand wall of the church a large memorial tablet can be seen. This commemorates the catastrophic flood of 1838, when the whole presentday inner city was under water. In some districts 90% of the buildings collapsed. Count Miklós Wesselényi, "the sailor of the flood", portrayed in action, was a hero of the rescue efforts.

KLOTILD PALACES **18C–18C** *V. Szabadsajtó út 5. and 6.* These twin palaces were built at the same time as the original Erzsébet híd. They are almost mirror images of each other (Flóris Korb, Kálmán Giergl, 1902). In the old days, this was one of the most conservative cafés of the city, where

18

A Franciscan Church of Pest,
B "Royal Block of Flats",
C Klotild Palaces, **D** Párisi udvar,
E Faculty of Arts, Eötvös
University, **F** Inner City
Paris Church,
G Elizabeth
Bridge.

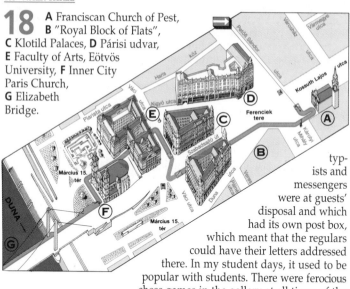

typists and
messengers
were at guests'
disposal and which
had its own post box,
which meant that the regulars
could have their letters addressed
there. In my student days, it used to be
popular with students. There were ferocious
chess games in the gallery at all times of the
day. The students disappeared when an expensive self-service restaurant
opened up. Then a posh, tourist-oriented restaurant-cabaret.

On the other side of the building there is an expensive furniture and fittings shop. Serval dozen such shops have opened in the last few years. It is very difficult to find good modern furniture.

A rest: Osiris Book Club — Veres Pálné utca 4-6.

PHOTOS BY GYÖRGY KLÖSZ *In the subway between the two parts of V. Váci utca.* In the pedestrian subway under the Pest end of Erzsébet híd you can see photos taken by a famous photographer who lived at the end of the last century. The photos were originally taken on 18x24 cm glass negatives. His studio used to be nearby, on the first floor of the first building after the Franciscan church. The photos exhibited in the subway portray the area around Erzsébet híd, before and after the recontructions made necessary by the building of the bridge. It is mostly Klösz's photos that can be found in a recently published illustrated book ("Budapest Anno..."), see the chapter "Reading". The graffiti and the beggars show how far we have come since.

INNER CITY PARISH CHURCH (BELVÁROSI PLÉBÁNIATEMPLOM) 18F

You may remember this church from our *First Walk*. Then we did not pause at the statue on the outer wall of the channel. This is the statue of St Florian, the saint who protects from fires. It was erected in 1723, after the great fires in Pest.

ELIZABETH BRIDGE (ERZSÉBET HÍD) 18G–19A

A suspension bridge, built between 1960 and 1964. (More thoroughly covered in the *First Walk*.) The vertical suspenders of the bridge are not fastened to the cables, only the weight of the bridge keeps them in place.

The beautiful location of Budapest is largely due to a 140-metre-high dolomite rock which descends steeply into the riverbed. The underground part of this rock is 1,000 metres under the surface at Városliget. The western slope is much more gentle. Its area, together with its northern slope, the Tabán, is almost 60 hectares. Naturally, the city tries to protect every single one of the 5,766 trees here. (Some fig trees were planted by the Turks.) According to the legend, the hill was the dwelling-place of witches, who arrived every night riding on the back of a human being, to get their daily wine. Nowadays there is no wine produced here — yet it was once covered in vineyards.

ST GELLÉRT MONUMENT 19C *Facing the Buda end of Erzsébet híd.* The bronze statue surrounded by a colonnade (Gyula Jankovits, 1904) is interesting not so much because of its own qualities but because of its location. St Gellért (or Gerald), the Bishop of Csanád, was pushed from the top of the hill by pagan Hungarians rebelling against Christianity, nailed into a barrel, as the legend goes (or, as most historians say, on a wheelbarrow) in 1046.

It takes 20-25 minutes to climb to the top of the hill. The trees hide the city on the way up so the panorama appears suddenly as you get to the top.

THE CITADEL 19E *On top of Gellért Hill.* The grim stronghold on the top of Gellért-hegy was built after the Revolution of 1848–1849; its military

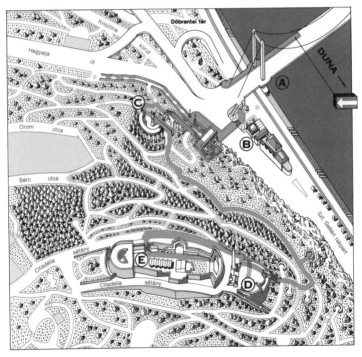

19 A Elizabeth Bridge, **B** Rudas Baths, **C** Statue of St Gellért, **D** Statue of Liberty, **E** Citadel.

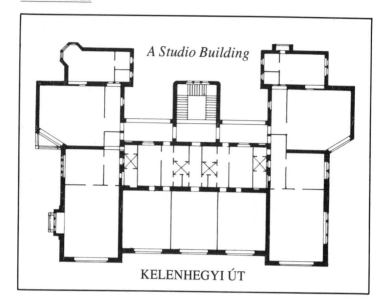

A Studio Building

KELENHEGYI ÚT

purpose was to control Castle Hill. It came into the possession of the capital in 1894, when it was symbolically demolished at some places. There have been plans to set up a Hungarian Pantheon or to make a relief map of Hungary here. It has been a prison camp, temporary accommodation for the homeless, the site of an anti-aircraft battery and finally, since 1961, a tourist attraction.

It is worth walking this far, if for nothing else, than to hire a telescope to look down on the city. On 20th August, Gellért-hegy is the site of the great fireworks display, with the rockets released from various parts of the hill. The 14-metre-tall statue of the woman holding a palm leaf in her hands is the Statue of Liberty, to commemorate liberation from Fascist rule. It has become the symbol of Budapest abroad so it is unlikely to be removed unlike the Red Army soldier in bronze, who used to stand guard at the base… It was erected in 1947 and can be seen from all parts of the city (by Zsigmond Kisfaludi Strobl, allegedly originally designed to commemorate the death of the son of the ultra right inter-war Governor Horthy).

Instead of the usual path leading to the foot of the hill, let me recommend an even more pleasant route, through the villas of the hill. Find Verejték utca, then follow Kelenhegyi út down to the Gellért baths.

A Studio Building *XI. Kelenhegyi út 12-14.* An art nouveau building made of traditional materials in a bold, functional way (Gyula Kosztolányi Kann, 1903). Painters and sculptors live here even today. Its architect is also better known as a painter. Of all his many building designs, few were actually built.

Hotel Gellért and Gellért Baths 20C *XI. Kelenhegyi út 4.* If you follow the route I recommend, you first see the open-air part of the baths which has recently been enlarged. The new part is uncommonly well made; the post-modern softness matches the heavy bulk of the art nouveau building which was completed in 1918 (Ármin Hegedűs, Artúr Sebestyén and Izidor Stark). The open-air swimming-pool stretches over to the other side of Kemenes utca and is connected to the main area through a subway.

"The Gellért Hotel looks like a huge white gem, which, unlike other buildings which get black with time, becomes whiter and whiter", claims a friend of mine, who is also the illustrator of this book. The hotel, together with the baths, was built by the city as part of a conscious policy to make Budapest into a city of baths. If you cannot spare the time to swim, at least walk into the hall through the entrance at the side of the building for the sake of the mosaic floor and the glass ceiling. From the back of the hall you can look into the roofed part of the swimming-pool. Try to slip in — you are supposed to have a swimming-pool ticket. Hotel guests have a separate lift at their disposal to come down to the baths.

The main entrance of the hotel looks onto the Danube. The lobby was rebuilt at the beginning of the 1960s, in the so called "Old Modern" style. Now it is beginning to look elegant in the way that the 1965 Opel Rekord which fascinated me in front of this hotel on an Autumn day, a long time ago. For this was the hotel where we could see all the latest models; for all I know Budapest schoolboys still go there car-spotting.

A rest: Grand Café Gellért — in the hotel

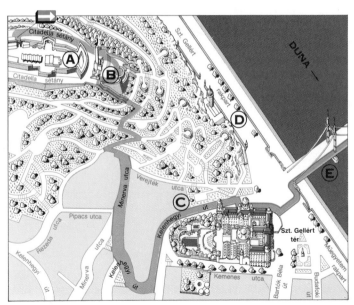

20   **A** Citadel, **B** Statue of Liberty, Rudas Baths, **C** Gellért Baths and the Hotel, Statue of St Gellért, **D** Pauline Monastery, **E** Liberty Bridge.

PAULINE MONASTERY 20D *XI. Szt. Gellért rakpart 1/a.* This is another pseudo-historic building which fits into the surroundings wonderfully. No one would think that it was built as late as 1932! (Károly Weichinger). A grotto chapel belonged to it as well. For forty years it was the student hostel of the Ballet Institution. I am not sure that the students felt at home in here.

The grotto that opens from the balcony nearby has recently been recon-sacrated.

LIBERTY BRIDGE (SZABADSÁG HÍD) 20E–21AF *Linking Gellért tér (Buda) and Fővám tér (Pest).* The third permanent bridge (originally Franz Joseph Bridge) was opened on the occasion of the Millennium celebrations in 1896. It was Franz Joseph himself who hammered in the last silver rivet. Not by hand, naturally: he pushed a button in a tent on the Pest side, which operated the 45 ton hammer. There are very few things around which give a better example of how much the people took pleasure in ornaments. It would be difficult to imagine what the bridge would look like if the designer (Virgil Nagy) did not stick to the following principles: "When designing the bridge, I had to obey the requirements of beauty, simplicity and economy". The bridge has a modular-structure, that is, if its middle were removed, it would still stand firmly (János Feketeházy).

On top of each pillar, standing on a golden ball, is a "Turul bird", the myth-ical bird of the Hungarians, stretching its wings, preparing to take off. Some would-be suicides still climb up here — most of them are rescued by the fire brigade. The famous silver rivet with the F.J. initials was stolen during World War I. So was its replacement. Today the rivet can be seen under a glass sheet. This one is not silver.

UNIVERSITY OF ECONOMIC SCIENCES 21B *IX. Fővám tér 8.* The neo-Renaissance building, originally the Main Customs Building, proved to be a trend-setter (Miklós Ybl, 1870–74), largely influencing construction along Andrássy út. It has housed the institution (formerly called Karl Marx University) since 1951. As a historic building it is protected; when the uni-versity asked to add a floor to the old building, the request was rejected and they were ordered to restore the building. Starting either to the left, or to the right from the main entrance, you come to an inner courtyard, which is now covered with a glass roof, under which there is Karl Marx himself sitting in bronze. A bridge arches over the courtyard, commonly known as the "Bridge of Sighs". The cast iron pillars have preserved the insciption "Ganz und Co. Ofen", the last word being the German name for Buda. It is well worth walking through at the elegant staircases.

Various beams of light break through the windows at the most surprising places.

This university has an especially lively jazz-life; concerts are held not here but in Közgáz Klub.

CENTRAL MARKET HALL (KÖZPONTI VÁSÁRCSARNOK) 21C *XI. Vámház körút 1-3.* At the end of the last century the city had five large, roofed markets all of which were built in a very similar style. All five were opened on the same day; the other four are in Rákóczi tér, Klauzál tér,

Hunyadi tér and in Hold utca. This is the largest of them (designed by Samu Pecz), along the sides of the 150-metre-long hall there are six aisles. The structure, the lighting and the coldstore were very modern in their time and work even today. Formerly, laden barges sailed right into exits; above its opening a notice says: "TUNNEL INTO THE CENTRAL MARKET HALL" (on the quay next to the ill-famed Matróz Csárda Restaurant).

The greatest attraction of the hall is the roof structure, which has resisted the ravages of time better than the plastered wall. Let's walk down from the main entrance to the end of the hall and go up to the galley on the right. This is where florists reign. The large notices warn that they cannot serve retailers. It is amazing how large the space is under the roof.

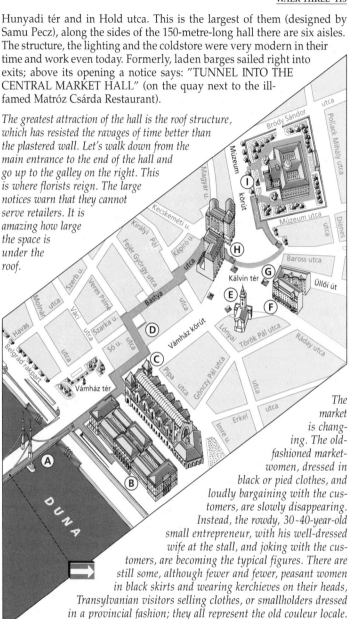

The market is changing. The old-fashioned market-women, dressed in black or pied clothes, and loudly bargaining with the customers, are slowly disappearing. Instead, the rowdy, 30-40-year-old small entrepreneur, with his well-dressed wife at the stall, and joking with the customers, are becoming the typical figures. There are still some, although fewer and fewer, peasant women in black skirts and wearing kerchieves on their heads, Transylvanian visitors selling clothes, or smallholders dressed in a provincial fashion; they all represent the old couleur locale.

21 **A** Liberty Bridge, **B** University of Economic Sciences, **C** Central Market Hall, **D** A part of the Medieval City Walls, **E** Calvinist Church, **F** Former "Two Lions Inn", **G** Headquarters of an Insurance Company, **H** Hotel Korona, **I** National Museum.

A rest: no name Salad Bar on the Gallery of the Market

BURGER KING IN BUTCHER SHOP IN FORMER HOTEL NÁDOR

V. Vámház körút 2. The building took its present form in 1840 and is now a residential block. There are quite a few classicist buildings, even though the others may not have such fine proportions, in the quiet parts of the City, that is in the area between the Danube, the inner boulevard and Kossuth Lajos utca. This area is more or less like the Reform-Age city used to be (before the 1848 Revolution).

On the ground floor, towards Vámház körút, there is a butcher's which has preserved its hundred-year-old, painted tiles. Here you can try the typical lunch of the simple clerks and old age pensioners in the area: have 100 grams of cooked sausage at the counter. Take some mustard or horse-radish and a slice of bread with it. If you want the crust, you have to tell the shop assistant.

A PART OF THE MEDIEVAL CITY WALL OF PEST 21D

V. Bástya utca, corner of Veres Pálné utca. The wall stretched in a semicircle from about the present Vigadó tér to Fővám tér. It was almost 2 kilometres long and a little more than 8 metres high.

A rest: Fatál Restaurant — V. Váci utca 67.

KÁLVIN TÉR AND THE EASTERN CITY GATE

V. Kálvin tér. This square was the site of one of the medieval gates of the city until it was pulled down in 1796. During the war as many as five buildings, the Calvinist church (József Hofrichter, József Hild, 1813–51) and the old Two Lions Inn, open until 1881 (Kálvin tér 9.) survived. You can still see the two lions cowering above the main entrance.

The silhouette of the city gate is hidden by the much-debated new hotel. You can have a look at it in New York-style café/salad bar/community space at the back of the left hand side part. The gate is also recalled by a marble statue suffocating in the subway, at the Kecskeméti utca end. The statue, some people feel, tries to symbolize the birth of the city, or rather a mother's lap. For others, it is an all too convenient public convenience.

A rest: Korona Passage Pancake Bar

NATIONAL MUSEUM (NEMZETI MÚZEUM) 22A

VIII. Múzeum körút 14-16. The largest museum in the country, built between 1837 and 1847, to the plans of Mihály Pollack. At that time this was so far from town that the weekly fair was held in Kálvin tér and some cattle sometimes wandered into the museum. It is almost 8,000 square metres in area, and it has five independent departments: the Archaeological Collection, the Medieval Collection, the Modern Collection, the Numismatics Collection and the Historical Portrait Collection. The slow, painstaking reconstruction gathered momentum in 1994–95, in order to house the new "History of Hungary" permanent exhibition.

It is a must for serious travellers. Despite the high standard of design, the bilingual inscriptions, the occasionally very imaginative multimedia programmes, the exhibition is quite old-fashioned. It makes people feel awe, much less think. Some critics say: it lacks context. But fortunately, hundreds of objects could be restored, and properly and safely exhibited. This exhibition could be made livelier later with programmable audio guides, possibly including minority opinions.

22 **A** National Museum, **B** Eötvös University, **C** University Church, **D** Károlyi Palace, now Museum of Literature, **E** Hotel Astoria, **F** East West Center, **G** Headquarters of the World Alliance of Hungarians, **H** Block of flats, **I** Synagogue.

My absolute favourite is in the long 19th-century room: the full display of all the screws of a factory, lovingly arranged on a large board. Look! We can produce all this!

My other favourite is a hidden part of the Exhibition, in the circular middle room. It is an unwanted memory of the Dark Fifties, when there was a temporary exhibition here, promoting the eternal and never ending (North) Korean-Hungarian Friendship. The decorators could not find a better technique of mounting the hundreds of letters, but to drive them in the stone. Now, despite the hundreds of millions forints invest-

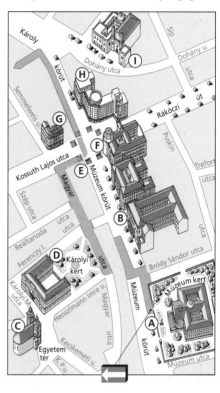

ed, these scars are still there, even the outlines of the letters can be made out. Can you make it out yourself, what I mean?

And one more, on top of all:

You should now return to Room 1, and have a quick look of the brick with an inscriptrion, the one that indicated the tomb of a monk in the 13th century. The insciption:

"What are you staring at me? The way I look now, it's your future fate. You'd rather say a Lord's Prayer".

The complete reconstruction of the National Museum is due to end in 2002, when the institution will have been 200 years old. Currently a request to cover the yard was turned down by the Monument Authority. And nearby Kálvin tér underground could not be rechristened as Kálvin tér — National Museum. No big thing, they thought. It has turned out to be a difficult one.

The museum played an important role on the first day of the 1848 Revolution. On 15th March a huge crowd of demonstrators gathered here to listen to the speeches of "the Youth of March", their leaders. The speakers were standing on the wall left of the stairs while the crowd listened to them, clutching their umbrellas. Not everyone recognized the importance of the day; the director of the museum wrote the following into his diary on that day: "Some noisy mob had their hurlyburly outside which disturbed me in my work so I left for home". To the left on the ground floor are displayed the Crown Jewels of Hungary. They have a particularly spectacular history, having been lost, stolen or misappropriated at various times in history. The crown was made in the early Middle Ages, but is probably totally different from the one which was placed on the head of King St Stephen, the founder of the Hungarian state, in the year 1000. The last king crowned with it was the last Hungarian king, Charles IV of the Habsburgs in 1916.

After World War II it was taken out of the country by escaping Hungarian fascists. Then it was held in the United States for decades until President Carter decided to return the crown to the Hungarian state. Secretary of State Cyrus Vance brought it back to Budapest in 1978, escorted by a large American delegation.

There are more than ten statues in the Museum Garden. There is even a column straight from the Forum Romanum, a donation from Italy in 1930. The garden is locked at 9 p.m.

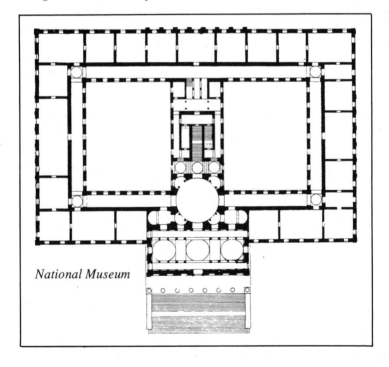

National Museum

director's choice • director's choice • director's choice

DR. FERENC SZIKOSSY, DEPUTY DIRECTOR GENERAL (60)

1. The Hungarian Coronation Regalia — because they are one of Europe's longest used such ensemble — from the end of the 1200s to 1916. (Exhibited in a purposefully built room.) **2.** The Gothic stallum of the St Egidius Church, 1483, with the coat of arms of King Matthias and his wife, Beatrix. The other coats of arms represent the lively foreign relations of Hungary. You can spot the Swedish, Norwegian, Spanish, British, French, and Cypriot coat of arms. (Room 5.) **3.** A tablet to invite people to join the Silversmith's Guild of Brassó, 1556. A miniature tour de force. (Room 7.) **4.** The Liberation of Buda: a wall-carpet, beginning of the 18th century. One of the very few pieces depicting actual historical moments in the history of Hungary. (Room 8.) **5.** Lajos Kossuth's formal Governor's Costume. Following family traditions, I am biassed towards Kossuth. (Room 12.) **6.** A Piece of the Iron Curtain, once operated in Hungary, because it was here that this awful product of captivity first tore apart here in Hungary.

Around Museum Garden are the most beautiful town houses built by the aristocrats of the last century. Some of them can be seen even today, like the one at Ötpacsirta utca 2., which is now the headquarters of the Association of Hungarian Architects, or another building on the corner of Múzeum utca and Pollack Mihály tér in line with the garden. Somewhat left of the latter there is a beautifully restored iron fence, which, however, hardly compensates for the sight of the glass blocks behind it. That is Radio Budapest.

At Múzeum körút 15. is the largest second-hand bookshop in Budapest. It has a wide range of antique books and foreign books. You may be lucky and find some surprising treasures, especially in German. Let's go back a couple of houses and go into No 21. It is a building with a passageway leading right through it and in the courtyard is the old city wall. On the other side there is a garden, Károlyi kert, where 15-20 years ago there used to be concerts in the Summer. People could hire cushions to put them on the uncomfortable chairs. The garden used to belong to a palace which was under reconstruction for years, and when it was ready, the tradition of the concerts was not revived. The streets around were already too noisy for music.

Behind Károlyi kert, Egyetemi templom (University Church) stretches its chubby spires. Since it has been surrounded by larger buildings, its fine proportions cannot be enjoyed. The best place to look at it is perhaps exactly here, at the entrance to the building we have come through. The peculiarity of the church is that its chancel is not directed eastward.

KÁROLYI GARDENS used to belong to an aristocratic family. It became a public park after World War I. It was not as nice as now, there was not even a fence around it. As I attended a nearby elementary school, we often came to play here. Watching the chess players and the pigeons, playing all kinds of games. It happened here, mid-April 1966, when I was beaten up for the first (and last time) because of a girl. It was a much smaller boy. And a much stronger one. I did not weep on the spot, just round the corner.

(By the way, I was beaten up two other times, but not any more because of a girl, or a woman...)

THE BACK YARD OF THE SCHOOL OF THE AUTHOR *Ferenczy István utca, the back of V. Reáltanoda utca 9.* When I was going to that school, there were no cars parking in the back yard. None of the teachers had a car. We had endless long jump practices there. The favourite quip of the old PE teacher, called Yousouf, who led generations of students to victory in high-school championships (in basketball, not long jump, and not with me) was: "My son, it is not worth running neither after a bus nor a woman: the next is coming soon."

KÁROLYI PALACE: FUTURE HOME OF THE HOUSE OF HUNGARIAN LITERATURE *V. Károlyi Mihály utca 16.* Count Mihály Károlyi lived here, before he had to emigrate for the first time in 1919. It was confiscated from him for his alleged high treason. He became ambassador of Hungary to France after WWII, but resigned when the totalitarian craze became evident in 1949. Now it houses the Petőfi Museum of Literature, and stores of some other museums. It will undergo a thorough renovation by 2000 and all kinds of literary associations, among them the most powerful Hungarian Writers' Union will move here. Also, there will be a café and a bookshop, and a state of the art library.

A rest: Café Talk Talk — Magyar utca 12-14.

HOTEL ASTORIA 22E *V. Kossuth Lajos utca 19.* This busy crossroads of the city has taken its name from the hotel which was built with an old fashioned touch (Emil Ágoston, Artúr Hikisch, 1912–14). The lobby of the hotel is luxuriously elegant. Before reconstruction the Café looked the same.

Astoria divides the inner boulveard road, Kiskörút, into two halves, which means that if you look towards the City, you will get to the Danube, no matter which direction you start walking, to the left, to the right or forward. The busy thoroughfare leading out of the City is Rákóczi út, which is a shopping street and ends where you can see the yellow façade of Keleti Railway Station in the distance. At Astoria, on one of the corners there used to be a large empty site: only one half of a large plan for a new complex has been completed (VII. Rákóczi út 4.: Béla Barát, Ede Novák, 1935; Rákóczi út 1.: Dezső Hültl, 1940). The war did not allow time and energy to finish the second half. The recent development doesn't really fit the environment — it's far too big and obtrusive, though it tries to echo the block opposite (Lajos Zalaváry, 1991).

This is where the National Theatre was once located — pulled down in 1908. The Astoria metro station on the Second (Red) Line is accessible from the subway although access is becoming more and more difficult. The way is often blocked by vendors. The people wearing their folk costumes are from Transylvania, they are Hungarians living in parts that have become Romania, who sell things they have brought from their villages. The men can easily be recognized by their straw hats, blue broadcloth jackets and black boots.

BROADWAY CINEMA *VII. Tanács körút 3.* This is the former cinema of the Institute of Cinematography, primarily showing old films and serious films, although sometimes box-office successes are not neglected. There are

23 **A** Headquarters of the World Alliance of Hungarians (former House of "Soviet Culture and Science"), **B** Block of flats, **C** Great Synagogue, **D** Pest Country Hall, **E** Former Design Center, **F** Budapest City Hall, former hospital for aged soldiers, **G** Main Post Office, **H** Servite Church, **I** Parking block, **J** Lutheran Church, **K** Blocks of flats, the beginning of a never completed avenue.

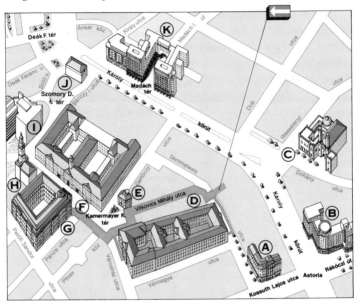

6-8 films on at the same time, not only those which are advertised on the façade, in a complicated but logical order. Above the ticket office a display shows when and for which films you can get tickets. If the light is on, the tickets for that performance are still available. Unfortunately it does not compare with the Cinemathéque in Paris or the N:F:T: in London in range of programming.

THE GREAT SYNAGOGUE 23C *VII. Dohány utca 2-8.* This is one of the largest synagogues in Europe (Ludwig Förster, 1844–59). The two onion-shaped domes are 43 metres high. Above the main entrance the Hebrew line reads: "Make me a sanctuary and I will dwell among them" (Exodus 25,8).

The building, which has three naves and a flat ceiling, holds almost 3,000 worshippers: 1497 men on the ground floor and 1472 women in the gallery. The nave in the middle was built with a 12-metre cast iron piece spanning the distance. Ferenc Liszt and Saint-Saens played the famous organ on several occasions.

The synagogue was originally built in an enclosed area. One of the buildings in the compound was the birthplace of Theodor Herzl, writer and journalist, who founded the Zionist movement (memorial tablet in the staircase of the corner building).

The arcade and the Heroes' Temple, which accommodates 250 people and is used for religious services on weekdays, were built when the building was enlarged (László Vágó, Ferenc Faragó, 1931). Outside hours of worship, the synagogue is open for visitors between 10 a.m. and 6 p.m. (3.30 p.m. in Winter) on weekdays.

The Holocaust Memorial in the back garden (Imre Varga, 1989) is directly over the mass graves dug during the 1944–45 Hungarian Fascist period. On every leaf there is the name of a martyr.

In 1944, after the Nazi occupation of Hungary, Budapest Jews were forced to move into a ghetto (they had never lived in one before) as a preparation to deportation. That finally — miraculously — didn't happen. But many died because

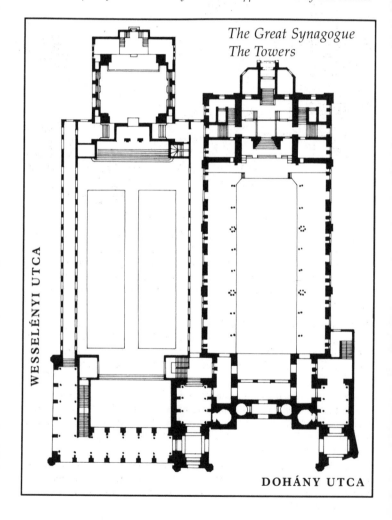

The Great Synagogue
The Towers

WESSELÉNYI UTCA

DOHÁNY UTCA

*of ill health, starvation and random murders. The pre-war percentage of 5%
dwindled to 0.5% of the country's population after the war. Practically all of
them live in Budapest.*

A rest: Fausto's — Dohány utca 5.

RÖSER BAZAAR *V. Tanács körút 22.* In Farsi the word "bazaar" means
marketplace, a broad street. In Budapest, it is usually a building with a
passageway full of shops and workshops. They have recently begun to
come to life again.

COUNTY HALL (PEST MEGYEI KÖZGYŰLÉS) 23D *V. Városház utca 7.*
If you follow the route in this book, you can go into the Country Hall from
the back, between 6 a.m. and 5 p.m. on a workday. You should pretend
that you belong here — then you are not stopped. The three-part building
was completed in 1811, 1832 and 1841. In this surprising oasis was also the
country prison and the prisoners'chapel. If you find the near gate locked,
walk round the building from the right, via Vitkovics Mihály utca.

A rest: Galleria Drink — Vitkovics Mihály utca 6.

BUDAPEST CITY HALL (POLGÁRMESTERI HIVATAL) 23F *V. Városház
utca 9-11.* The construction of the building started in 1711 and it was intended to be a home for disabled soldiers and to have an area of 189×189
metres. In the end only the eastern wing was built by 1747 (by Anton
Erhard Martinelli, Court Architect) and gave home to two thousand soldiers. Maria Theresa found it more beautiful than her own palace in
Vienna. The rest of the building was never built, simply because permission was not given to break through the city wall. Later it became the
Károly Army Barracks, and it has been the Town Hall since 1894. There
are 47 windows in each row of the façade. The statues above the main
entrance have been freshly sculpted.

MERLIN THEATRE AND CLUB *(Entrance from V. Gerlóczy utca 4.)*
Originally it was conceived by City Hall masterminds as a drama school
round the year and an English speaking theatre in the Summer, the profits from the latter activities spent on the drama school... Then the two
founders quarrelled, it was only the drama school that remained. And a
very lively egghead hangout, a club and a restaurant, with sophisticated
video equipment to follow things from all the tables simultaneously.

Actor/director/teacher/fundraiser Tamás Jordán, originally trained as an
engineer, then spending almost two decades as the ever better star of a
successful country theatre in Kaposvár, came to Budapest less than ten
years ago. It is his radiating personality that lures people here, his fun and
amiable personality. Until quite recently you could listen to his breathtaking one man show: "The Apology of Socrates" by Platon.

There are plays in English occasionally, but rarely the lighthearted, funny
entertainment tourists or even travellers might be hooked on.

MAIN POST OFFICE 23G, 24A *V. Városház utca 13-15. Back door
V. Városház utca 18.* This is the building which blocks the view of the Town
Hall (Antal Skalniczky, 1875). Let's walk through the building on the ground

24 A Main Post Office, **B** Hotel Taverna, **C** Fontana Department Store, **D** McDonald's, **E** Hotel Marriott, **F** Vigadó, **G** Gerbaud, **H** Luxus Department Store, **I** Office block, **J** Parking block, **K** Servite Church, **L** Budapest City Hall, **M** Lutheran Church.

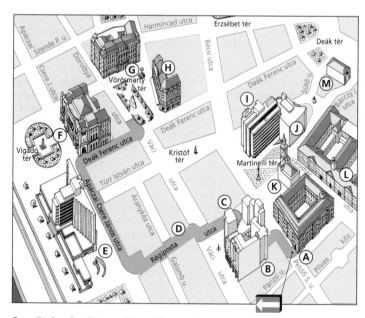

floor. Right after I entered I could count four types of marble and six types of painted marble at the foot of the stairs. This is where the Poste Restante letters are held. Since the post office bought a Japanese lettersorting machine a few years ago, non-standard envelopes need stamps of double value.

A BLOCK OF FLATS FROM THE EARLY FORTIES *V. Párisi utca 6.* Only a few inhabitants of the city raise their heads to inspect the vivid, elegant façade of this building from Párisi utca. It was built in the middle of the war (Gedeon Gerlóczy, 1942–44).

HOTEL TAVERNA 24B *V. Váci utca 20.* We have seen its front façade on the First Walk. Now let's walk just as far as the crossing in the inner yard, and there, at the small clock tower, we turn right. On the four sides of the tower, four marvellously fusible small statues show the pleasures of relaxation (Géza Stremeny, 1985).

A ROW OF LAMPS *V. Régiposta utca 10., between ground floor and first floor.* Art nouveau neglected the cult of lions in Pest, these lamps are a rare exception. Rescue teams have been organized to save and repair the old lamps. In Váci utca there are too many of them — too much antiquarianism is as bad as none.

A rest: Pierrot in Pest — Aranykéz utca 2.

ARANYKÉZ UTCA 2. *The corner of V. Régiposta utca.* The bold imagination of the design had the Vigadó in mind (Miklós and Ernő Román, 1930). The ground floor is occupied by offices, the lift starts from the level of the mezzanine. The City Protection Association has a separate group which specializes in lifts, attempting to save as many old lifts as possible.

Apáczai Csere János utca was on the river before the building of the quay; now it is overshadowed by the back of the Marriott Hotel. The street is homogeneous, all Classicist buildings, all built with taste and all have their own surprises. At No 3. there is a half-naked beauty in marble, musing in the staircase, trying to hide one of her breasts behind a colourful and inadequate bunch of flowers. (Her name is Persephoneia.) At No 5. there are some exceptionally pretty iron gratings, wooden and stone ornaments protecting the corners of the building. Into No 7. a building company has moved in. Behind the gate the surprise is another door and some fine statuary.

This walk took me four and a half hours and that was without going into the National Museum. I collapsed on the terrace of Dunacorsó. This café existed at the time of the old Promenade. Then I went to the Hyatt hotel to inspect the airplane. I would have liked to go to the top floor by lift, but this is now only usable by those staying at the hotel. Even the cheapest room's price seemed to be too much for a ride in a lift.

WALK FOUR

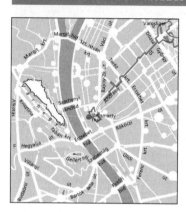

Andrássy út and Városliget follows "Radial Avenue" at first. We shall look into two apartments here. We will take a bird's-eye view of Városliget and if you wish, you can row on the lake (or skate in Wintertime). We shall visit a castle which is not part of the Amusement Park and we return by the underground built for the Great Exhibition. Time: approximatchy 5 hours.

"MERINO" TEXTILE SHOP *V. Petőfi Sándor utca 20.* The older generation simply call it "Brammer's". Ödön Brammer, the textile merchant built the shop in 1924, when he had to move from a shop which he had been running successfully for years. His materials with their red, white and green labels were to be found in most large department stores in Western Europe at the beginning of the century. The English mahogany decoration of the shop is under a preservation order which means that not even a nail can be hammered into the walls. During the decades the shop was owned by the state, the restorer wished to emphasize this by adding the state coat of arms in several dozen places on the old plaster decoration on the ceiling.

FORMER TÖRÖK BANK BUILDING *V. Martinelli tér 3.* The façade is an architectural battle field between art nouveau and modernism (designed by Ármin Hegedűs, Henrik Bőhm, 1906). This building is typical of the City, the first two or three floors are occupied by offices and above these are flats. The title of the large glass mosaic is "The Apotheosis of Hungaria". The modern elements seem to dominate now, perhaps because the astonishingly heavy Atlas statue, which used to crown the building, has been removed. Unfortunately the bank's owner was not a relative of mine.

RÓZSAVÖLGYI HOUSE *V. Martinelli tér 5.* The building was commissioned by a tailor's (Béla Lajta, 1912). "In Hungary the buildings... speak French, German, Spanish, English but not Hungarian", wrote the designer of the building. Few were able to find such a modern way of speaking Hungarian! The building takes its name from the music shop, established 1850, which is still there. The original interior was destroyed by fire on August 14, 1961, as a note mentions, placed almost invisibly high, only in Hungarian. They have a marvellous range of scores and old records.

The new buildings in the square unfortunately are out of place with the old. A government building and a multi-storey car-park, which criminally make the square smaller, and the telephone exchange, clashing with the church, were all built in the 1970s.

I̶N̶ M̶EMORIAM C̶AFÉ Q̶UINT *V. Bárczi István utca 1.* Behind the modest sign and the shopwindow there used to be a uniquely preserved interior. It was probably from the end of the 1950s, which did not differ largely from the style of pre-war Budapest. You could drink one of the best coffees in Pest here, which was made with the antique instruments displayed on the counter. Even the waitresses were conservative in their dress and manners. The caricatures on the wall commemorated the fencing victories of the proprietor, Mr. Kovács, world and Olympic champion in sword. In the middle there were plastic boxes with transparent lids — good cookies in boxes you were sold spare parts for sewing machines. The champion died soon after the shop was sold. Luckily, he didn't see what was coming.

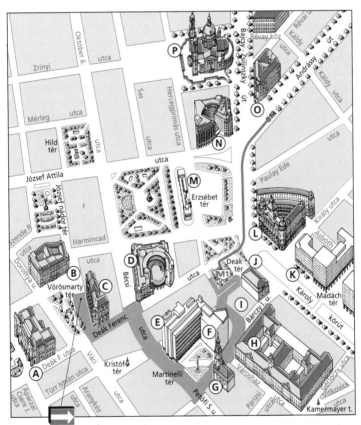

25 **A** Vigadó, **B** Gerbaud, **C** Luxus Department Store, **D** Grand Hotel Corvinus Kempinski, **E** Office block, **F** Parking block, **G** Servite Church, **H** Budapest City Hall, **I** Lutheran Museum, **J** Lutheran Church, **K** Block of flats, **L** "Anker" palace, former Insurance Company, **M** Coach station, the youngest of Hungary's architectural monuments (1949), **N** Trade Center, **O** Office block, **P** St Stephen's Church.

Stop here for a moment to think about vanishing Budapest. Inside there is one of the naffest interior — with soulless service. The Champion died not long after he had sold the shop.

There are not as many types of coffee in Budapest as in Vienna; people simply ask for "kávé", "fekete" or "dupla", which all refer to exactly the same: black espresso coffee. (The word "dupla" has survived from about twenty years ago, when "szimpla", a smaller portion, still existed.) For a cup of strong, Italian espresso-type coffee about 6 grams of pure ground coffee is used, and people drink it with or without sugar, milk, cream or whipped cream. In lager cafés you can order two different types of white coffee: one is made of real black coffee, the other from coffee substitute. Decaffeinated coffee is on the rise, especially in hotels. Most Hungarians still find it as an affectation. We live only once, they think, and then Hungarians don't live very long. Best coffee these days is to be found in the tiny shops of the COQUAN'S chain in Nádor utca or Ráday utca, for instance.

LUTHERAN CHURCH AND MUSEUM 25I, 25J *V. Deák Ferenc tér 4.*

A memorial tablet says "Sándor Petőfi, the romantic poet was educated here." The church attracts attention with its unornamented, spireless dignity. I remember there was a rather gigantic bust of Luther in the tiny courtyard, standing there as if it had grown out of the ground. It is not here any more. I went into the Lutheran Museum to ask about it. In the classrooms of the former school a touching exhibition has been arranged. Old clergymen, now pensioners, show visitors around and answer question (in German as well). When examining one of the treasures of the collection, an altar-cloth from 1650, I had two questions put to me. Why do the disciples have red noses in the embroidered cloth and which of the disciples is missing?

The church (Mihály Pollack, 1799–1808), did have a spire originally but this had to be pulled down, when the roof structure, which, out of necessity, had been built of cheap material, could no longer bear it. The inside of the church is amazingly simple, even by Lutheran standards. The choir was built only to diminish the echo. It is open only at times of religous services. The church is a vivid musical centre and the events are advertised on the front gate.

The Luther-statue, I learned, had been left unfinished because of the war. Recently it was finished and set up in front of the Theological Academy, in the XIVth district.

UNDERGROUND RAILWAY MUSEUM *In the subway at Deák tér.* When building the Metro station, a short section of the first line became redundant. Some old carriages are exhibited here beside the old platform — and that is the whole museum. A tablet near the entrance in four languages gives a short history of the "Franz Joseph Underground Railway", which was opened in 1896. There are more than the usual number of mistakes in the English version. If you walk to the end of the museum, it is there that the story really begins. The little museum has preserved the smell of the old line as well. Unfortunately, you cannot go into the old carriages. (I've seen rare exceptions made, however.) Entry into the museum is with a tram ticket.

After the museum, let'go one stop by the underground, which is now the First (Yellow) Metro Line (or, as people refer to it, the little Metro), in the direction of Mexikói út.

When you come up out of the station, you can see Andrássy út, originally Sugárút, or "Radial Avenue" in front of you, a masterpiece of the bold city planning of the last century. It was finished in 1885 and took 14 years to build in the course of which 219 houses, mostly one-storey, had to be demolished. Although few of the individual buildings stand out from homogeneous impression, it is one of the finest streets in the eclectic style in Europe. Not that everyone shares this opinion: an American guidebook claims that the buildings of the road are "an architectural hodgepodge, although most of them are described as neo-Classical". I would call it neo-Renaissance (or eclectic), and not neo-Classic, which is called Classicist in Hungary.

The city was so anxious to preserve the character of its beloved Sugárút that no form of public transport was allowed to ruin it. They did permit an underground line of 3 kilometres to be built underneath between 1894 and 1896. This was the second underground railway in Europe, after the London tube. The terminus at the far end was not where it is now: it was originally in Városliget, above ground. Long ago at the entrances to the stations there was a light on the street showing when a train was coming.

The name changes of Andrássy út are instructive: Sugár (Radial), Andrássy (after the 19th-century statesman), Stalin (after the wise father of the world's proletariat), Hungarian Youth (in the days of the Revolution of 56), and Népköztársaság (People's Republic, 1957-89) and, now again Andrássy — the name that real Budapesters nevers stopped using.

AN UPPER-UPPER MIDDLE CLASS APARTMENT — THE POSTAL MUSEUM *VI. Andrássy út 3. First floor.* The building used to be a residential block (Győző Czigler, 1886), and is typical of the more decorative buildings on Sugárút. There are frescoes on the staircase (Károly Lotz).

The Postal Museum is in what used to be the owner's seven-room private apartment. His initials: A.S.(Andreas Saxlehner), can be seen all over the flat and the house. Apart from the portable furniture, everything is intact; the bath tub has only recently been sent to another museum.

The individual items of the collection can be put into operation by the attendants. You can see a section of a pneumatic exchange. From the window can be seen the dome of the Basilica from another angle.

DUTCH INSURANCE COMPANY HEADQUARTERS (HOLLAND BIZTOSÍTÓ SZÉKHÁZA) **26B** *VI. Andrássy út 9.* The unusual outcome of the recent renovation cannot be seen from street level. As if the Lord Almighty had dropped a huge drop on the roof, to make room for the Board of Directors. You can walk up, and look up, at the covered courtyard. The basement is painted black: a sort of Hades.

The block behind was pulled down, and an entirely new buiding was erected.

By the way, I was called by the firm at least four times, very aggressively. But considering the new construction, this technique must work with certain people.

ÚJ SZÍNHÁZ (NEW THEATRE) *VI. Paulay Ede utca 35.* The fin-de-siècle cabaret has been modernized a couple of times since it opened in 1909. (Designed by Béla Lajta.) During a recent facelift, the façade was restored in an exemplary way. (By Kőnig & Wagner Associates, Budapest, 1990.) As the designer told at a press conference, the restoration of the façade cost only 1/75 of the total budget. The foyer is somewhat controversial, reminding some of

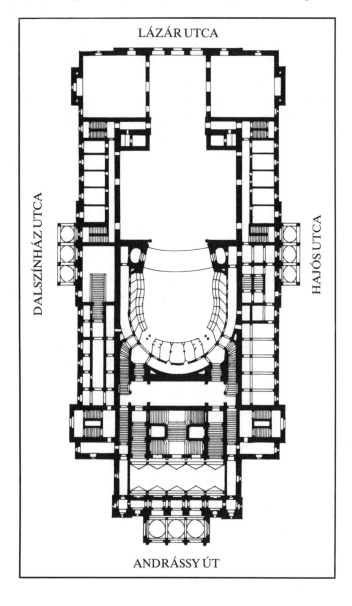

LÁZÁR UTCA

DALSZÍNHÁZ UTCA

HAJÓS UTCA

ANDRÁSSY ÚT

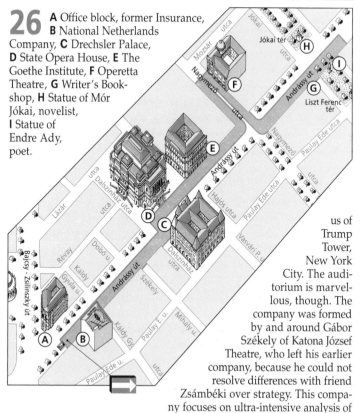

26 **A** Office block, former Insurance, **B** National Netherlands Company, **C** Drechsler Palace, **D** State Opera House, **E** The Goethe Institute, **F** Operetta Theatre, **G** Writer's Bookshop, **H** Statue of Mór Jókai, novelist, **I** Statue of Endre Ady, poet.

us of Trump Tower, New York City. The auditorium is marvellous, though. The company was formed by and around Gábor Székely of Katona József Theatre, who left his earlier company, because he could not resolve differences with friend Zsámbéki over strategy. This company focuses on ultra-intensive analysis of characters, situations. Kleist, Lorca, Shakespeare, Chekhov were their authors during the first two seasons. They are also notorious for painstaking stage designs.

A rest: Picasso Point — Hajós utca 31.

STATE OPERA HOUSE 26D *VI. Andrássy út 22.* This is the most important building on this walk and, one of the most important buildings in the history of Hungarian architecture (Miklós Ybl, 1884). Work on the building lasted 9 years; the architect, who also directed the construction work, is said to have checked every cartload of bricks.

The huge building, perhaps because of the nature of its character, does not look that large at all, except perhaps when viewed from Gellért-hegy. On the right there is the stage-door, on the left the carriage-way and entrance to the Royal Staircase. The auditorium sits 1,289 people. It is decorated by hundreds of statues and paintings both inside and out. It was lovingly restored in the 1980s.

In the niche to the right of the carriage-way a statue of Ferenc Liszt, to the left one of Ferenc Erkel, the father of Hungarian opera. In the niches at the corner of the building at the first-floor level are statues of the muses of opera: Terpsichore, Erato, Thalia and Melpomene.

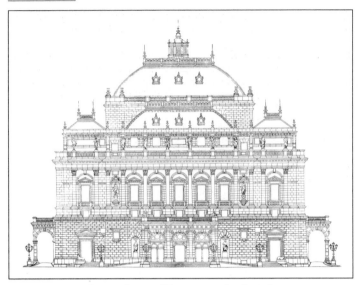

State Opera House — the façade

On the stone cornice of the terrace above the second-floor level are the statues of (from left to right) Monteverdi, Alessandro Scarlatti, Gluck, Mozart, Beethoven (on the left); Rossini, Donizetti, Glinka, Wagner, Verdi, Gounod, Bizet (in the middle); Moussorgsky, Tchaikovsky, Moniuszko and Smetana (on the right).

The Opera House quickly became one of the leading musical centres of Europe. Gustav Mahler was the director here for three season and personally staged two Puccini operas. (After the first night of Madame Butterfly, the composer made drastic cuts in the score on this friends' advice.) After World War II, Otto Klemperer was director of the company for a short time. At present they have a repertoire of about 90 operas, a number unique in the world. The Erkel Theatre, seating 2,400 people, also belongs to the Opera.

The box-office is on the left-hand side of the building and is open between 10 a.m. and 7 p.m. from Tuesday to Saturday (lunchbreak between 2 and 2.30 p.m.) and between 10 a.m. and 1 p.m. on Sunday. The decoration around the office is in harmony with the building. The brass bars are intended to ensure civilized queuing. Some tickets are usually available on the day of the performance, although these are for the worst seats. When I last went to buy a ticket on a November morning I had no difficulty in getting one for the same evening. However, stamped on the ticket was: "Warning! The stage cannot be seen from this seat".

Seats like that (all in the upper circle) are accessible from a separate staircase, through a side entrance. In fact I could not see anything of the stage although I could hear everything perfectly. I was sitting quite close to the fresco on the ceiling showing Olympus and all the Greek gods (by Károly Lotz) and closer still to the stalls. You can usually go down and take one of these seats in the interval.

There is an Opera Shop to the right of the main entrance, with very good books, collectibles & CDs. You can collect what you have bought after the performance.

DRECHSLER HOUSE 26C *VI. Andrássy út 25.* The apartment block opposite the Opera House took its name from a large café which used to occupy the ground floor (Ödön Lechner, Gyula Pártos, 1882). Six successive owners went bankrupt or committed suicide; this is not necessarily the reason why the café disappeared.

Now the building houses the State Ballet Institute, whose students are on the move in and out at all times of the day. You can walk through the inner courtyard of the building which has an enchanting atmosphere (in Wintertime only one of the gates is open). The graffiti indicates the time of the last renovation: BREAK.

GOETHE INSTITUTE 26E *VI. Andrássy út 24.* As a plaque at the gate commemorates, here, to the right of the gate used to be the Café Three Ravens (Három holló), where that genius of early twentieth-century poetry, Endre Ady spent many a night. The Hungarian government offered the premises for a Romanian Cultural Centre to be opened on the same day, when a Hungarian one opened in Bucharest. But all that was kept in secret. This did not happen for 15 years. Meanwhile, the ground floor was vacant. Then Goethe Institute bought the space and launched their attractive programmes. An Internet café was planned to open soon, when this book went to press.

MŰVÉSZ CONFECTIONER'S *VI. Andrássy út 29.* It opens early in the morning, at 8 (10 on Saturday). This intimate middle-class place is rather noisy early on because of the staff but later their chatter is overcome by the hum of the customers. I like sitting in the inner room, left of the marble lady, who has an intense charm from the front. At around 9 a table would form of old show-business hands. At around 10 a very old, solitary man arrives and sits at his "törzsasztal" (regular customer's reserved table), in the right corner. He is the doyen of men of letters, a prolific author of dozens of historical novels. He has got an ancient, wooden coathanger in the self-service cloakroom, with the initials E.J. on it. Don't use it.

Fresh pastry arrives around half past eight. I usually order a white coffee, a French brioche and the chandelier. They are reluctant to turn on the chandelier in the middle. Closed on Sundays.

Andrássy út is cut in half by a market place, which used to be at Nagymező utca. The part which is now to the left of the road is nicknamed the Broadway of Pest. It has three theatres, a nightclub and the famous former Arizona nightclub, hence the name of the theatre next door. The short section to the right has a theatre, a cinema, an exhibition hall and a "little green house", an old public lavatory.

A con-man at the end of the century one morning started taking measurements at the upper end of Váci utca, attracting a great deal of attention. Finally a shopkeeper came out of his shop and asked him what he was doing. He replied that he was going to put up a "green house" there. The shopkeeper gave him some money to build it ten metres down the street, away from his door. There another shopkeeper came out and the whole story started all over again...

A VERY NAFF INTERIOR INDEED *VI. Andrássy út 37.* "Alles was gut und teuer": (everything that is good and expensive) as the ironic Budapest saying goes. Marble and mirrors all over the Corinthian columns, a standard telephone and four monitors on the walls, with the MTV programme on three. Remarkably ostentatious: singular in Budapest.

The cakes are outstanding, despite the heavy hand with the sugar. Service is attentive and quick. For the sake of American readers: "naff" in British English means something like "tacky". In Hungarian:"ciki". A word that spread like prairie fire in the seventies.

DIVATCSARNOK DEPARTMENT STORE *Andrássy út 29.* This seven-storey building, housing the old Parisian Department Store, opened its doors in 1911. Before there had been a casino on the site. The architect succeeded in persuading the commissioner to preserve the large ball room, which is now called "Lotz terem" (Lotz Hall) and can be seen at the back of the department store between the first and the second floors. Sales and Christmas toy sales are held there. The roof garden, however, can no longer be visited, which is a pity since a splendid view is to be had from there. Now there is nothing to recall the slogan that appeared on handbills the year the department store was opened: "The oldest European-standard department store in the country".

At the crossing of Andrássy út and the Nagykörút, the buildings form an octagonal square, hence its name, Oktogon, used during all those 40-odd years when the signs showed "November 7 Square". There is an old café in the square, rebuilt in appalling taste, a shop where you buy various drinks, a Burger King shop (the biggest in the world) which is one of the most refreshing modern spaces in town today — it would make a perfect Amsterdam-style "grand café".

At this point the road widens and makes room for four rows of trees. Between the trees, where there is now a pavement, used to be a track for horse-riding. The

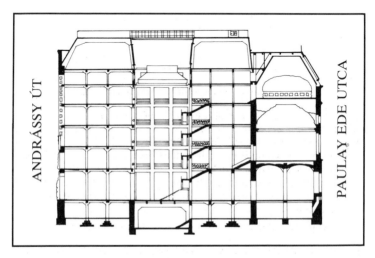

Divatcsarnok Department Store

27 A Statue of Mór Jókai,
B Statue of Endre Ady,
C An unattractive Café,
D A stamp shop,
E Ferenc Liszt Memorial
Museum, F Academy
of Fine Arts,
G Lukács
Confec-
tioner's.

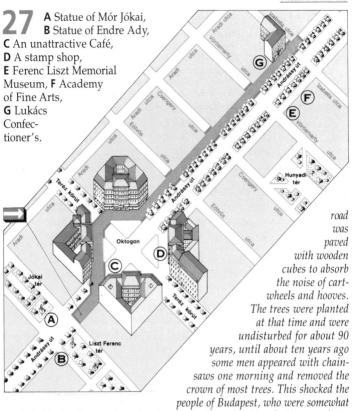

*road
was
paved
with wooden
cubes to absorb
the noise of cart-
wheels and hooves.
The trees were planted
at that time and were
undisturbed for about 90
years, until about ten years ago
some men appeared with chain-
saws one morning and removed the
crown of most trees. This shocked the
people of Budapest, who were somewhat
comforted by the Parks and Gardens Department's explanation that it was a choice
between pruning the trees or watching them die. But that didn't prove to be
enough. Most of the trees had to be replaced since then. The new-old, recast lamps
have recently been set up, entirely from donations. The big ones cost 150,000, the
small ones 45,000 forints. (About 3000 and 9000 dollars, respectively.) A small
plaque commemorates the donors' name — mostly corporate ones.*

A rest: Falafel Faloda upstairs — Paulay Ede utca 53.

THE FORMER SECRET POLICE BUILDING *Andrássy út 60.* This is
where the secret police of the ultra-right wing inter-war regime operated.
Many left-wing activists and Communists were detained, beaten and tortured here. After World War II, during the Communist "dark fifties", their
secret police kept on using that headquarters. Many left-wing activists and
Communists were detained and tortured here. Some of those who had
already been there. They were "persuaded" by the same equipment,
inherited from the previous regime...

Some people would like to turn it into a museum of Stalinism.

FERENC LISZT MUSEUM AND MEMORIAL BUILDING 27E *VI. Vörösmarty utca 35.* It is only in our time that Ferenc Liszt became acknowl-

edged as a composer although he always had a cult in Hungary and, although he did not speak the language, he always declared himself to be Hungarian. His concerts at home were always great events. After his years in Paris, Weimar and Rome, he settled in Pest in 1875, partly because he wanted to found a Hungarian Royal Academy of Music in his own house. He moved into this building in 1879, into the first floor where the museum is situated. In the hall you can see the copper plate which was on the door of one of his apartments. The inscription says in Hungarian and in German: "Ferenc Liszt is at home between 3 and 4 p.m. on Tuesdays, Thursdays and Saturdays". Visiting hours are now longer: between 10 a.m. and 6 p.m. from Monday to Friday and between 9 a.m. and 5 p.m. on Saturdays. In the flat most of the original pieces. There are many portraits, beautifully decorated rare musical instruments, even his travelling keyboard and his glass piano. Andrássy út can be viewed from the window.

At the entrance Liszt records and various editions related to the composer can be bought. There are several small concert and rehearsal halls in the building and the sound of rehearsals can usually be heard. The building resounds with music. Through a window on the ground floor you can peep into a wind instrument workshop where the instruments of music students are repaired.

THE OLD EXHIBITION HALL (KÉPZŐMŰVÉSZETI FŐISKOLA) *VI. Andrássy út 69*. This building, which was erected by public subscription, tries to summarize all the architectural delicatess (Adolf Lang,

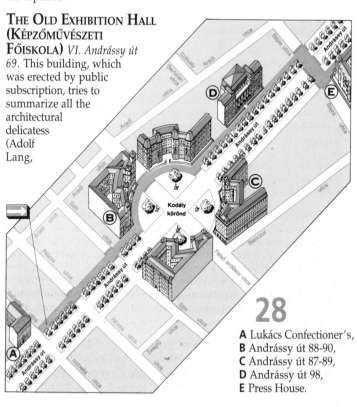

28

A Lukács Confectioner's,
B Andrássy út 88-90,
C Andrássy út 87-89,
D Andrássy út 98,
E Press House.

1877). Now it houses the offices of the College of Fine Arts, and has recently started to organize exhibitions again. Everything inside, even the ceiling, is of painted and genuine marble. In the basement the State Puppet Theatre gives performances.

CAFÉ LUKÁCS AND CIB BANK HEADQUARTERS 27G *VI. Andrássy út 70.*

The imaginative conversion of the building put an end to a decade of stagnation in the life of this nicest of the few grand cafés. It once belonged to the Lukács family. It was confiscated in 1949 and closed to the public — it became the cafeteria of the secret police.

When I was a student, you could choose between the Baroque splendour upstairs and the elegance of the 1930s on the ground floor. Service was considerably slower upstairs but one could admire the naked porcelain lady combing her hair on the marble fireplace. You can still buy a copy in most large souvenir shops, in different sizes.

The down floor used to have some furniture, in the corridor, leading to the service area, that evoked the times of Jean Cocteau. This is all gone now. But there is new life. The times they-are-a-changing... we were singing with Bob Dylan, when I was twenty. But changes then in Hungary did not change at all. Now they do, with Chicago pace, again, at this second exuberant fin-de-siècle of Budapest. The new café is a typical showcase.

Kodály körönd is one of the finest circuses of the city. It is enclosed by four town houses which used to be rented out and which by their shape form the circle that gives the circus (körönd) its name. Of the four, architectural experts usually prefer the one at No. 88-90; my favourite is No. 87-89, perhaps because of its rambling turret-rooms. In one of these rooms is the studio of Jenő Barcsay, the recently deceased master of modern Hungarian painting. In the same block, where the composer used to live, there is a Kodály Zoltán Museum now.

Further along from the Kodály körönd, the road becomes even more airy. The houses are further apart, hiding behind front gardens. After a while a row of detached villas line the road. Unfortunately, after the last war, permission was given to build four modern buildings on this part of the road. Two of them are especially out of place and of the road. Two of them are especially out of place and of strikingly inferior quality.

HUNGARIAN PRESS BUILDING 28E *VI. Andrássy út 101.* The plans for this building are missing from the archives, all we know about this fine example of an art nouveau villa is that it was built sometime between 1900 and 1903 for the "Timber-king of Szolnok" (a country town) and it housed the Turkish Embassy for a short time. No two windows are the same on this building. My favourite ornaments are the bird figures under the windows on the first floor and the stairs to the twin chimney. Above the birds you can see some strange, totally unfunctional iron consoles. They used to support a large sign saying "Huszonötödik Színház" (25th Theatre), which was the 25th professional theatre company in Hungary. In the early 1970s I frequently came here to watch their progressive, modern performances.

MILLENNARY MONUMENT 29E *XIV. Hősök tere.* The monument was erected in 1896 to celebrate the 1000th anniversary of the Hungarian settlement (designed by the sculptor György Zala and the achitect Albert Schickedanz; completed in 1929). On a 36-metre pillar, exactly on the axis

of Andrássy út, stands the Archangel Gabriel, who, according to the legend, appeared in a dream of King St Stephen, founder of the Hungarian state, and offered him the crown. Standing opposite the angel, it looks a bit rigid, theatrically solemn. It was awarded the Grand Prix at the 1900 World Exhibition in Paris. Facing the statue, the wings cover the angel's hands, holding the crown. Looking at it from the side, from outside one of the museums you will see how the angel balances on a ball, nearly floating in the air, and how affectionately he hands over the crown, with almost the whole of his body.

At the pedestal are the statues of the legendary "Seven Chieftains" who led their tribes on the conquest of present Hungary. The colonnade has two semicircles and is 85 metres wide, 25 metres in depth. Notice the symbolic figures on top of the corner pillars. The two in the middle are especially remarkable. On the left War whips his horses into an even more frantic gallop, opposite him Peace calmly rides at a slow pace, carrying a palm leaf in his hand. His calmness has apparently communicated itself to the horses.

At the left end of the left colonnade are the figures of Work and Welfare, on the other end those of Knowledge and Glory. Some of the statues of kings on the colonnade have been changed after World War II. Those of Habsburg rulers (Ferdinand I, Charles III, Mária Theresa, Leopold II, and Francis Joseph I) were replaced by Hungarian champions of freedom. Here is also the cenotaph for the Unknown Soldier. The pavement has recently been relaid and is now as smooth as glass. This turned the square into a meeting place for roller skaters and skateboarders overnight.

MUSEUM OF FINE ARTS 29B *XIV Hősök tere*. The building to the left at the end of the square was completed in 1906 (designed by Albert Schickedanz and Fülöp Herzog), with the pupose of housing the city's fine art collection, which by that time was quite remarkable. In the pediment above the main entrance the relief shows the fight of Centaurs and the Lapiths. The scene is a completed copy of a fragment on the Zeus Temple at Olympia.

Behind the attractive façade, the monumental staircases and spaces paid no heed to the practical needs of the museum, which had to be rebuilt several times. Since 1957 the National Gallery has been responsible for the Hungarian Collection. This museum has the following sections: Egyptian Collection, Antique Collection, Old Paintings (a very rich collection), Old Statues; Old Hungarian Collection, Graphic Art Collection and Modern Paintings and Statues. After WWII the right-side building of the musem had so large wholes in the wall, that kids could get into the museum easily. They could not pass internal doors, true. (By courtesy of my editor, who was one of the kids.)

At the moment large-scale renovation of the building is under way. The "arts robbery of the century" took advantage of this. One night in November 1983, the robbers climbed up the scaffolding and into the museum, rendering the primitive alarm system harmless. Seven priceless paintings, two Raphaels among others, were stolen. It took ten weeks to find the paintings in the garden of a Greek monastery and to arrest the criminals in their homeland, Italy. Since then they have been sentenced to prison,

29 **A** Press House, **B** Museum of Fine Arts, **C** Tomb of the Unknown Soldier, **D** Archangel Gabriel and the Seven Chieftains, **E** Millennary Monument, **F** Restaurant Gundel, **G** Zoo, **H** Palm House in the Zoo, **I** Bird House in the Zoo, **J** Exhibition Hall.

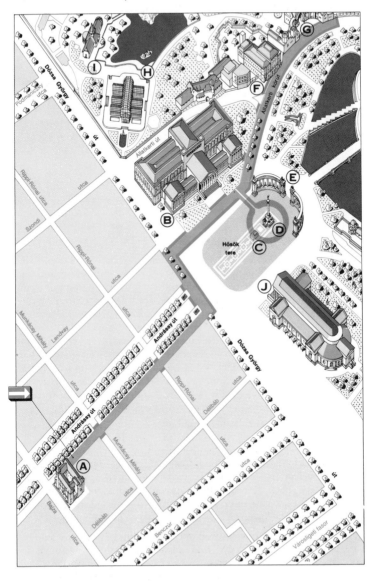

the paintings have come home and the alarm system has been modernized. These paintings were restored then exhibited separately to a public that never before showed such an interest.

director's choice • director's choice • director's choice

MIKLÓS MOJZER, GENERAL DIRECTOR (68) *(no places given, since the collection is being moved around, because of the extensive renovation. Find them...!) The dual main staircase, with the Marble Hall between them: a formidable space, designer a designer Schikedanz' highly original, genuine way up to the collections. • Ionic Hall — that most cheerful space of the building, a herald of the fact that the building was designed to be a showpiece of architectural styles, as well. • Lombardian Renaissance Hall, with the altarpiece "Madonna of Lod", by Boltaffio, and a series of outstanding pieces from the immediate circle of Leonardo. • "Apostle St Jacob is defeating the Moors" by Tiepolo. There is not a single more triumphal piece in the entire Italian Collection. • The small bronze equestrian statue of Francis I, by Leonardo. The chef d'oeuvre of the Renaissance collection. • Maria Magdalen, by Greco. One of the undoubted masterpieces of the painter.*

Városliget, with an area of about 1 square kilometre, is the largest park of the city. It does not take long to walk across it. Our route takes you down Állatkerti körút, past the Gundel Restaurant (which has one of the longest traditions in Budapest), past the Zoo (full of small buildings in a Hungarianized version of art nouveau) and past the Circus. Then we come to the

GUNDEL RESTAURANT 29F *XIV. Állatkerti körút 3.* T: 321-3550, F: 342-2917. Open 7 p.m. to midnight, every day. 102 years old, it has regained its unprecedented leadership after it reopened in 1992. Budapest-born restaurateur George Lang (of worldwide fame) did not spare his painstaking care to find the materials that fit the best traditional restaurant between Paris and San Francisco (this is an authentic guest statement — mine). What is really unusual is the first-rate collection of Hungarian masters on the walls. The last page of the menu tells you about the collection, and gives an exact location with a ground plan of the room. So you can just have a look from the corner of your eyes. Mind you, the new logo and the stationery was designed by one of the most famous designers in the world, Milton Glaser. (See his posters in the bar, reminding you of the Art Deco 20s in Chicago.)

Mr Lang told me that the elevation in one third of the main room has no structural cause, it is just a trick, to preserve some intimacy in a basically very large room. Above the Dining Room there is Elisabeth Room and Andrássy Room, the scene of the most elegant banquets of Budapest (a maximum of 260 people can be seated in the two rooms). Mr Lang, or when he is out, his right hand, Mr Gábor Budai expect a lot from the 120-odd staff. Gundel has his own, self-produced wine list by now, and a very serious wine-cellar, in the building — a frequent destination to end the dinner with.

By the way, when Mr Lang invited me for a dinner, he asked for Table 8, a strategically located table, from where you can see everything. He knows best. This must be the best table.

THE ZOO (ÁLLATKERT) *Officially called: Municipal Botanical and Zoological Gardens — Fővárosi Állat- és Növénykert (XIV. Állatkerti körút 6. Open: 9 a.m. to 6 p.m.; Autumn to Winter closing at 4 pm.)* Originally established as a pri-

30 **A** Zoo: main entrance, **B** Artificial Cliff, **C** Elephant House, **D** Municipal Circus, **E** Carousel in the Amusement Park, **F** Amusement Park: main entrance, **G** Széchenyi Baths, **H** Vajdahunyad Castle, **I** Statue of Anonymus, medieval chronicler, **J** Ice Rink, **K** Exhibition Hall, **L** Millennary Monument.

vate corporation, it opened on 16 hectares of land donated by the municipality of the (then still independent) city of Pest in 1865 — only for animals. It presents plants as well since 1872. From the 1880s it hosted peculiar "live shows" — red Indian, black, Tamil, Arctic aboriginal families were invited to live in for some months, to publicize their way of life.

In the early 1900s the Zoo went bankrupt, and the City took it over and reestablished it in 1907. A great number of characteristic new buildings were added, the ones we like so much these days, by trend-setting National Romantic architects Károly Kós, Kornél Neuschloss and Dezső Zrumeczky. It reopened in 1912. Its musts are obvious: the main entrance, with the stone elephants at street level, and the twelve polar bears around the top, the Elephant House, the Bird House, Palm House, and other buildings with character. An eternal favourite of kids is the "Animal Kindergarten", where newlyborn animals are kept together (at least those ones who do not eat the others).

Energetic, conspicuously young general director Miklós Persányi, the first *non-biologist* first man in many decades managed to have the buildings from the 1910s listed as **monuments** in 1997. (Mr Persányi, an economist, read the job advertisement abroad where he had worked for years then. He confessed to me that to become the director of the Zoo was a childhood dream for him. Generally speaking, Hungary tends not to be the land of childhood ambitions fulfilled.) The general director and his staff works in the painfully obtrusive 1960s Bison House, a blatant example of the modernist craze raging then, so insensitive to the immediate (and larger) environment. A problem Communists couldn't only be blamed for.

The Zoo is quite often the venue of fundraising events — I once attended a concert *inside* the Big Rock. Outside the big gate at the corner of Dózsa György út and Állatkerti körút, there is a very funny, obviously untranslatable slang sentence of self advertisment: "Állati jó hely!" Literally: This is an "animally" (i.e. terrifically) good place.

You can adopt all kinds of animals, and support the place in many imaginative ways. After many aborted attempts, the adjacent Amusement Park might in the end be relocated to the Xth district of Pest, then the area of the Zoo might be doubled relatively soon.

AMUSEMENT PARK (VIDÁMPARK) 30F XIV. Állatkerti körút 14-16.

This incredibly worn-down, ramshackle fun-fair is a sympathetic, sad place for those of us who cherish happy childhood memories of it. A full view of Városliget can be had from the FERRIS WHEEL. It is very wise to hold on tight when the creaking construction starts moving. If there are only a few visitors, only every second gondola can be used. There is always a very long queue for the ROLLER COASTER, but you should not have to wait more than 20-25 minutes for your turn. Almost one third of the wooden structure is replaced every year.

The SLOT-MACHINE HALL has probably the most worn out American and Soviet machines in the world. If one breaks down, you have to turn to one of the gentlemen wearing a blue coat, chatting in the middle of the hall. They will open the machine but usually just shake their heads and say "Play it on the other one", and point to a similar machine. Near the entrance is the octogonal building of the CAROUSSEL. Children, some not so young, go mad with indecision over the ride to choose: the fiery horse, the luxurious triumphal coach or the spinning box. There is a fresco above and the operator peeps out from behind the organ. The other treasure of the fun-fair, the ENCHANTED CASTLE, was set on fire by an employee some ten years ago. His explanation was that he wanted to gain distinction by reporting the fire quickly. Only the exit of the castle, the "Barrel" survived. Its totally modernized successor naturally lacks the old atmosphere.

(From 1 st October to 1 st April the Amusement Park is only partially open. Most of its attractions, like the Roller Coaster or the Ferris Wheel are closed.)

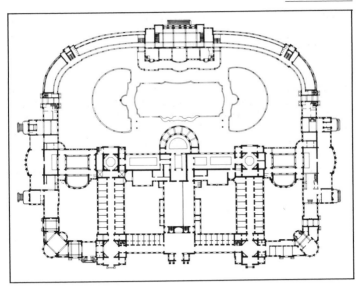

Széchenyi Baths

SZÉCHENYI BATHS **30G** *XIV. Állatkerti körút 9-11.* This, one of the largest of such buildings in Europe, is visited by 2 million people annually. It has two separate parts, two different worlds of architecture, which attract two different types of regulars. You have to go round the building to see the Medicinal Baths, which were the first to be built (Győző Czigler, Ede Dvorzsák, 1909-13). It is one of the most relaxed buildings of the turn of the century. The dome of the main entrance, which looks so light from the outside, has such a huge art nouveau mosaic inside, that it keeps visitors busy admiring it for long. The tiles on the floor, the lights, the door-frames, every fitting has been made with exceptional care. You may also walk a bit to the left or to the right, as far as the two side-domes. This is where guests can have a thermal bath in a tub, in a very luxurious environment. The numbers chalked on the doors show what time the guest started his bath.

Of the flood of notices in the entrance hall, those written only in Hungarian tell guests where to find the Complaints Book, or who and on which conditions can use the baths through the National Health Service.

The northern wing of the building was opened in 1927 (designed by Imre Francsek), and its neo-Baroque interior already shows a very modern use of space. The entrance hall has largely preserved its original condition; the newly added parts seem to be glaring mistakes (like the softdrink machines) and only emphasise the original charm. The atmosphere is quite different here from that of the other wing. This part is always busy. Behind the entrance hall there is a battered but lively restaurant, from where you can see the pools.

In Winter the pools are reached through a heated corridor. The water temperature in the large pool is 27, in the warm-water pool 38 Centigrade.

31 A Vajdahunyad Castle, **B** Petőfi Csarnok — Metropolitan Youth Centre, **C** Fuit stone, **D** Former Metropolitan Museum (1885), **E** A pavilion from the time of the Budapest International Fair, **F** Statue of George Washington.

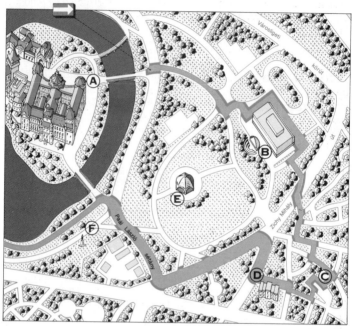

A unique local sport is featured here: water-chess, which is played on floating cork chessboards with the normal rules.

The 1,000 years of the Hungarian state was celebrated in 1896 with a huge exhibition, which took up the whole area of Városliget. A popular attraction of the Millennary Exhibition was a group of buildings, set up temporarily with the purpose of showing the various architectural styles of those 1,000 years. Some of these were copies of real buildings. This mixture of buildings, however absurd the idea may now seem, met with such success that the city authorities commissioned a stone version to be built after the exhibition. Its popular name is:

VAJDAHUNYAD CASTLE **30H** *XIV. Városliget.* Part of it was modelled on a Transylvanian castle of that name by the architect Ignác Alpár (finished by 1904). The complex consists of four main parts: the Romanesque, Gothic, the Transitional and the Renaissance/Baroque.

This bizarre notion was carried out by an architect of exceptional talent and imagination; the impression is rather that of a fairy tale than of kitsch. Naturally, no two turrets are the same, yet the many contrasting forms seem to combine into a unit. In Winter the boating lake is turned into an ice rink. The permanent stone building was planned for the purposes of the Agricultural Museum which still occupies the Castle. Opposite the main entrance is one of the most popular statues in Pest, that of Anonymus, he was the first medieval Hungarian chronicler whose epochal work was modestly signed with the words that appear on the pedestal of the statue: GLORIOSISSIMI BELAE REGIS NOTARIUS. ("The notary of the most glorious King Béla.") This would be suffcent had not four kings been called Béla in the 12th and 13th century. His identity is still disputed by scholars. The sculptor has given him a hood so that his face cannot be seen (Miklós Ligeti, 1903).

A rest: Restaurant Anonymus — in the Castle

PETŐFI HALL 31B *XIV. Zichy Mihály út 14.* This youth centre was opened in 1985 after rebuilding an older exhibition hall. It is now the stronghold of Hungarian rock and pop music. But it also has a fleamarket, theatrical performances for children, a Roller Skate Club and on Saturday evenings the Csillagfény Disco. In Summer there is also an open-air cinema, but they have organized a new-wave fashion show, an underground theatrical performance, a disco-dancing competition, a "hairshow" too. In brief, it caters for and has caught the imagination of the young who flock to it.

Their 142-4327 telephone number is an important one for you if you want information on what's happening in Budapest and they can usually help you in English or in German. Or you can do what the young do: just turn up and see what's happening.

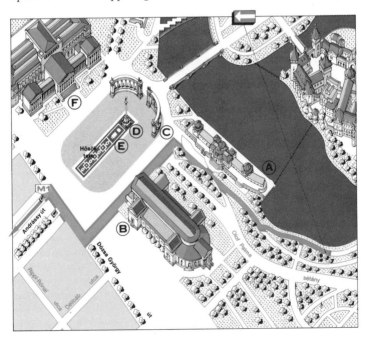

32 **A** Ice Rink Building, **B** Exhibition Hall, **C-D** Millennary Monument, **E** Tomb of the Unknown Soldier, **F** Museum of Fine Arts.

STATUE OF GEORGE WASHINGTON 31F *XIV. Városliget.* According to official American statistics, between 1871 and 1913, three and a half million immigrants from Austria–Hungary arrived in the United States, half of them Hungarians. Many came frome Bohemia though — hence "Bohunk" in old American slang. The funds to erect this statue were collected by them (Gyula Bezerédi, 1906).

EXHIBITION HALL (MŰCSARNOK) 32B *XIV. Hősök tere.* The largest exhibition hall in the country was opened in 1896, at the time of the Millennary celebrations. It was designed by the same architects as the Museum of Fine Arts opposite it. The ground plan shows the influence of the late Renaissance, as does the fine ornamentation of the façade. These were made from "frost-resistant pyrogranite", a contemporary Hungarian invention. Funds ran short when it came to decorating the pediment, the mosaic of "St Stephen, Patron of the Arts" only being put in place in 1941. During World War I it housed a military hospital.

The Exhibition Hall began as a stronghold of conservatism and remained as such until the early 80s, when the era of opening to the world took place, still with more or less adequate funds.

Then a total facelift came. Műcsarnok reopened in January 1995, with a crisis of leadership. Its much criticized lady director became the victim of a sort of political tug of war. She was demoted, obviously not at the best moment. The present director is criticized again, for a bias in his policy towards international trends, while at the same time grossly neglecting Hungarian roots. It is Műcsarnok director László Beke who is the Commissioner for the Hungarian exhibition at the Venice Biennial. Have you ever visited the beautifully restored pavilion, just right of Italy's one? If not, it is long overdue.

A rest: Café Műcsarnok & Bookshop

Along the side of Városliget there is a wide concrete pavement which is called Felvonulási tér (Procession Square). It is here that celebrations involving huge crowds of people, such as those on 4th April or 1st May, were held, and was also the scene of the military parade, which took place only in every fifth year. On such occasions there was a fly-past of fighter planes. In 1990, April 4 ceased to be a holiday — it celebrated the liberation of Hungary by the Red Army — to the sorrow of many a boys, since there would be no more military parades.

Opposite Városligeti fasor there stood the huge statue of Stalin, pulled down by the Revolution in 56. It was from the pediment of this statue that the Communist leaders waved to the crowds that were passing by in their ten thousands. It was pulled down, just like the statue of Lenin, wich was taken away to be repaired, because of "metal fatigue", just when the anicent regime was collapsing. It never returned, of course. (It used to stand near the Exhibition Hall.)

This is the end of our walk in Városliget. As I have promised, we shall return to Vörösmarty tér by the Millennary underground. You have to get off at Deák tér.

DANUBIUS FOUNTAIN 33B *V. Erzsébet tér.* A fountain with three basins, with a male figure symbolizing the Danube on the top. The women

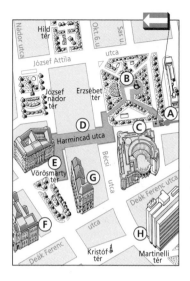

33 **A** Coach station,
B Danubius Fountain,
C Grand Hotel Corvinus
Kempinski, **D** British Embassy,
E Gerbaud, **F** Vigadó,
G Luxus, **H** Office block.

sitting on the rim of the lower basin stand for three of the Danube tributaries the Tisza, Dráva and Száva. The lower basin was carved out of a single piece of rock weighing almost 100 tons. Transporting a rock of this size presented quite a problem at the beginning of the 1880s (Miklós Ybl, Leó Feszler, 1893). This is a copy of the original, destroyed in World War II.

This walk took me five hours but I did not even look into the Museum of Fine Arts or the Exhibition Hall.

WALK FIVE

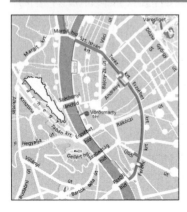

Along and behind the Nagykörút It takes us all the way down the Nagykörút, (or Great Boulevard) from the Danube to the Danube. We shall look into some side-streets and peer behind the plastic cover of the Corvin department store. We shall pay our respects to the site where the National Theatre used to be, visit the Royal Waiting Room, a handsome railway station and see something of Új-Lipótváros and return.

Time: Six hours plus. From Vigadó tér, we board a 2 or 2/A Tram coming from the right. This will take us to the south end of the Nagykörút. While waiting you will probably notice how expansive the river panorama is. Budapest is made up of two equally important parts, of totally different character.

Right opposite us is the large building of the Bazaar at the foot of Castle Hill. The intention was that small shops would occupy the ground floor, now this houses sculptors' workshops. On the upper level the legendary rock concerts of the 1960s were held. These concerts affected the foundations of the building which is now awaiting restoration.

We get off at the fourth stop, that is, at the third bridge down from where we boarded the tram. Let's walk to the southern end of the bridge. On the opposite side of the river is Lágymányos, a part of the XIth district, which was once a marsh. Over there on the riverbank stands the campus of the Technical University, to the left is the railway bridge (1873–76, designer unknown). The bridge was so far away from the city itself that the designer presumably felt no obligation to any aesthetic principles.

Behind the railway bridge you can see the tip of Csepel Island — the proposed site for some ambitious development. Some planners dream of a miniature Manhattan, or Défense there. There is a lot of talk about an express train to Vienna that would

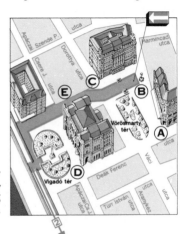

34 **A** Luxus Department Store, **B** Fountain with lions, **C** Gerbaud, **D** Vigadó, **E** Shipping company headquarters, with sirens.

only take 53 minutes. Also of incoming Hong Kong businessmen, who are on the way by the thousand to Hun Kong. The centre of the island can be reached in 13 minutes, by way of this commuters'train HÉV. Its terminus is next to the bridge.

Walking through the subways we come to the beginning of our "Fifth Walk".

LÁGYMÁNYOS BRIDGE AND UNIVERSITY TOWN was long overdue, and was built on an obvious location. It finishes the Outer Boulevard in Pest and used existing pillars — that of the Southern Railway Bridge. The Buda side roads leaving the bridge were protested against by the inhabitants of every single proposed line. Finally probably the worst solution was chosen — together with a scandal.

Anyway, most Budapest people like the bridge, especially admire the big mirrors that throw an even light on the road.

Meanwhile University Town is taking more and more definite shape on the 1996 Expo Site (The idea was dropped in 1994, when it was clear that the state should have funded it altogether.)

The Science Faculty of Eötvös University moves here, establishing a long-awaited symbiosis with Budapest Institute of Technology, less than a kilometre away.

NAGYKÖRÚT (GRAND BOULEVARD) This is the longest thoroughfare of the city, measuring exactly 4,114 metres. At this point the site was once a backwater of the Danube. By the end of the last century, the narrow streets of an unorganized suburb had developed here. Construction began in 1872, at the same time it did on Sugárút, and lasted 35 years. A total of 251 buildings were pulled down and 253, much larger than original ones, were built. Nagykörút, with a sewerage system running underneath, is 45 metres wide at every point and crosses through 5 districts: hence its sections have different names — Ferenc, József, Erzsébet, Teréz (so named after Habsburg kings and queens) and Szent István körút.

The Nagykörút helped to connect parts of the city which, before its existence, had been separate and socially very distinct. The boulevard was planned to run from the suburb at Boráros tér, through better-off districts, to the ill-famed slums of the Margit híd area, which became a fashionable, well-off district as a consequence of the city settling itself around Parliament. So when the boulevard officially opened in 1906, it led from a poorer suburb towards better and better-off districts — just as it does today.

Blocks of flats along the Nagykörút are very similar to one another. Their façades are all eclectic, showing elements of all sorts of architectural styles and usually have mortared walls decorated with plaster ornaments. The designs of the buildings imitated those of the townhouses along Andrássy út. On the street-side, light and spacious flats with at least two bedrooms (and a bathroom) were placed. Their kitchens are large, with a small room opening from them, which was once the maid's room. The flats at the rear of the buildings, opening from the inner courtyard access balcony.

After World War II, when flats were nationalized, the larger front-facing flats were broken up into smaller units, often quite illogically. However, many flats at the rear acquired a bathroom. In the early 1980s the façades all along the

Nagykörút were restored and the interiors of some buildings, such as that at Ferenc körút 5., were renovated. Rents are low compared to the cost of maintenance. If you go into any building, you will see that they have two separate staircases: the main staircase leads to the front-facing flats and the one at the rear was used by tradesmen and servants. The main staircase is usually much more ornate, though sometimes, as at Ferenc körút 5., it looks just the same as that at the rear. Today everyone uses the main staircase or the lifts which have been since installed, the rear stairs are frequently not even cleaned properly. Inside, in the courtyards, a busy social life used to go on. A reminder of those times is the wooden frame on which carpets were beaten, called the "poroló". Maids and later housewives used to take their carpets down to the courtyard and beat them there with a cane carpet beater (the "prakker" which was also what children were threatened with for misbehaviour). Everyone had to have an agreed upon time for beating their carpets and this gave rise to many arguments. When the ladies made peace, they used to gather in the yard to chat. Sadly, the general use of vacuum-cleaners, which had occurred by the mid 1960s, brought this busy social life to an end.

Ferenc körút *divides Ferencváros, the IXth district. It was named after Emperor Franz I in 1792 when he came to the throne. This area was agricultural in the last century, but by the end of the 1800s important mills and meat plants had been established here. This soon multiplied the number of the district where the inhabitants are working class and artisan. The modernization of the district was interrupted by the recession before the war.*

This can be seen on a detour into Angyal utca, a street which could symbolize Ferencváros as a whole. Some buildings try to imitate those in the Nagykörút, but on a smaller scale, others are single-storey buildings occupied by one family and the third type are single-storey buildings containing a courtyard and housing several families. And finally there is the only modern block built the way the city authorities had planned.

SECOND HAND FURNITURE STORE 35G *IX. Tűzoltó utca 14-16.* If you follow Angyal utca, it will lead you straight to this building which, with a slight exaggeration, could be called the museum of forgotten furniture. The ground floor is packed with wardrobes, the upper level with chairs and beds. Usually the furniture comes from older and poorer people without a family to leave it to. Many of the local households are furnished in this way. People who like home carpentry, slumming intellectuals or quite simply the poor come here to buy. If someone comes often enough, they are bound to find something they want among the trash — on the cheap. I once paid 30 Ft here for an armchair — having it recovered cost me 700 Ft.

MUSEUM OF APPLIED ARTS (IPARMŰVÉSZETI MÚZEUM) 35I

IX. Üllői út 33-37. In contrast to where we have just been, this place contains a collection of objects well worth preserving (Ödön Lechner and Gyula Pártos, 1896). There is an immediate clash between the exterior and the ceiling of the main entrance with the white interior; the aula is covered with a steel-framed glass ceiling. Some years ago a pendulum was hung from here to show the rotation of the Earth as part of the exhibition on the history of measuring time.

director's choice • director's choice • director's choice

DR. ZSUZSA LOVAG, DIRECTOR GENERAL (57) 1. The colour-
ful ceramic walls outside the main entrance (so-called Zsolnay technique) **2.** The fancy hole that breaks through all the levels of the
building, and looking upwards through which we can glance the
small coloured glass dome. (We call it by a local nickname: "The
Well".) **3.** Lady's Dress: dark red and striped velvet, dark and satin
and tulle embroidered with pearls. Braided with lace fringes. Paris,
circa 1875. (Ground Floor, right corner.) **4.** Silver dish, chased,
punched, by Paul Grill, Augsburg, 1680-85. Together with the silver
maquette by Péter Varga, from our staff, that explains how the dish
was made, phase by phase. (1st Floor, Arts and Crafts permanent
exhibition.) **5.** A 13-piece silver make-up kit, with copper inlaid
ornaments, imitating fish, birds and insects. Louis Confort Tiffany,
New York, 1902-1907 (1st Floor, left corner). **6.** Peacocks on a "Halas-
type" lace, sewn out of flax. Design by Árpád Dékány, realized by
the Halas Lace Workshop, led by Mária Markovits, Kiskunhalas,
circa 1906.

FORMER ARMY BARRACKS 35H *IX. Üllői út 49-51.* This large yellow
building is the only one that was already here when the Nagykörút was
being marked out (József Hild, 1845–46). It presently contains offices, ware-
houses and temporary housing for people whose home is under reconstruction.

**A DETOUR: HUNGARIAN MUSEUM OF NATURAL HISTORY —
MAGYAR TERMÉSZETTUDOMÁNYI MÚZEUM** *VIII. Ludovika tér 3.* The
newcomer on the museum scene, a sort of new sensation in Budapest, specially for kids, is well worth a detour, possibly one stop by underground,
from Ferenc körút to Klinikák station, and a five minute-walk, most of it
through a park.

As most major museums, this one has also seceded from the National
Museum, in 1934. It took, however another 63 years to have a building of
its own. The building used to be the riding school of the Ludoviceum, the
Hungarian military college, after WWII it was converted into a cinema,
caled "Alfa". Inside the museum there is a history of the site as well, with
a photo of the cinema burning. It could not be saved, and it stood there
deserted for over a decade.

The elegant Classicist monument (Mihály Pollack, 1834) was fully reconstructed from the outside, while an ingenously designed high-tech/post-
modern interior was built inside (István Mányi, 1996).

In front of the musem there are two dozen big pieces of stones, presents of
the stone quarry businesses to the museum, arranged chronologically (note
the small plaques on the rocks.) The entrance is from the side (they did not
want to spoil the original, protected facade.) On the reception level there is
not much to see, if not, under the stairs, the skeleton of an elephant
deceased recently in the Budaest Zoo. The first floor hosts the temporary

director's choice • director's choice • director's choice

DR. ISTVÁN MATSKÁSI, DIRECTOR GENERAL, HUNGARIAN NATURAL
HISTORY MUSEUM (54) *The marble mangers in the Lecture room, recall-*
ing the historical function of the building (Hall, Lecture room). • The
mummy dissected by a pathalogist in the 18th century revealed in the
crypt of the Dominican church in Vác. (Groundfloor, left side). • The cave
of the Neaderthal woman with "kitchen" utensils and prey (Gallery, left
side). • The majestic diorama displaying the legendary game richness of
Hungary (Gallery, far end). • The modern kitchen with its undesirable
animals, in contrast of the Neaderthal cave (Gallery, right side vis-a-vis the
cave). • Noah's Ark symbolising the efforts to preserve the threatened
species of the Earth (Gallery).

BUDAPEST BESTS : : BUDAPEST BESTS : : BUDAPEST BESTS

Péter Lengyel, Novelist, Short Story Writer, a Reclusive Cult Figure

My city is such a city. (Among the men and women in my books, she is
always to be found.) Her visitors had better walk and walk and walk.
We, aboriginals have no better idea, either, I mean if one of us wants to
get close to her, intimately close.

Sacrifice your entire day. Avoid Tárnok utca and Szentháromság tér up
in the Castle, the place to meet the other guests and pseudo-peasants —
possibly computer mechanics at night. Avoid everything that was created just to impress you — they are unreal things, never genuine. If you
crave for the bustle, travel along the metropolitan underground to
Eastern Station, and tread the streets around Garay tér. Visit Mátyás tér
in District Eight, and have a look at the city that is never boasted to foreigners with. Slip into her subways, and feast on the bazaars of seven
nations.

Nyugati tér, Astoria, Batthyányi tér. Put your money in your most
secure of your secure pockets, if you do not happen to have any,
madame, sew one somewhere inside, right away. The pickpockets'
favourite hunting grounds are Váci utca and Petőfi Sándor utca, and the
tramway line on Nagykörút (for you: Grand Boulevard.) Beware of those
who offer their services, whether their bodies or their bank rates —
you'll find fault with them in the end.

Take a 17 tram from the Buda side of Margit híd all the way to Old Buda.
Get off at Szépvölgyi út. Have a look at the enclosure of the small car
park, and try to imagine that on that couple of inches of concrete there
used to be a market, complete with vegetables, fruit, food, with some
rows of stalls, a well, with a street, a narrow alleyway, a sort of chaotic
Urban Eden, steaming with perspiration and heavy secrets. From Lajos
utca cross Evező utca, turn into Uszály utca and stroll among the
Bauhaus-style buildings, amid the three-story high trees. From
Dereglye utca go up to the banks of the Duna river. Sit quietly on a

exhibitions, and a discovery room, to feel and touch things, a very welcome addition to the somewhat retarded Hungarian museu scene, still more or less dominated by professors interested in schorarly publications, much ess in community outreach and educating and even entartaining of the public. Not this one, though, it emanates the latest approaches of the American museum scene. occasionally I felt myself in the Field Museum of Chicago, Illionois. (Not the design of the museum exhibits nd the signs, though. My all-out favourite is one of the tens of thousand miserably, nondescript, small kitchens of the prefabricated, ten-story buildings, rebuilt here, with the "undesirable companions", magnified a bit, for better visibility.

There are exciting plans to expand the museum to the adjacent former military college main block, (through an underground tunnel), and Orczy park, beyond the museum will, sooner or later be incorporated into the institution, as a sort of ecological park. (On Botanical Gardens, 200 meters from here, see "For Serious Addicts", section "Twelve Impressions".)

---

bench in Small Park under the tallest of the hollow willow trees and try to contemplate the Uszály utca of the 1950s. The trees are not taller than humans yet. Street kids like me play foot tennis at the top of the street. "*Autó!*" they shout no more than three times a day altogether, and the game stops until the car has passed. Three cars a day. Not a bad life, to be a street kid then and there.

At the northern side of the park turn back towards the city. To the right there is, within a couple of steps, the Military Amphitheatre of the ancient Roman times. We are on the eastern frontier-rim *(limes)* of the Roman Empire, just like at other times on the western limes of other empires (Ottoman, Soviet), Old Buda alone has two amphitheatres, the other one, farther away, is the one for civilians. It was this one where we left for in the breaks between classes from nearby Árpád Grammar School, that's where our gym classes were held by Master Iglóy, the trainer of the national athletic team, whose disciples then held *every single* world record of the middle and long distance events.

Then, following the heavy work of imagination, you can have a rest, in a street parallel with Duna river, bumpy, cobblestone-covered Bokor utca, in tiny Café Kiskorona. Order some soft drink. The lady owner knows everything you should ever know about popular medicine. From your table you can have an unobstructed view of a site where a small block was recently pulled down. That was the house, where a hero in one of the books of the author of the present lines, a certain Rókus Láncz, the eminent fence of stolen goods was committing his recurrent crimes. And lo, now it was life that has hurried to imitate fiction. The company that operates in the new building on the same site, bears the name of the heroine of the same novel*: "Bóra BT". Remember: Hungarians do read books — every now and then.

---

* His celebrated book, **Macskakő** ("Cobblestone") is now available in English, by Readers International, London.

35 **A** Petőfi Bridge, **B** Memorial Column, **C-D-E** Blocks of flats, **F** Ferencváros Parish Church, **G** Furniture Hall, **H** Former Barracks, **I** Museum of Applied Arts, **J** Corvin cinema.

CORVIN BUDAPEST FILM PALACE 35J *VIII. Corvin köz.*

The first cinemas in Budapest were usually installed on the ground floor of residential blocks; this is a rare exception (Emil Bauer, 1923). It used to have a lobby not smaller than its

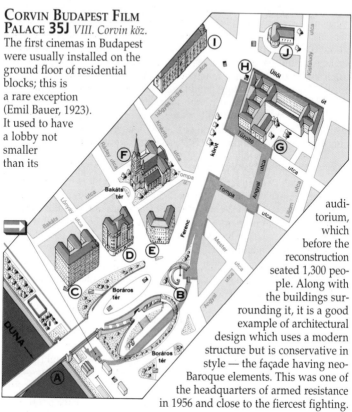

auditorium, which before the reconstruction seated 1,300 people. Along with the buildings surrounding it, it is a good example of architectural design which uses a modern structure but is conservative in style — the façade having neo-Baroque elements. This was one of the headquarters of armed resistance in 1956 and close to the fiercest fighting.

In 1996 it was converted into a multiplex cinema with 6 rooms. The rooms have all names of legendary film directors, the interiors are decorated with old posters. On one side there is a pleasant café, on the other an Art Video Rental Shop called Odeon.

Quite a good place to be in — only the entrance is too narrow. But that was one of the few constraints of the original design that was impossible to change.

József körút. The next section of the Nagykörút is thus called because it crosses the VIIIth district, Józsefváros. It was named in 1777 after Emperor Joseph II, who was then heir to the throne. Behind the row of buildings towards Kálvin tér, the area becomes more and more elegant (the aristocrats had their town-houses, "palota" in Hungarian, built around the National Museum); to the right, however, it is rather less grand with many single-storey houses. A lot of cloak and dagger films have been shot around here and there are whole streets where nothing has changed since the beginning of the century (Futó utca, Nagytemplom utca or another one, blasphemously called Leonardo da Vinci utca). Standing on the corner of Nap utca you can see a stately old

hospital building to the left, at the end of the small street on the other side of the Nagykörút, to the right there is a new housing estate. A drastic method of inner-city renewal was adapted here: some ten highrise blocks were built on the site of the old single-storey houses.

The area along the Nagykörút on the city side and as far as Baross utca was called "Cérnakorzó" (Thread-promenade) before the war. It was only here that needle-women used to walk after work to become acquainted with the craftsmen in the area. The ladies promenading here now are looking for less long-lasting relationships.

JÓZSEFVÁROS PARISH CHURCH

VIII. Horváth Mihály tér 7. This Baroque church, re-built several times, has a fine location as the gateway of József-város (József Thalherr, 1798). In front of the church there is a statue of Péter Pázmány, the scholarly priest who began the Counter-Reformation in Hungary (Béla Radnai, 1914).

Further down József körút the number of small shops increases: a watchmaker's, a pipe shop, a souvenir shop disguised as a tobacconist's and the like. Souvenir shops have been flooded with things like quartz watches from the Far East or key cases which bleep when you whistle to them — it is difficult to find something which is typically Hungarian. Perhaps the plastic donkey which produces a cig-arette from its backside when you pull its tail. That I have never seen anywhere else…

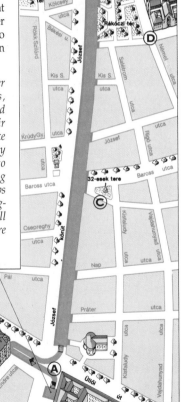

36 A Former Barracks, **B** Museum of Applied Arts, **C** War Memorial, **D** Market Hall.

Rákóczi tér is known not only for its market hall and the secondary school that trains dressmakers. It is also the centre of low prostitution. Since 1947 any form of "selling a woman's body for money" has been illegal in Hungary. After years of desperate and vain struggle to end prostitution, the aim now just seems to be to keep it under control. As everywhere in the world, prostitution is interwoven with crime. Women satisfying the needs of fastidious customers can be found only in expensive nightclubs or luxury hotels.

The buildings here look the same as anywhere else. The value of flats, however, because of the notoriety of the location, is much lower around here. The area beyond the Nagykörút is, if possible, an even more pathetic sight than at other sections. If you peep into the ground floor flats in the dark, narrow streets, although it is not a nice thing to do even here, you can see that the lights have to be on in broad daylight and that some lightbulbs in the chandeliers are gone. A lot of lonely, hopeless, old people live here.

When I lived in this area for some years, I had the impression that alongside the old there lived a lot of young Gipsies settling there from the country — Gipsy musicians with a number of kids or second-hand dealers. The courtyard my flat shared was in a five-storey high cauldron and no one could keep any secret from the others. Everyone reached their flat by walking down the long access balcony and in so doing had to walk past the other flats that shared it. In Summer, when people left windows open you could hear the baker's alarm clock go off at three in the morning and then, at 15 minute intervals, one after the other. Every district has a couple of pubs or restaurants where you can sense the atmosphere and all the distress of the area. In Józsefváros, it is the Góbé restaurant (József körút 28., on the corner of Bérkocsis utca). The regulars here are some of the girls working at Rákóczi tér, family men, often in tracksuits, as they pop in after (or before or even instead of) work and women of unidentifiable ages. The furnishings are quite worn and you have a feeling that should anything new be put in here, it would soon take on the look of the miserable surroundings. I did not try any of the food, though the lamb dishes have a certain reputation. On the other side of the Nagykörút there are computer shops, on this side small shops of various kinds: a ballet-shoe maker, an old-fashioned hairdresser or a fountain-pen shop with long traditions. And there is a Totó-Lottó betting office as well. **Lottó** is a form of lottery, you buy a ticket and you tick off 5 numbers of the 90; **totó** is the Hungarian football pools where you have to find the final results of 13 +1 football matches.

Blaha Lujza tér is one of the central squares in the city. It bisects the Nagykörút, which crosses Rákóczi út at this point. At one end of Rákóczi út there is Erzsébet híd, on the other you can see the great yellow mass of Keleti Railway Station. On the square was the old Nemzeti (National) Theatre and the famous clock standing in front of it, the standard rendezvous spot for ages. "I'll meet you at seven at the Nemzeti, where the number six tram stops", went the old song. The older generation still refer to the spot as the "Nemzeti". It would have been a nice gesture to call this stop of the Metro "Nemzeti" since it was partly due to the constrution of the Metro that the old theatre building had to be demolished in 1966. Architects did not consider rebuilding it as at that time the eclectic style that dominates the Nagykörút was held as next to nothing. This was the area of modernization which favoured angular and zig-zag lines.

The editorial offices of the once dreaded Communist party paper *Népszabadság* used to be here in the corner block (37A). Now it's by far the most

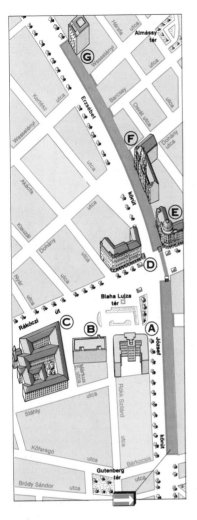

37 **A** The former *Népszabadság* House, **B** Corvin Department, **C** Rókus Hospital, **D** Block of flats, **E** Block of flats, with a supermarket on the ground floor, **F** New York Palace and the Café, **G** Madách Theatre.

successful and readable daily, independent even of the left wing Socialist Party. It now has a very democratic setup and German capital.

The "new" façade of the Corvin department store (Ferenc Battka, 1966) is the memorial of this wild rage of modernism. If you want to know what the original façade looked like, turn to the left side of the building, the one which did not get its share of plastic cover. This store can no longer use its not wildly original slogan which went "The largest store — the largest choice" for there is now a larger department store.

Its customers are mainly people from the suburbs. I can hardly wait until the plastic façade is taken off and the old wall is painted out of some postmodern inspiration. It would be a perfect wall for that (37B).

In the subway you can buy newspapers day and night and in the early 1960s the first automatic food dispensers were placed here. If you were tall enough, you inserted the coin — but often nothing happened.

You then had to bang on the machine, whereupon the person who filled it with food from behind, unwillingly came up and gave you your chosen cake with his own hand or gave your money back. Now the said person sits behind a window. At New Year's Eve at midnight the carnival-like procession reaches its climax in streets around here; days before vendors invade the Körút selling the props: the parking restrictions are set aside on this day and even flowerboxes are taken away from the corners, whose purpose is partly to stop pedestrians from crossing.

The buildings of the Nagykörút are not of much aesthetic value individually but there is an exception:

THE NEW YORK PALACE 37F *VII. Erzsébet körút 9-11* can be seen from afar as it is situated on the bend in the road. It faces three streets. Built as the headquarters of the New York Insurance Company (Alajos Hauszmann, 1891–95), it used to house Budapest Fleet street. The neo-Renaissance building was built of fine, long-lasting materials and in a tasteful, unique mixture of styles, which already hinted at art-nouveau (especially in the formation of the tower). The building is a little worn inside. Now its up for sale. You can ask in the café if it has already been sold. Mr. Bitai, the scrouge of young waiters, a retired manager will surely know about it.

CAFÉ NEW YORK 37F

CAFÉ NEW YORK 37F On the ground floor of the New York House. Budapest had more than 400 cafés at the turn of the century, but this was the most beautiful, the busiest and the one with the liveliest atmosphere. When it was opened, the playwright Ferenc Molnár and his friends threw its key into the Danube so that it should stay open night and day. As the saying goes, at that time every writer had his own café and every café had its own writer. The New York had many: virtually all the literary men of the era since those who were not regulars here often dropped in. Many of them came to work here from dark, unheated rooms they rented nearby to fill themselves on the "writers' plate" (cold meat, cheese and bread — with a discount for writers) and because paper and ink was free. The "literary headwaiters" knew everybody's habits and latest works; better still, they could dine on credit. A lot of them wrote here but some also sold their books or looked for a job and everyone read the latest papers. The titles of the papers the café had, were set on a huge noticeboard: "all the dailies and arts journals of the world". Of course, it was not only writers and journalists who came here but people of all kinds, depending on the time of day. Actors, journalists and cinema staff early in the morning, retired actors later, elegant groups came to dinner, card players, circus artists and waiters from other places enjoyed the nights. The clock above the door to the basement restaurant called "Mélyvíz" (Deep water) must have worked in those days.

The café had its golden age in the early 1910s, the second in the second half of the 1920s and in the early 1930s. It was here, up in the gallery that the most influential journals were edited. Caricatures of the old editors are still to be seen on the walls. After World War II, through the windows of the shelled and burnt out café potatoes, and later, shoes were sold. Still later, as the café was seen as the symbol of the old, useless world, a sports shop was opened within the walls. It reopened as a café again in 1954. Writers came here again for a while but disappeared for good. The New York is listed in all guidebooks and has become the scene of tourist pilgrimage. Nowadays you find just a few newspapers here, but athough the Venetian chandeliers were replaced by out-of-style modern ones during a renovations, the interior still retains its splendour. Now it is only open between 9 a.m. and 10 p.m. and the "Mélyvíz" restaurant from 11.30 a.m. to 3 p.m. and 6.30 p.m. to midnight.

There are some relentless customers, though. A pensive soft drink small business owner, in his late forties (?), always in grey suit seems to be here every afternoon standing at, or leaning on the counter of the beer bar, the nearer the blond bartender lady, the better.

Some writers and men of letters have returned. I used to spend my Thursday afternoons here from 2 to 4, on the gallery. We did not have a proper editorial office back in 1989 Spring when we established "2000", the influential egghead literary and social journal, a sort of a cross between the New Yorker and the New Republic. It still flourishes, and my friends — those ones who were not lured into government service — are happy and are here on Thursday afternoons. And though the waiters apparently don't read the high-brow literary and social monthly they own and publish, they have a "literary toilet-attendant", a senior lady who does read our paper, and refuses to let us pay if we use her facility.

HORIZONT CINEMA *VII. Erzsébet körút 13.* Most cinemas in Budapest were built in the inter-war period and were quite modern for the time. This cinema opened in 1938 and looks exactly as it used to, only the films have changed. It no longer has a one-hour continuous programme, which started with a newsreel; it still has, however, the two reliefs depicting the history of mankind on either side of the screen.

The Horizont is situated on the next section of the Körút, called **Erzsébet körút.** *It runs through the VIIth district, Erzsébetváros, named, like the bridge, after Franz Joseph's wife. It is the most densely populated part of the city; 55 thousand people per square kilometre. You can find a number of single-storey buildings in this area, too. Along the Nagykörút itself, there are innumerable new, small shops, especially in the entrances of the buildings and some even on the upper levels. Anyone can get a licence to run such a shop (providing there are no sanitary or professional objections)*

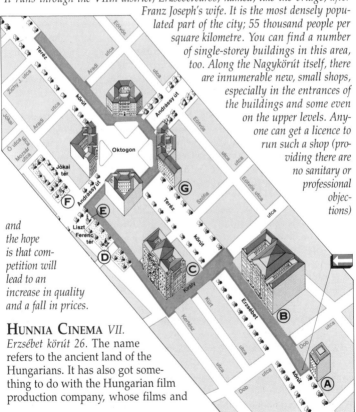

and the hope is that competition will lead to an increase in quality and a fall in prices.

HUNNIA CINEMA *VII. Erzsébet körút 26.* The name refers to the ancient land of the Hungarians. It has also got something to do with the Hungarian film production company, whose films and

38 **A** Madách Theatre, **B** Grand Hotel Royal, **C** Academy of Music, **D** Statue of Ferenc Liszt, **E** Statue of Endre Ady, poet, **F** Statue of Mór Jókai, novelist, **G** Copy of Palazzo Strozzi, Florence.

other Hungarian movies and art movies are shown here. It has also got something to do with the Hungarian Film Club Association. There is a pleasant café inside. A trendy place, full of intellectuals.

A rest: Kék Ibolya — Wesselényi utca 45.

MADÁCH THEATRE 37G *VII. Erzsébet körút 31-33.* This was built on the site of the old Orfeum between 1953 and 1961 (designed by Oszkár Kaufmann). It is very successful in terms of attracing audiences; since in Hungary almost all the theatres belong to the state, box-office success does not mean large profits. It is a repertory theatre, that is, they have several productions on at the same time. After running *Cats* for years, they are now scoring with *Joseph and his Technicolour Dreamcoat.*

HOTEL ROYAL 38B *VII. Erzsébet körút 49.* When it was opened, this hotel was one of the largest in the whole Austro-Hungarian Empire (Rezső Ray, 1896). The four cast iron statues on the façade (the Four Seasons) were brought from Paris. In 1915 its luxurious ball room was converted into a cinema, which is still going strong, the Apollo (for 40 years called the "Vöröscsillag", i.e. Red Star.) Originally the building had a ground plan in the shape of an E but the two courtyards were closed in the early1960s. The modernized portal has recently been rebuilt in its original form.

LISZT ACADEMY OF MUSIC 38C *VI. Liszt Ferenc tér 8.* The official name of the institution, "Liszt Ferenc Zeneművészeti Főiskola", is to be found between the two genii at the top of the building. Music teachers and performing musicians are trained here — about 300 students in all. The building was completed in 1907, after three years to the plans of Flóris Korb and Kálmán Giergl. Above the main entrance the bronze statue of Ferenc Liszt can be seen (by Alajos Stróbl). Main Hall ("Nagyterem" in Hungarian) is 25 by 17 metres and has 1,200 seats, the best of which is obviously the 1st seat left in the 8th row — a former director of Hungaroton, the national record company, used to get his complimentary ticket for this chair. The "best" just means that you have the best view of the stage from here, the acoustics in the hall are extraordinarily good, you can hear everything even from the back row of the second gallery. These seats are usually taken by music students who loudly express their opinions on concerts from there.

If more than twelve hundred people are interested in a concert, the seats behind the stage are sold. If even more, then some chairs are placed on stage as well, as it happened last time when Maurizio Pollini played here.

On both sides of the Walcker organ there are two inscriptions in Latin. One of them is: "Sursum Corda": Raise Your Hearts (to your left), the other is "Favete Linguis": Hold Your Tongue, or Be Quiet. There are hundreds of other details to notice on the walls and on the ceiling. At the right bottom corner of the organ there is a cavity of a grown-up sized human. This is where radio commentators perch and introduce concerts from, unless a special need forces them to leave for a time, like on the occasion of a recent Vespro by Monteverdi, when the "Echo" tenor solo was sung from here.

The Small Hall ("Kisterem" in Hungarian), which you can reach from the first floor, seats 400 people. It too has good acoustics, but sometimes you can hear what is going on in the Main Hall, as well. This is the venue of examination concerts for music students. Here happened that I threw a reasonably large bouquet of roses to the alto girlfriend of mine on stage after her graduation performance, not realizing that the contemporary pieces she sang towards the end were less than perfect, and were rewarded by a grade Three, more than she deserved, analysts commented. Everywhere in the building you can see the signs of an exceptionally careful and loving

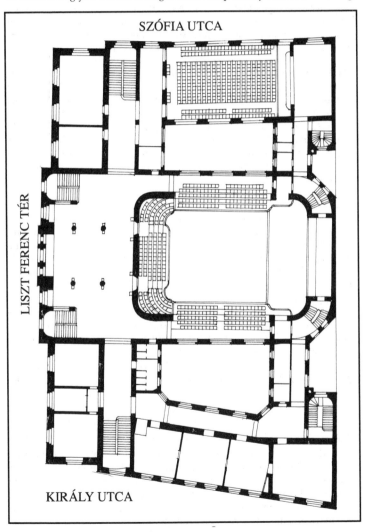

Liszt Academy of Music — the first floor

shaping of surfaces. This is generally true of most art nouveau buildings, but here the presence can also be felt of a special tranquility. As if this art nouveau building had grown straight out of eclecticism — fire out of water. This reminds me: you should be careful with the marble basin between the ground floor doors — it is always full of water, it is just too clean to be noticed. During term-time you can always walk into the building through the side entrance in Király utca. It is worth buying a ticket for a concert that may not be first class just for the sake of the Main Hall.

CHILDREN'S LIBRARY *VI. Liszt Ferenc tér 6.* This is the library I joined at the age of 10 although it was a long way off from both my school and our home. The library was exactly like that of the adults, only everything was smaller, including the chairs and the tables. It has a reading room facing the square and many catalogue cases. There used to be a big lady with red hair, who helped us find what we wanted. Above one shelf there used to be the notice: "A selection of adult literature". The red-haired lady has now retired.

THE NEW LISZT STATUE *VI. Liszt Ferenc tér.* The statue was erected to commemorate the 100th anniversary of the composer's death, although there are two full-figure Liszt statues within a distance of a few hundred metres (László Marton, 1986). The statue aroused considerable resistance in musical circles. Critics denounced it as "lukewarm-modern". Passersby ask each other who might the bald man on Liszt's lapel be. (It is the sculptor.)

A rest: Café Incognito — Liszt Ferenc tér 2.

"PALAZZO STROZZI" **38G** *VI. Teréz körút 67.* Another work of Alajos Hauszmann, the architect of New York Palace, this one from 1884.

The original in Florence is larger and better. It houses offices and on the ground floor there is a richly decorated wedding-hall, perhaps the most fashionable in the whole city. Marriage services are conducted at district councils and at such central offices. The bride usually wears a white dress and the bridegroom a dark suit. The young couple are taken to the ceremony in cars decorated with flowers. There is a small photo gallery in the basement, with occasional historical shows.

In the next section of Teréz körút you will have to forget my promise that we shall walk through better and better-off areas, although the boutiques are of better quality than those in Király utca.

The Kőműves Restaurant ("The Bricklayer") is an extension of the world behind Teréz körút. Around here there is a huge hard-ware store which stretches as far as the other end of the block, called "Kátai's" after the ex-owner of the shop (Teréz körút 28.), and also the Béke Hotel Radisson, which has been modernized a number of times — the last occasion being just recently. The pattiserie of the hotel is very popular with businessmen for its good coffee, desserts and ice cream. The chubby gentleman wearing a suit deals with an order as if everything there were his own. On the façade two sitting lions hold a torch in their paws. Opposite the hotel there is Játékszín, a small theatre which does not have its own company (VII. Teréz körút 48.). Rather unusually for Hungary, here the casts are put together only for the individual productions.

39 A Hotel Béke Radisson, **B** Post Office, **C** Western Railway Station, **D** Skála Department Store, **E-F** Blocks of flats.

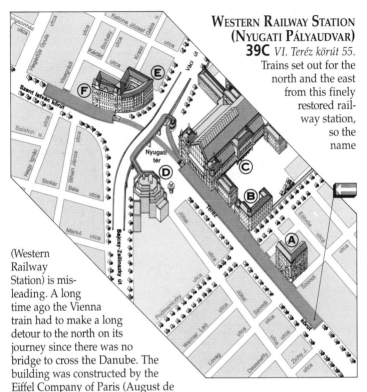

WESTERN RAILWAY STATION (NYUGATI PÁLYAUDVAR)

39C *VI. Teréz körút 55.*
Trains set out for the north and the east from this finely restored railway station, so the name (Western Railway Station) is misleading. A long time ago the Vienna train had to make a long detour to the north on its journey since there was no bridge to cross the Danube. The building was constructed by the Eiffel Company of Paris (August de Serres, 1874-77) in such a way that the old railway terminal was able to function undisturbed underneath. Over the next 100 years the 25-thousand-square-metre hall deteriorated and plans were made for a new building. Fortunately the conservationists won and most of the old iron structure has been re-cast; only the paint has been changed to light blue, the favourite colour of post-modernism. Towards the end of the hall on the left there is a large closed door, above the lintel is carved in marble: VIRIBUS UNITS (With Unity Strength). This used to be the door to the Royal Waiting Room. Although pretty from the outside it is not in use. The new wing has been occupied by a row of 26 shops, the Westend Bevásárló Udvar, where you can have a good idea of what sort of things people put their money into. The elegant glass screen of the station's main façade lets trains become part of the city's traffic. Once, about twenty years ago, a train actually came through, when the brakes failed, and stopped at the tram stop.

The giant restaurant room to the right of the main entrance has been turned into a McDonald's. The interior is quite a success. Note the elegant, unobtrusive post-modern tower at the corner. Sometimes I come here to smell the odour, it reminds me of my first visits to Western Europe — my youth.

A rest: big Mac's biggest — Teréz körút 55.

SKÁLA METRO DEPARTMENT STORE 39D *VI. Marx tér 1-2.* In the 1970s and the 1980s the Skála Shopping Chain was perhaps the most dramatically developing company in the country. So said TIME magazine in full page they devoted to this company with the headline "Marks and Spencer of the East". Their store in Buda took over the title of "the largest store" from Corvin. This store in Pest (György Kővári, 1984) is much smaller, occupying only the first and second floors of the building. The one-time CEO of this chain is now part of the international jet-set. Sometimes in Canada, sometimes in the Ukraine. He has just built a very large Shopping Center along M3 Motorway, called Pólus Center.

But apart from that, there is a veritable shopping mall craze now in Hungary — retail trade is being transformed. People simply love the new shopping malls, even if they find them expensive.

The old and the new character of the square is reflected in the two clocks. On the façade of the railway station, just below the copy of the crown, a traditional clock shows the time; in front of the department store, however, there is a digital clock. The time of the two clocks rarely coincide.

*Under **Nyugati tér** you find an entrance to the Nyugati Pályaudvar Metro station (Third [Blue] Metro Line). It has another entrance from the ticket office of the railway station. The last section of Nagykörút, Szent István körút, stretches from Nyugati tér to the Danube. This part of the road leads through two elegant, residential districts, the 19th century Lipótváros and its extension to the north, Újlipótváros, built in the 1930s.*

VÍGSZÍNHÁZ 40A *XIII. Szent István körút 14.* When the theatre was built in 1896 this area was so much out of town that the constructor was laughed at: who on earth is going to walk such a long way to see a play? The theatre, however, became very popular through some contemporary naturalist plays and French comedies. This is where Ferenc Molnár started out on his way towards international recognition.

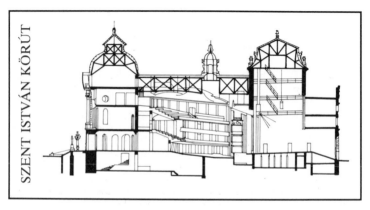

Vígszínház — a cross section

40 **A** Vígszínház, **B** The block "with the electric switches", **C** Block of flats, **D** Margaret Bridge, **E** "White House".

In hardly any other theatre company do actors enjoy a star status such as those of the Vígszínház do. The present management is trying to establish a balance between popular plays and restrained experiments. There have also been produced several musicals. When the building was constructed by the Viennese Fellner and Helmer Company, much simpler and smaller scenery was used for the plays. Nowadays scenery is stored behind the building, in a large container or in the open air, as can be seen from the window of the Művész restaurant behind the theatre building.

A rest: Pampalino Salad Bar — Hollán Ernő utca 7.

At the end of Nagykörút art nouveau has left more traces, as in the buildings at numbers 12 and 10 of Szent István körút. The latter is nicknamed the "electric switch building" by children because its white, square stone decoration brings modern switches to mind. The bus-stop for the number 26, which serves Margitsziget, is in front of this building. These buildings may look pleasant and interesting, from the inside they are just the typical Nagykörút blocks: narrow and dark. The part of Újlipótváros near the river has quite different buildings. On the site of an old industrial district dozens of modern blocks of flats were constructed in the 1930s. These blocks, although they seem to be massive, closed structures, enclose large inner courtyards where only the windows of the kitchens and of the maids' rooms opened to. The flats had modern, practical features built in and were all supplied with central heating. Almost every room has a balcony and the flats receive a lot of light through the large windows. The buildings which were strange and unusual at the time, were moved into by young, progressive sections of the middle class. The area was described by one of the residents, Antal Szerb, the writer, in his book, A Guidebook to Budapest for Martians (1935): "Nowadays you find the flattest modern palaces here. Inside the palaces young psychoanalists are laying out each other's souls on the sofas, splendid amazons of bridge games are daydreaming in snow-white bathrooms, extraordinarily intelligent clerks tune their radios to the broadcast from Moscow... Everything is modern, simple, objective and uniformed here. The whole

41 A Thonet House, B Vigadó, C Gerbaud, D Luxus Department Store.

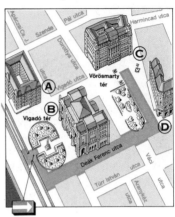

district is made up of two-room flats with a small sitting room and its residents are stubbornly, youthfully and energetically trying to conceal the only reality in their lives: none of them has any money at all." The main street of Újlipótváros is Pozsonyi út, which has as its centre the elegant Szent István park. The residents, who once were modern, young people, cling to the area they live in as is clear from the advertisements for changing flats. The value of these flats is almost as high as of those in Buda. Vígszínház draws its audiences from this area. In the auditorium, just as in the shops of the district, there are many elderly people: energetic, talkative, widowed ladies wearing much jewellery and neatly dressed gentlemen.

Their children often live somewhere around here, at most, in the housing estate built further north on the riverbank. There are a lot of new cars and pretty small shops around. The whole district apparently enjoys its sparkling life. If you decide not to finish your walk in Újlipótváros or in Margitsziget, just board the number 2 tram at the bridge; the fifth stop is Vigadó tér.

It was the longest walk, leading a long way away from the fine marble tables of the Gerbaud café. Not that you cannot discover anything new just by sitting around in the café. Only after completing this route myself and dropping on a chair there, did I first notice that the surface of the tables fall into two groups: some are homogenious some seem to have several layers — like the Gerbaud cakes. Surely you have noticed already that the legs of the tables are of three different kinds: bronze, copper and with curved legs... If you wish to make even more profound observations and have some more time to spend in Budapest, go on to the chapter For the Second Time. You can find some distressingly non-touristic tips there — even less touristic ones than in Walk Five. To those, leaving the city, may I say "Jó utat" — Bon voyage. I hope you will come back sometime.

FOR SERIOUS ADDICTS

This chapter is for those who are already past the "beginner's stage" in Budapest. It recommends various things to see off the traditional tourist routes.

TWELVE BUILDINGS

ENTRANCE TO THE ROYAL GARDENS *I. Groza Péter rakpart.* Built in 1872, at the foot of the gardens of the Royal Palace. Two elegant lions guard the gates, the premises, originally planned as shops, are now used by sculptors as workshops. The separate "kiosk" building was built to cover the chimney of the boiler-house, heating the Palace. Both buildings were designed by Miklós Ybl, whose statue is nearby.

THE MUNICIPAL LIBRARY (KÖZPONTI SZABÓ ERVIN KÖNYVTÁR) *VIII. Szabó Ervin tér 1.* The neo-Baroque palace of a baron's family from 1889. Exept for Wednesdays, it is open daily between 9.00 a.m. and 1.00 p.m. On the ground floor to the right some lines from a poem hang in the cloakroom: "Oh, what a burdensome life / dressing and undressing every morning and night!" (János Arany).

THE CHURCH IN REZSŐ TÉR *VIII. Rezső tér.* This Catholic church, which has a central arrangement with a dome, is situated on the main square of an eighty-odd-year-old housing estate. Only Classicist plans could be submitted for the competition. The church was finished in 1928; the ornamentation recalls the time of the Hungarian settlement (towards the end of the 9th century). The huge bulk of the building can be seen far off from Üllői út, the main road leading south-east (and to the Airport), though only few people go near it.

MONUMENT TO THE MARTYRS OF 1956 — PARCEL 301 *X. Új Köztemető (New Public Cemetery).* This is the monument erected from public donations, by the winner of the design competition, sculptor György Jovánovics. The site is the remotest part of the cemetery, covered by weeds until 1989, where the martyrs of the revolution, among them Prime Minister Imre Nagy was buried, far away from visitors, in unmarked graves, with face down — an intentional disgrace.

The monument is a very complex work of art, relying in its symbolism on the will of one of the executed revolutionaries, István Angyal, who mentioned a "big white piece of stone". In the center of the monument there is a column exactly 1956 mm high.

"NEW" CITY HALL IN VÁCI UTCA *V. Váci utca 62-64.* The southern, less elegant part of Váci utca was just converted to a pedestrian zone. Here stands, somewhat hidden in the narrow street that building where the 66-member City Council has its session, usually the last Thursday of the month. It is open to the public. Sometimes it is noisy and disorderly, but I don't agree with an old friend, who works there, and once described the Council with the following words: "A Flea Circus, isn't it?"

GOZSDU UDVAR *Between VII. Dob utca 16. and VII. Király utca 11., near Deák tér.* A long row of buildings with a passageway leading through them forming inner courtyards, between Dob utca and Király utca, with small shops and workshops. There is a bend in the middle of the passageway so you cannot see where you started out from if you look back. The area has preserved the atmosphere of the one-time Jewish quarter, which it is in the heart of.

THE FORMER HOUSE OF REPRESENTATIVES *VIII. Bródy Sándor utca 8.* The palace, overlooking Museum Gardens, was commissioned by Emperor Franz Joseph on 5th August 1865, the representatives had their first meeting here as little as five months later. During this time the site was assigned, plans drawn and the work done. This kept 800 workers busy day and night. Today it houses the Italian Cultural Institute.

KELETI RAILWAY STATION *VIII. Baross tér.* This main railway station of the city was at first planned to be built in line with the Nagykörút-like Nyugati Railway Station, which was still Austrian property at that time. In spite of its name (Eastern Railway Station) this is the terminus for the major express trains going westward. It was commissioned by Hungarian Railways (MÁV) and planned by Hungarian architects (Gyula Rochlitz, János Feketeházy, 1884). On each side of the glass main entrance there are the statues of George Stephenson and James Watt.

THE NAPOLEON COURTYARD *VI. Hajós utca 25.* This art nouveau block, overlooking three streets, needs to be seen from a large perspective, but it is built in a very narrow street. Notice the fine glass windows and the interesting small details of the building. High above, in the middle of the façade, a Napoleon–figure looks down in contempt at the little traffic moving in the street. No one walking there would ever guess that the Emperor is watching him.

VIII. NÉPSZÍNHÁZ UTCA 16. A typical block in the Józsefváros distric, with two inner courtyards, in which I had the pleasure of living for two years. The structure requires wooden timbers for support, enough to make up a forest. The tenants in the rear court are especially dependent on each other. The moving spirit of the building is Mr. Laci, who accepts all sorts of duties, even delivering packages in his old Volkswagen. Naturally he would also bring sodawater bottles up for the tenants and let repairmen into the flats.

THE MOST SCAFFOLDED BLOCK IN CENTRAL EUROPE *VIII. Pollack Mihály tér 1.* Behind the scaffolding there is the Institute of Sociology, Eötvös University. Behind: Hungarian Radio, now a Corporation. To the right: a beautiful gate that does not lead to anywhere. To the back: The National Museum, with the Crown Jewels.

THE WATER-LEVEL TOWER *Opposite I. Bem rakpart 3.* An ornamented iron tower of a man's height which keeps a diagram record of the water-level of the Danube. Now it works with electricity. At the Buda end of Lánchíd.

TWELVE STREETS AND SQUARES

VII. BARÁT UTCA The short street has only a few houses and looks as if it has been left behind from the 1930s. Uniform buildings with trees in front of them and mostly with their original signboards. It was rumoured that factory owners bought small flats here for their girlfriends, hence the name "Friend Street".

VIII. BAROSS UTCA This is the main street of the Józsefváros district, leading from elegant Kálvin tér through increasingly poorer parts to the suburbs. Many joiners and upholsterers opened workshops here and their typical products are often mocked by the name "Baross utca style". This nickname refers to a richly ornamented, old-fashioned furniture, which has not changed for years and years and is bought almost exclusively by the tradespeople living in the area. From Horváth Mihály tér on, the street looks like the main street of a provincial town.

VII. DOB UTCA This street leads through the whole Erzsébetváros district from Károly körút to Rottenbiller utca. The rows of buildings are never in line with each other, there is a wide variety of houses here, from ramshackle one-storey to large, four-storied buildings. The area between Kazinczy utca and Klauzál tér is "block 16", which is where a complex rehabilitation experiment was carried out. Soon after the successful reconstruction, a number of fashionable shops opened here and a post-modern building went up, in perfect harmony with its surroundings. It seems that the deterioration of the area was successfully stopped here.

II. ENDRŐDI SÁNDOR UTCA Symbol of the new Rózsadomb. In the early 1980s large villas, breaking with the tradition of being laid out at a right angle, mushroomed on this part of the hill. Large vacant sites bordered by this street, Törökvész út, Fullánk utca and Kapy utca seem to have received building permission at the same time, giving the character of a German suburb to the whole.

See Rómer Flóris utca for an example of the old Rózsadomb.

II. GARAS UTCA One of the most pleasant streets in Buda, between a park called Városmajor and Fillér utca. This where the fashionable Rózsadomb area begins. There are some carefully built apartment blocks in the street, which are higher than the villas built at the beginning of the century, and many tall trees. It looks somewhat like the XVIIth arrondisment of Paris.

VI. VÁROSLIGETI FASOR (FORMER "GORKHY" LANE) One of the most attractive streets in Pest, which leads from Lövölde tér to Városliget, that is, it runs parallel to Andrássy út — though it is much quieter. The rows of horse-chestnuts grow unharmed too. There are old and modern villas, embassies, schools and even a factory in the street. And on the corner of Bajza utca there is the legendary Grammar School of the Lutheran Church where a dozen later Nobel-prize winner émigré scientists were educated. (The school was reopened in 1989, still struggling to regain its reputation.)

II. GÜL BABA UTCA A steeply rising, picturesque cobbled street, near the Buda end of Margit híd. This street leads to the tomb of the 16th century Turkish holy man Gül Baba. The "Father of Flowers" died in Buda in 1541. His memorial is the northernmost Islamic holy place kept up with subsidies from the Turkish government. Next to the tomb there is a small look-out tower.

XV. DRÉGELYVÁR UTCA The main street of a housing estate called Újpalota, all ten-story blocks. Now they already have a good confectioner's and even a second-hand bookshop. Unfortunately the trees are growing slowly and may never become as high as the tenth floor. Recently hundreds of small shops opened on the ground floors, changig hands and characters all too often in this Budapest of a million small business enterpreneurs.

VIII. MÁTYÁS TÉR A square with a unique atmosphere in the heart of the Józsefváros district, a sort of a Budapest Harlem. It is surrounded by single-storey and six-storey buildings, workshops and pubs. The atmosphere perhaps comes from the fact that the traditional Jewish middle-class lives here together with gypsies, who have come from Koszorú utca and Tavaszmező utca; there is a touching statue of a tin-plate Christ.

II. NAPRAFORGÓ UTCA Called the "experimental housing estate" and of real interest to those who like architecture. It was built in 1931, with the support of the city, by a building entrepreneur. The twenty-two small buildings are on a small site but in a very clever arrangement. On one side, the back of the buildings overlook a small stream called Ördögárok. The names of the architects can be seen on a memorial column in the middle of the plot.

XIV. ABONYI UTCA This is an elegant, expensive short street between City Park and busy thoroughfare Thököly út. Almost totally free of noise and dirt. Blocks built in the 1920s, for diplomats and generals. Halfway there is a landmark redbrick school building, the former Jewish Secondary School (Béla Lajta, 1934.) Now it bears the name of Miklós Radnóti, the poet. (Jewish by birth, killed by Fascists in forced labour service in 1944.) This is a rare school for kids from 6 to 18. It has an atmosphere that is both inspirative and funny. Both my daughters attend that school. They sweated through the hellish 4 and a half hour test exams to get in, both of them.

Between 7.20 and 7.45 you can spot some of the best cars and some of the most concerned Jewish mothers, plus a couple of state secretaries, driving their company Volkswagen Passats. Also, some adolescents looking down on fellow-students being brought by cars. (Corner of Cházár András utca.)

XIX. KÓS KÁROLY TÉR Construction work on this working-class housing estate started in 1909, and was named after the Prime Minister who initiated the work, hence the name: Wekerle-telep. 650 single-storey and 270 one-storey houses were built here in very varied formations. Its centre, Kós Károly tér, can be approached through four ornamented gates, which were built in a style common in Transylvania. The whole gives the impression of a large village which has been swallowed up by the city. This square can be visited on the way to Ecseri Market.

TWELVE OLD SHOPS AND WORKSHOPS

A BUTCHER'S IN THE LEHEL MARKET *XIII. Lehel tér.* This shop, entirely of wood, is at the southern edge of the market, near Váci út. The walls are blue and from the ceiling hangs a huge metal fan which I have never seen in operation. The butchers, just like their predecessors must have done a hundred years ago, produce their pencil stubs from behind their ears to write the price of the meat on the wrapping paper. The diploma hanging above the door certifies that it is an "Excellent shop". The better-looking a lady-customer is, the better the meat she gets — as everywhere, butchers are great admirers of the gentle sex.

CSIZMADIA CAR ELECTRICS *VI. Podmaniczky utca 75.* The tall, bespectacled, good-humoured man, Master Csizmadia, is always surrounded by 4-5 busy assistants. He is the guardian angel of taxi drivers and gives his help immediately if he can. He also gives an immediate and accurate diagnosis, free of charge. The workshop is partly equipped with 50-60-year-old instruments and, at the back, he also has a classic American rolltop desk, always full of piles of documents.

FLEISHER SHIRTS *The corner of VI. Paulay Ede utca and VI. Nagymező utca.* There are very few people who still buy their shirts bespoke. This shop has remained here, almost unchanged, from the 1920s. Between the shopwindow and the shop itself the partition is made from the traditional, vertically striped engraved glass.

GLASS SCULPTURE (ÜVEGSZOBRÁSZAT) *V. Váci utca 68.* A very clumsy, awkward shop that partly produces useful objects, partly kitch ornaments. Like an overweight adolescent that left for a wedding in the next village, but found herself instead at a ball in the royal court. Funny and moving, a bit ridiculous.

LÁSZLÓ KLEM, FURRIER *XIII. Sallai Imre utca 18.* The small shop was modernized in the early 1960s and it still has the curved plastic letters. The notice "Latest models" must have been there since that time. At the entrance to the right a puppet dressed in a tailcoat offers notepaper and the card of the shop.

LAJOS LIBÁL, OPTICIAN *V. Veres Pálné utca 7.* Some of the furniture might well be a hundred years old — the small drawers for example. Contact lenses are now increasingly common. Several new shops have computers to examine their customers' eyes. They also have lenghty queues.

SÁNDOR PUSKÁS, SIGN-PAINTER *VI. Podmaniczky utca 18.* A traditional sign-painter's workshop very near Nyugati Railway Station. Everything is done by hand here, the brushes are put against a stick to measure the spacing. Behind the shopwindow, to the left of the entrance, one or two ageing assistants work. In the shopwindow a display of samples can be seen, not much influenced by changes in fashion.

A TOBACCONIST *XII. Márvány utca 24/b.* The usual, run-down tobacconist with everything under the sun in the shop from shoelaces through fresh wafers to magnifying glasses fastened on pens.

But there are hardly any souvenirs, which makes it different from the tobacconists in the City area, which have been flooded with various bits of kitsch, electronic games and expensive perfumes.

DÉNES VÁNDORFFY, FEMALE BUTTONS *V. Váci utca 75.* This shop is in the southern end of Váci utca, the section towards Szabadság híd. The bespectacled gentleman in a white coat, belying his age, briskly moves about his small shop. There are some quite extraordinary buttons in his drawers. If he needs some special material, he goes and gets it even "from under the earth", as the saying goes. If you stay long enough, and buy enough he tells you about his young years. Together with a group of boyscouts he visited an infamous German totalitarian leader with a mustache. He specializes exclusively in women's buttons.

THE VELVÁRT BICYCLE REPAIR WORKSHOP *VII. Wesselényi utca 56.* Nándor Velvárt was a champion cyclist in the 1920s, winning several big international races. There are old photos, drawings and newspaper clippings in the shopwindow. Everybody thinks that it is the ex-cyclist, a famous one-time cyclist. Every year the word goes around that he is retiring but then he changes his mind. He simply cannot stop working. His workshop is a fine example of poetic disorder.

LAJOS ZSUREK, CABINET MAKERS *V. Irányi utca 9.* You can peep into the workshop through the door and the window. "Contemporary" furniture is made here. There are torsos, unfinished pieces on the gallery. The light is always on until late at night.

ÁGI GYÜMÖLCS GREENGROCERS *XIII. Tátra utca 20. (Corner of Raoul Wallenberg utca).* A family venture of greengrocers, offering the freshest and best quality produce in the area. It is a small corner shop, with entrances to both streets. Inside, there is stern-looking Ági in her sixties (do not call her Aunt Ági, never!), who does not pamper her customers. A lot of family pictures on the wall, children and grandchildren — most of them are occasionally working in the shop. And there are motorcycle ads, too. But the hallmark of the shop is beyond doubt a poster — bought in Western Europe in the late sixties. It shows a very small boy, who is lifting the very short skirt of a very tall young lady, and peeping upwards. The outside of the shop witnesses the same shameful visual pollution that happens all around Budapest: the two biggest soft drink producers of the world want to win the decisive battle here in New Leopold Town. Both are here, on the façade. They are bigger than the original, clumsy sign.

TWELVE IMPRESSIONS

THE "ECSERI" SECOND-HAND MARKET *XIX. Nagykőrösi út 156.* The market, which has been driven out further and further of town, step by step, is more interesting and varied than fleamarkets in many Western cities. It is rather like an antique shop crossed with a junk store, having all sorts of tit-bits some Western treasure hunters are looking for. There are silver pocket watches, Thonet chairs, re-cast copper lamps; there are also trendy Italian jeans, the latest pop records and plastic carrier bags just for the price of 3-5 litres of milk. There are folk costumes, art nouveau blankets, "Everything-for-20-Forints" piles of clothes and all sorts of goods which may not be available in the town. Although foreigners are usually over-charged, they can usually find something which is in fashion again at home but is still rubbish here. Bauhaus furniture is now becoming fashionable here but that from the 1950s still counts as trash. As it is quite difficult to get good quality modern furniture, some of the young furnish their homes from here. They fight over a piece with property men from theatres or with dealers over from Austria. The market is a museum of man-created forms, where there is a mixture of old and new, poor and rich; fine and chaotic. Nobody likes being photographed here but you can get old pictures and postcards.

The Ecseri Market can be found at the opening of the E5 motorway, coming from the city, next to the first footbridge over the road. Accessible by Bus 54.

THE WALLED-IN LADY, AWAITING HER HUSBAND *XIV. Thököly út 61*. On the side-wall of a yellow apartment block a strange, life-size statue is watching the street. According to the legend, this woman, her hair in a bun, spent many a day on this balcony, waiting for her husband's return from the Great War. She died of the Spanish influenza, two days before he arrived home. The husband had the statue erected in honour of his wife's fidelity.

THE "FUIT" STONE *XIV. Városliget, between Olof Palme sétány and Hermina út*. A simple tomb stone with the one Latin word carved into it: FUIT (was). A lawyer in Pest, who wished to remain unknown, left a large amount of money to the city and asked in return to be buried here and in this manner. On All Souls Day, November 1st, many people light candles at his stone, remembering their own loved ones. Near the Museum of Transport, in the direction of Dózsa György út.

BOTANICAL GARDENS (HORTUS BOTANICUS) *VIII. Illés utca 25. T: 133-4333*. A pathetically neglected garden, full of the scents of the six thousand types of plants. The octagonal, glass-covered palm-houses in the middle (József Drescher, 1867), are in an awful state, some of them used as dwelling places for families. Buying tickets is not taken seriously, nor is closing time. The huge, old, white dog hardly moves. Plants can be seen in taxonomical arrangement, from 9 a.m. to 4 p.m. on weekdays and from 9 a.m. to 1 p.m. at the weekend. The city has not protected this treasure. A large high-rise block now stands right next to it.

THE SECOND-HAND SHOP IN HERNÁD UTCA *VII. Hernád utca 7*. The shop offers things like bronze chandeliers, used prams and cheap china-ware. They have probably the widest range of the products of the East-European souvenir industry: glass fish, tapestry, plates to hang on the wall. There is no danger of being accused of smuggling art treasure on leaving the country if you buy anything here.

THE LUKÁCS'S GARDEN AND THE THANKSGIVING TABLETS *II. Frankel Leó út 25-29*. There has been a spa on the site of this 100-year-old building since the 16th century. It is also since then that those cured have placed tablets here to express their gratitude. The tablets on the wall praise the medicinal power of the spa itself. It is frequented by many senior journalists close to the Establishment, and other leading lights.

THE TOTALITARIAN STATUE THEME PARK *XXII. Balatoni út, corner of Szabadkai utca. T: 227-7446*. The debate what to do with the Lenins, Marxes and local versions in marble and bronze (to let them stay where they are or to destroy them) ended in a wise compomise: they were relocated to the outskirts of Budapest. Most of them are bad artwork, but not all. The park is hardly visited by anyone, its derelict, neglected atmosphere adds to the experience in an unintentional way. A must for the serious addict of Budapest. A very nice outing, which takes about 30 minutes by car from the centre. On the way home it is stylish to have lunch or dinner in the theme restaurant called Marxim's (II. Kisrókus utca 23. T: 115-5036. Open 11 a.m. to 1 a.m. Mon-Sat, 6 p.m. to 1 a.m. Sun.) This place became famous, when they were tried for violating the law that bans using totalitarian insignia. The lady judge who were given the case then visited the place and dropped the charge, declaring that "the social danger it poses on society is negligible".

THE MAIN HALL OF THE POLYCLINIC IN PÉTERFY SÁNDOR UTCA *VII. Péterfy Sándor utca 8.* The hospital was built by the Insurance Company for Civil Servants in 1934. Seeing the gaunt outside of the building, you would not guess how elegant the two-floor high hall is inside, with its glass roof that could be opened. In the hospital wing there used to be sitting rooms and kitchenettes on every floor. Even a roof garden was built for sunbathing and the wards had only 3-5 patients. Not any more, when the author of this book was born here.

XIV. ÖRS VEZÉR TÉR — THE EASTERN GATE OF THE CITY The Örs vezér tér terminal of the Second (Red) Metro Line decants people by the thousand into the subway. Some are hurrying towards the housing estate, some are travelling on to neighbouring villages by suburban train. 300,000 people use this subway every morning. This is where one of the funniest newsagents in the city can be found. His most famous shout is: "Ma még van még" (Some more left, just today). Here they shout out real or made-up headlines. The popular, bearded newsagent collects about 60-70 kilogrammes of coins every single day. One of his famous "headlines" is: "The wandering knife-grinder drank himself to death".

XIX. KÓS KÁROLY TÉR Construction work on this working-class housing estate started in 1909, and was named after the Prime Minister who initiated the project, hence the name: Wekerle-telep. 650 single-story and 270 one-story houses were built here in very varied formations. Its centre, Kós Károly tér, can be approached through four ornamented gates, which were built in a style common in Transylvania. The whole gives the impression of a large village which has been swallowed up by the city. The square is easy to visit on the way to the Ecseri fleamarket.

XV. PÓLUS CENTER SHOPPING MALL *XV. Nyírpalota utca, corner of Szentmihályi út, off Motorway 3.* The biggest of the recently built shopping malls, the inside of which imitates a wild west frontier town — and it appeals to the visitors. Several hundred small shops, ice-rink, a multiplex cinema. Occasionally you can meet an imaginative name of a business. I liked a bonds and shares vendor called "Góg" there, which is a clear hint to a poem of giant early 20th-century poet Endre Ady. Budapest Chief Architect István Schneller keeps on explaining that shopping malls will soon erode the traditional shop-network of the inner city, and attempts a crusade against new malls, but the 23 districts of Budapest are independent fiefdoms, and Budapest is a really loose Commonwealth.

TWELVE STYLES
The most typical buildings of the city are listed here, some of them have already been mentioned in our Walks. No styles are mentioned from the times before the 18th century, only those which have contributed to the present face of the city.

BAROQUE *(especially its Austrian version)* St Anna Church (I. Batthyány tér), Egyetemi templom (The University Church — V. Eötvös Loránd utca 5.), Orthodox Serbian Church (V. Szerb utca 4.), Franciscan Monastery and Church in Buda (II. Mártírok útja 23.), the Town Hall in Buda (I. Szentháromság utca 2.), Endrődy palace (I. Táncsics Mihály utca 3.), the Semmelweis-house (I. Apród utca 1-3.), the Central City Hall, previously a hospital for disabled soldiers, "Invalidusház" (V. Városház utca 9-11.), the Castle in Nagytétény (XXII. Csókási Pál utca 9-11.).

CLASSICISM The National Museum (VIII. Múzeum körút 14-16.), the former Valero Silk Factory (V. Honvéd utca 26-30.), the Synagogue in Óbuda (III. Lajos utca 163.), the Country Hall (V. Városház utca 7.), the former Ludovika Academy of Military Sciences (VIII. Ludovika tér), the Trattner-House (V. Petőfi Sándor utca 2.), Károlyi Palace (V. Károlyi Mihály utca 16.), the former István Főherceg szálló (Archduke Stephen Hotel — V. Akadémia utca 16.).

ROMANTIC The Vigadó in Pest (V. Vigadó tér), the Synagogue (VII. Dohány utca 2-8.), the Unger-house (Múzeum körút 7.), the Pekáry-house (VII. Király utca 47.), the Kauser-house (VIII. Gyulai Pál utca 5.), Toldy Grammar School (I. Toldy Ferenc utca 9.), Nyugati Railway Station (VI. Nyugati tér), the former House of Representatives (VIII. Bródy Sándor utca 8.).

ECLECTIC *(We have seen so many examples of this style during the Walks that here only some lesser known, but fine buildings are mentioned:)* The new Town Hall (V. Váci utca 62-64.), the Palace of Alajos Károlyi (VIII. Pollack Mihály tér), the Parish Church in Ferencváros (IX. Bakáts tér), the Parish Church in Erzsébetváros (VII. Rózsák tere), the Ádám-house (VIII. Bródy Sándor utca 4.)

ART NOUVEAU The Museum of Applied Arts (IX. Üllői út 33-37.), the Parish Church in Kőbánya (X. Szent László tér), a block of flats (V. Honvéd utca 3.), Gresham Palace (V. Roosevelt tér 5.), the Geological Institute (XIV. Stefánia út 14.), the Academy of Music (VI. Liszt Ferenc tér 8.), the Post Office Savings Bank (V. Hold utca 4.), the Gellért Hotel and Baths (XI. Szent Gellért tér).

FOLKLORISTIC-MODERN ("NATIONAL ROMANTICISM") Elementary School (XII. Városmajor utca 59.), a residential block (VIII. Népszínház utca 19.), the Nerve Surgery Institute (XIV. Amerikai út 57.), a residential block (XIII. Váci út 36.), the Calvinist Church in Városligeti fasor (VI. Városligeti fasor 4.), the Palatinus-houses (XIII. Pozsonyi út 2.).

NEO-NEO-BAROQUE ("CORVIN-CINEMA STYLE") The Corvin Cinema (VIII. Kisfaludy köz), Kaffka Margit Grammar School (XI. Villányi út 5-7.), the former Cistercian Grammar School (XI. Villányi út 27.), the block of flats built for a mining company (V. Kossuth Lajos tér 13-15.), the former Cyclop Garage (VII. Kertész utca 24.), the new part of Széchenyi Baths (XIV. Állatkerti körút), the original façade of Corvin Department Store (VIII. Blaha Lujza tér).

BAUHAUS The row of apartment blocks lining XIII. Szent István park, the Atrium-houses and the cinema (II. Mártírok útja 55.), an apartment block (V. Régiposta utca 13.), the airport in Budaörs, the bell tower of the Catholic Church in Városmajor (XII. Csaba utca 7.), an apartment block (VII. Rákóczi út 4.), the Post Office headquarters (VII. Hársfa utca 47.), Calvinist Church and office buildings (V. Szabadság tér 2.), the housing estate in Napraforgó utca (IInd district).

THE STYLE OF THE 1950s The Council House of the IInd District (II. Mechwart tér), the Dubbing Film Studio (II. Vöröshadsereg útja 68.), the College of Applied Arts (II. Zugligeti út 9-25.), a building complex (XIV. Pákozdi tér area), the Party Headquarters in Óbuda (III. Flórián tér), a student hostel (XI. Bercsényi utca 28-30.), the MOM Cultural Centre (XII. Csörsz utca 18.).

THE STYLE OF THE 1960s An office building (V. Bécsi utca 3.), a transmission station (IX. Csarnok tér 3.), Trade Union Centre (XIII. Váci út 73.), Kőbánya Cinema (X. Szent László tér), an apartment block (V. József nádor tér 8.), the Budapest Hotel (II. Szilágyi Erzsébet fasor 47.), the headquarters of the Hungarian Automobile Association (II. Rómer Flóris utca 4.), the staircase block (I. Gellérthegy utca 35.), the temporary National Theatre (VII. Hevesi Sándor tér 4.), the false façade of Corvin Department Store (VIII. Blaha Lujza tér), the Aluminium Indrustry Trust Building (XIII. Pozsonyi út 56.).

THE STYLE OF THE 1970s Skála Budapest Department Store and the market (XI. Körösy József utca 6-10.), office building and car-park (V. Martinelli tér), Duna Intercontinental Hotel, University of Horticulture, the lecture-hall wing (XI. Villányi út 35.), Conference Centre (XI. Villányi út 35.), the central buildings of the Medical University (IX. Nagyvárad tér 1.), Athenaeum Printing House (X. Kozma utca 2.), Domus furniture store (XIII. Róbert Károly körút 67.), Hilton Hotel (I. Hess András tér).

BUDAPEST BESTS : : BUDAPEST BESTS : : BUDAPEST BESTS
Peter Doherty, Translator, Teacher, Virtuoso of English

The riverscape, the finest in Europe. The Danube scurries through Vienna, avoiding eye-contact, like an elderly aunt who lives with relatives who are ashamed of her. But she parades through the heart of Budapest in grace and beauty, boldly returning the admiring looks she draws. There are many vantage points to admire her from. In Autumn one of the best is from the Pest side of the Margaret Bridge: Parliament rises from the curve of the river, the Castle lies aslant opposite and Gellért Hill looms over all the gray stillness.

The Budapest markets, better than any calendar. Budapest people, so many still with their roots in the country, have the countryman's appreciation of fresh produce. And follow the progress of the year through their tables.

Fő utca, stories in stone. The history of a city is encompassed in this one street, every building a talkative witness of what is past, passing and to come.

Jókai bean soup, a Hungarian variation on a Central European theme. A supper for a Winter evening, to dispel the cold outside, to warm the heart. Like almost all the delights of home cooking, ignored by the luxury restaurants — but can be savoured in those scruffy, over-heated, cheerful places that the locals know and treasure.

Hungarian folk music. An atavistic experience, especially when the solo voice is that of a woman.

The Holocaust Memorial by Imre Varga, the poetry of pity. Varga is the creator of some of Budapest's finest modern public sculptures. When near any of them, there are many who steer themselves so as to pass by. This, in the courtyard of the Great Synagogue, thunders in quiet remembrance of Hungarian Jews murdered by Nazism.

BUDAPEST BESTS : : BUDAPEST BESTS : : BUDAPEST BESTS

Iván András Bojár, Art Historian, Professional Passer-By, A Castle District Kid

What I especially like in my native city is its transitional character. These days I prefer those corners, quarters and buildings that were reshaped by economic and social change in the funniest way. The former "Stalin Baroque" style workers' hostel in Fehérvári út, for instance, that was converted into a cheap hotel by some smart guys (called Hotel Ventura now.) The stern Classisism of the one-time dictatorship was diluted in some tacky postmodern shapes.

Another building I like is witnessing an attempt at reversing the times. Architectural progress (or "progress") reawakened the ideals of an earlier epoch. In Váci út (No. 202/a) there was a featureless, 70s style building: ten stories of modernistic, flavourless boredom. Now, when the former Main Street of the Dictatorship of the Proletariat is being radically revamped by multinational developers, a native real estate businessman wanted to be included in the pack, among the recent trade centers. He bought this block, detested by others, and had it redecorated inside. Outside, he commissioned half-columns (so-called pilasters) on the hitherto bare facade, that perfectly fit the older buildings around, most of them from the 50s. He managed to have it painted it with the most vulgar of the pinks, and let Coca Cola paint on the side of the building its biggest ad in Central Europe.

A third of my "favourites" is the Trade Center on the corner of József Attila utca and Bajcsy-Zsilinszky út, designed by József Finta, who is a definitive architect of present-day Budapest. This dusty, by now grey building was one of the first trade centers built for foreigners. Its perplexing hodgepodge of forms is a most charming visual impact of the crisis of identities in an age of transition.

These buildings, no doubt, will be hard to interpret in thirty years time. Appreciate, please, the added value. Now, and in thirty years time.

THE END OF MODERNISM The Novotel, Penta, Forum and the Hyatt Hotels, the Institute of Haematology (XI. Daróczi út 24.), the Recreation Centre in Almássy tér (VII. Almássy tér 6.), the Krisztina Telephone Exchange (XII. Városmajor utca 35-37.), Skála Metro Department Store and office building (VI. Nyugati tér 1-2.), the new section of the Museum of transport (XIV. Városligeti körút 11.), Waste Re-cycling Works (XV. Szántóföld utca 119-121.).

POST-MODERN The Taverna Hotel and Trade Centre (V. Váci utca 20. and 19.), a block of flats (VII. Klauzál tér 12.), the Villa District in Endrődi Sándor utca (IInd district), the Bartók memorial building (II. Csalán utca 29.), the Ady Endre Cultural Centre (IV. Tavasz utca 4.), Hotel Kempinski Corvinus (V. Bécsi utca), International Trade Centre (V. Bajcsy-Zsilinszky út 12.), Hotel Liget (VI. Dózsa György út 106.), Office block (I. Hegyalja út 21.), National Police Headquarters (XIII. Teve utca 1.).

WHO WAS WHO

PERIODS OF HUNGARIAN HISTORY

895–896	THE SETTLEMENT (Hungarian tribes reach the Carpathian Basin)
955	Raids and incursions into Western Europe
1000	ST STEPHEN CONVERTS HUNGARY TO CHRISTIANITY
1000–1541	INDEPENDENT HUNGARIAN KINGDOM
	1241-42 Mongolian Invasion
	1458-1490 King Mátyás (Matthias)
	1526 Utter defeat of the Hungarian army by the Turks
1541–1686	TURKISH OCCUPATION
1686–1867	THE HABSBURG DYNASTY
	1703-1711 War of Independence led by Ferenc Rákóczi II
	1848-49 Revolution and War of Independence
	1867 The Austro/Hungarian Compromise
1867–1918	AUSTRO/HUNGARIAN COMPROMISE
1918–19	HUNGARIAN REPUBLIC
	1918 Revolution
	1919 Hungarian Soviet Republic
1919–46	KINGDOM WITHOUT A KING
	Admiral Miklós Horthy as Regent
	The Versailles Treaty of 1920 assigned 3/5 of the country to successor states
1941	Entry into the war as an ally of Germany
1944	Attempts to negotiate an armistice
1944	GERMAN INVASION
1944–48	HUNGARIAN REPUBLIC (Multi-party parliamentary democracy)
1948	"Year of the Turnover": Communist coup d'état.
1956 23 Oct	REVOLUTION
1956 4 Nov	János Kádár returns in Russian tanks.
1956–58	The Revenge. Over 400 executions, including Imre Nagy and his circle
1963	Amnesty to most political prisoners
1968	New Economic Management
1972–73	Reform refrozen
1979	Stagnation starts
1984–86	Debts doubled — but boosting policies fail
1988 May	Ailing, outmanoevred Kádár deposed after 32 years in power
1990 25 March	First democratic elections

NAMES ON STREETSIGNS AND STATUES

This is a selective list of people whose names we have met in street names. Law does not permit the naming of a street after people deceased less than 5 years before.

ADY, ENDRE (1877-1919) Poet, journalist, founder of modern Hungarian lyric poetry; central figure of intellectual life at the beginning of the century.

ANONYMUS (late 11th century — early 12th century?) Chronicler, author of the earliest Hungarian historical work, Gesta Hungarorum. See "Walk Four", Vajdahunyad Castle, about him and his statue.

APÁCZAI CSERE, JÁNOS (1625-1659) Hungarian theologist in Transylvania, writer, teacher. Author of the Hungarian Encyclopedia.

ARANY, JÁNOS (1817-1882) The greatest Hungarian epic poet. His statue is in front of the National Museum.

ÁRPÁD, PRINCE (?-907?) Leader of the alliance of tribes which conquered the territory of present-day Hungary, chieftain of the "Magyar" tribe. Ancestor of Hungarian kings.

AULICH, LAJOS (1792-1849) General, Minister of Defence during the 1848 War of Independence. One of the 13 generals executed after the defeat.

BABITS, MIHÁLY (1883-1941) Poet, literary translator and novelist. Major influence on literary life.

BAJCSY-ZSILINSZKY, ENDRE (1886-1944) Political writer and politican, a leader of the resistance during World War II. Executed at Christmas 1944.

BALASSI, BÁLINT (1554-1594) Great poet and womanizer of the Hungarian Renaissance. One of the first to write poetry in Hungarian, not Latin. His statue is in Kodály körönd.

BAROSS, GÁBOR (1848-1892) Politician, the Iron Minister. Initiator of the nationalization of the railway system and the organization of cheap transport. His statue is in the square named after him.

BARTÓK, BÉLA (1881-1945) Composer, pianist, musicologist and teacher. A major figure in 20th-century European music. Died in New York. He declared in his will that no street can bear his name until there is a Hitler Square and a Mussolini Square in Budapest.

BÁTHORI, ISTVÁN (1533-1586) Prince of Transylvania, from 1576 King of Poland.

BATTHYÁNY, LAJOS (1806-1849) Landowner, politician. The first Prime Minister in 1848. Executed after the defeat.

BEM, JÓZSEF (1794-1850) Polish army officer, Hungarian general, leading figure in the 1848-49 War of Independence.

BLAHA, LUJZA (1850-1926) Leading actress and prima donna, the "Nightingale of the Nation".

BORÁROS, JÁNOS (1755-1834) Chief Justice, later Mayor of Pest. He opened Városliget to the public.

BRÓDY, SÁNDOR (1863-1924) Writer, dramatist and muckraker journalist. Helped naturalism to be accepted in Hungary.

CLARK, ÁDÁM (1811-1866) English architect, directed the construction of Lánchíd, designed the Tunnel. Settled in Hungary.

CSOKONAI, VITÉZ MIHÁLY (1773-1805) Poet, dramatist, teacher. The major figure in the Hungarian Enlightenment.

DEÁK, FERENC (1803-1876) Politician, lawyer, the "Sage of the Nation". Had a decisive role in the Compromise with the Habsburgs (1867). His statue is in Roosevelt tér.

DÜRER, ALBRECHT "Ajtósi" (1471-1528) German painter and graphic artist. His father immigrated to Nürnberg from a Hungarian village called Ajtós. The "Dürer" name is a literal translation of the name of the Hungarian village.

EÖTVÖS, JÓZSEF (1813-1871) Writer, poet and politician. Introduced Public Education Law. His statue is outside the Forum Hotel.

EÖTVÖS, LORÁND (1848-1919) University professor of physics, minister, son of József Eötvös, inventor of an important instrument named after him and still used in geological research.

ERKEL, FERENC (1810-1893) Composer, conductor and pianist. Founded the national opera and composed the music for the national anthem.

ERZSÉBET (Elizabeth), Queen (1837-1898) Wife of Franz Jozeph Austrian Emperor and King of Hungary. She learned the Hungarian language and spent a great deal of time in Hungary.

GÁRDONYI, GÉZA (1863-1922) Writer, poet and teacher. Still one of the most widely read writers.

HUNYADI, JÁNOS (1407?-1456) Regent and army leader. His victories over the Turkish army temporarily held up the Turkish onslought. Father of King Matthias. His statue is on Halászbástya.

INNOCENT XI, (1611-1689) Benedetto Odescalchi as Pope; called for the liberation of Hungary from Turkish rule. His statue is in the Castle District in Hess András tér.

JÁSZAI, MARI (1850-1926) Great Hungarian tragic actress. Played many leading Shakespearian roles in the National Theatre.

JÓKAI, MÓR (1825-1904) Prolific novelist, the greatest figure of Hungarian romantic prose. Hero of the 1848 Revolution, keeping the spirit of the revolution alive later, he was Member of Parliament for a while.

JÓZSEF, ATTILA (1905-1937) Poet, the greatest figure in 20th century Hungarian poetry. His statue is near Parliament, at the bank of the Danube.

JÓZSEF, Palatine of Hungary (1776-1847) Austrian regent, who helped the development of Pest. His statue is in József Nádor tér, the square named after him.

JULIANUS THE MONK (?-1289?) Hungarian monk and traveller who, on his journey in Asia, found the original home of the Hungarians and warned of the Mongolian invasion. His statue is behind the Hilton Hotel.

KAPISZTRÁN (Capistrano), (St) János (1386-1456) Monk, inquisitor and army leader. Had a major role in the victory over the Turks in 1456.

KARINTHY, FRIGYES (1887-1938) Writer, poet, classic Hungarian humourist, legendary jester.

KÁROLYI, MIHÁLY (1875-1955) Landowner, politician, the first President of the Hungarian Republic (1918). His ashes were ceremoniously brought back to Hungary in 1962. His statue is to the right of the Parliament.

KODÁLY, ZOLTÁN (1882-1967) Composer, musicologist, teacher of music. Colleague and friend of Bartók's.

KOSSUTH, LAJOS (1802-1894) Lawyer, journalist, politician. Outstanding figure in the Reform Age just before the 1848 War of Independence, then Hungarian leader during the War as Regent. Died in exile in Torino.

KOSZTOLÁNYI, DEZSŐ (1885-1936) Poet, novelist, literary translator, journalist. One of the first to use urban life in large cities as a subject for novels. See "Reading".

LECHNER, ÖDÖN (1845-1914) Architect, philosopher of architecture, master of the Hungarian art nouveau.

LISZT, FERENC (1811-1886) romantic composer, pianist, founder of the Academy of Music.

MADÁCH, IMRE (1823-1864) Dramatist who lived in isolation in the country. Writer of "The Tragedy of Man", the classic Hungarian drama. His statue is on Margitsziget.

MIKSZÁTH, KÁLMÁN (1847-1910) Novelist, polemicist on social iusses. The prolific literary figure who revived popular prose.

MUNKÁCSY, MIHÁLY (1844-1900) Realist painter, well known in Europe. His paintings are in the National Gallery.

NAGY, IMRE (1896-1958) Communist politician turned revolutionary. See more of him in "Walk Two", under his statue.

PÁZMÁNY, PÉTER (1570-1637) Archbishop of Esztergom, cardinal, writer. Leading figure of the Counter-Reformation in Hungary. Budapest University used to bear his name.

PETERMANN, JUDGE (late 13th century — early 14th century) Justice in Buda of Hungarian nationality between 1302-9, when the citizens of Buda excommunicated the Pope.

PETŐFI, SÁNDOR (1823-1849) Prolific romantic poet, revolutionary politician. His statue is on the bank of the Danube.

RÁKÓCZI, FERENC II (1616-1735) Hungarian prince who became the Regent, led the War of Independence between 1703 and 1711. Died in exile in Turkey.

SAVOY, EUGENE of (1663-1736) French-Austrian prince, army general, liberator of Hungary. His statue is in front of the Royal Palace.

SEMMELWEIS, IGNÁC (1818-1865) Professor of Medicine, the "Saviour of Mothers". The surgeon to first realize the importance of antisepsis.

SZÉCHENYI, ISTVÁN (1791-1860) Hungarian count, politician and writer, called "the greatest of Hungarians". The prime mover behind innumerable Hungarian public institutions and enterprises. His statue is in Roosevelt tér.

SZENT ISTVÁN, St. Stephen (?977-1038) King, founder of the Hungarian state, converted to Christianity in 1000. His statue is on Halászbástya.

SZONDI, GYÖRGY (?-1552) Soldier, commander of a castle which he defended with a garrison of 150 Hungarians against 10,000 Turks. He fell there with all his soldiers. His statue is in Kodály Körönd.

TÁNCSICS, MIHÁLY (1799-1884) Politician, journalist. Imprisoned for his ideas several times in the street which now bears his name. His portrait is on the wall of his former prison.

VAK BOTTYÁN, JÁNOS (?1643-1709) Legendary military leader of the Rákóczi War of Independence, a talented strategist. In a battle he lost one eye, hence his nikname of "vak" (blind). His statue is in Kodály körönd.

VÖRÖSMARTY, MIHÁLY (1800-1855) Romantic poet, author of one of the most influential patriotic poems in the last century. His statue is in the square named after him in the City.

WESSELÉNYI, MIKLÓS (1796–1850) Political writer, reformer, the "Hero of the Flood" of 1838. One of the leaders of the anti-Austrian opposition before the Revolution.

YBL, MIKLÓS (1814-1891) Leading Hungrian architect, designer of the Opera House, the Basilica and many other public buildings, master of the neo-Renaissance style. His statue is on the bank of the Danube, at the foot of Castle Hill.

ZICHY, MIHÁLY (1827-1906) Painter, graphic artist, welcomed in serval European royal courts. He died in St Petersburg.

ZRÍNYI, MIKLÓS (?1508-1566) Hungarian nobleman, who was killed at the siege of Szigetvár, defending the castle. His statue is in Kodály körönd.

ZRÍNYI, MIKLÓS (1620-1664) Army commander, poet, the "Hero of the Sword and the Lute". Wrote a famous epic on the heroic deeds of his afore-mentioned great grandfather. His statue is in front of the Vígszínház.

A CITY TO ENJOY

EATING WELL AND NOT TOO MUCH

Those with long memories speak nostalgically of the Budapest restaurants of the inter-war years. In what was "the most peaceful, easygoing and least expensive city in Europe", an enormous number of restaurants competed for the discerning customer. Then came the war and the lean years that followed. In a dictonary of mine, published in the fifties, the entry at "banana" is an illustration with minimal attempt at explanation of a phenomenon so outside ordinary experience. Like many other children of the sixties I felt that things were getting better, improving all the time. The exception, however, was eating out. My childhood memories are of rows with waiters and of food left barely touched on the table. I later came to understand that all restaurants had the dead rigid hand of large catering companies on them. The new hotels that went up in the seventies brought new standards with them and they attracted the talented and ambitious. Eventually in the early eighties a system of contract leasing whereby restaurants were let out on three to five year leases to the highest (sealed) bid, came into being. This has led to a proliferation of privately run restaurants — often in impossible locations, for example in a street famous only for its courts of justice and rows of ambulances parked on standby alert. Over the past five years establishments ranging from those serving hamburgers to those using silverware have joined together to provide good home cooking for their delighted neighbours.

Who remembers that now, just after the restaurant revolution?

HUNGARIAN COOKING The predominant influence on Hungarian cooking has long been Austrian and thus, indirectly, French. Interestingly enough it was French chefs, mainly employed at the great houses, who "liberated" Hungarian cooking from the Austrian. Just as French cuisine turned to peasant and traditional dishes for inspiration, so too did these chefs look to Hungarian peasant cooking and brought it into the mainstream of European tastes.

The basis of Hungarian peasant cooking is heavy "rántás", a roux of rich flour and pork lard. This naturally requires rich spicing and gets it from red paprika. Yet the use of paprika, now thought of as a defining feature of Hungarian cooking, only dates from the latter half of the eighteenth century. Ground paprika, however, is a Hungarian innovation. Slowly the eating of the fiery pepper became a Hungarian virtus and as the saying goes, "a real Magyar can handle his strong paprika well". Another feature of Hungarian cooking is the use of sour cream. Soups and pasta also figure strongly — the latter because of the excellence of our flour. Our traditional cooking was only "Europeanized" about a hundred years ago: this conjoinig is Hungarian cooking.

The heyday of hospitality and eating out was that commonly evoked European golden age — the two decades before the outbreak of the First World War. In Hungary it has its own chronicler: the novelist and short story writer, Gyula Krúdy (1878-1933, his statue is in III. Szentlélek tér).

His work, still as popular as ever, abounds in the sensuous evocation and celebration of food and its eating. His name has been bequeathed to more than 100 dishes, all of which are worth trying.

It would be only a slight exaggeration to say that Hungarian cooking of today is his meditation of the peasant cooking already referred to. For many of us Krúdy's name evokes a marrowbone. Let me explain. Zoltán Huszárik's film Szindbád (1971) was based on Krúdy's stories of the same name. (The film deservedly features high on a recent critics' poll of the twelve best Hungarian films ever, see "Entertainment".) It contains a scene in which the eponymous hero — and the camera — gaze lovingly on a golden coloured bowl of soup. Szindbád expertly cracks the marrowbone and the camera closes in onto the marrow as it shimmers on the surface of a crispy slice of toast. Audiences inevitably and involuntarily gasped with pleasure. The scene has passed into the subjective consciousness of the nation and may well have contributed to the revival and rejuvenation of traditional dishes.

This process has gone far, even though Budapest can still not bear comparison with a French or an Italian city for the range and quality of its cooking. (Hungarian cooking has not encompassed a wide usage of herbs or vegetables and the recent revolution in French taste is still in the offing.) Nevertheless I doubt that anyone will be seriously disappointed in any of the establishments I list below. They have all been checked personally and in consultation with two restaurateurs. This selection from the more than 5,000 eating establishments should provide sustenance and more to the visitor.

For good cookery books see "Reading".

ELEGANT RESTAURANTS *Listed below are those which do not cater for block-booked tourist groups — hence the omission of one or two wellknown names. This is not to say their food is bad, but I feel that the individual customer tends to have difficulty in getting reasonable attention from a staff busy with and harrassed by these groups. Nor are restaurants of the major hotels included since what they serve is, in general, standard international hotel fare. I am told that the restaurants of the Gellért, the Intercontinental and the Forum enjoy a high reputation within the profession.*

AMADEUS *V. Apáczai Csere János utca 13. T: 118-4677.* Open: 12-24, weekdays; Sun-Sat: 18-24. No credit cards. Capacity: 50. A recently enlarged chic place with designer décor. No printed menu, just the blackboard over the counter. Everything, except for the superb salads, is cooked over charcoal, — that's why it takes ages. They shamefully overcharge for bottled mineral water. A favourite of Hungarian intellectuals in the fast lane.

BAROKK *VI. Mozsár utca 12. T: 131-8942.* Open: noon to midnight. Capacity: 45. A theme restaurant, a good one. Waiters wear a costume and serve the period dishes very attentively. They really mean the style, but the décor does not stand up in the light of day.

BELCANTO *VI. Dalszínház utca 8. T: 111-8471.* Open: 6 p.m. to 2 a.m. Capacity: 100. Another theme place, a curious one, 50 metres from the Opera House. The waiters stop and sing an occasional quartet or quintet, with the aid of some opera singers. Understandably overpriced. Always tourist-

and celebrity-packed. It is doomed to be naffness, still, it isn't for reasons I don't know. (Maybe because the waiters really love the opera? Or the closeness of the most beautiful opera in the world?) A welcome addition to the restaurant scene.

CYRANO *V. Kristóf tér 7-8. T: 266-3096.* Open: 11 a.m. to midnight. Capacity: 40. A favourite of the trendy Budapest business community: a place to stay for a long time. The idiosynchratic décor includes a big chandelier that was the stage prop during the shooting of the Cyrano film (the Dépardieu version), hence the name. Considering all that, reasonably priced. The small balcony has pleasant tables, but not all. The picture of the horse on the wall (the one that looks like a Fellini Roma discovery), is of course a fake, designed by the restaurateur, an amateur designer, who conceived the whole place.

FAUSTO'S *VII. Dohány utca 5. T: 122-7806.* Open: Noon 3 p.m., 7 p.m. to 11 p.m. Mon-Sat. Capacity: 60. An outstanding, unpretentious place, where it is pretty impossible to park. Come by taxi or by your chauffeur-driven company car. The Venetian kitsch décor is too grades lower than the food. Booking is of course essential. Called simply the best Italian food in Central Europe — no small feat, considering the supply.

GARVICS *III. Ürömi köz 2. T: 168-3254.* Open: 5 p.m. to midnight. Closed on Sundays. Capacity: 45. A sort of grey eminence on the Budapest culinary scene: hardly advertised, and not every nouveau riche robber baron knows about it. In the III. district, in a quickly gentrifying neighbourhood called "Újlak", in a building by a contemporary star architect of the "National Heritage School".

GUNDEL *XIV. Állatkerti körút 2. T: 321-3550.* Open: Noon to 4 p.m., 7 p.m. to 12 p.m. daily. The crowned king of the scene, with prices according. See "Walk Four" in detail, pp. 124.

LÉGRÁDI *V. Magyar utca 23. T: 118-6804.* Open: 7 p.m. to 1 a.m. Capacity: 35. An almost secretive luxury restaurant, never advertised. Incredibly elegant — almost a stately home of an eccentric baron from the beginning of the last century. It is to be found in a cellar in a winding street in the non-touristic part of Inner City, just opposite one-time "Maison Frida", a former red-lamp house. There are oil-paintings on its white walls and antique furniture provide the décor. Herend china, silver cutlery, tailcoated waiters and the white-tied Légrádi brothers who have given their name to the establishment watch over quiet unhurried service. Seems an age-old established place. Essential to book. Quiet live music. Ladies get menues without prices.

LE LÉGRÁDI ANTIQUE *V. Bárczy István utca 3-5. T 266-4993.* Open: noon to 3 p.m., 7 p.m. to midnight, Mon-Fri. On the outer wall of the side of City Hall, camouflaged by a luxury antique shop downstairs, which you actually have to go through, when entering the elegant-but-not-posh place which is known only to the initiated, or those invited by Mayor Demszky or one of the deputy mayors with style. Really attentive, smooth, impeccable service, you can feel in a French small town aristocrat's mansion at least 150 years ago. Hardly known to Budapest nouveau riche community, maybe because they want to be seen.

MÚZEUM *VIII. Múzeum kert 12. T: 138-4221.* Open: 10 a.m. to 2 a.m. Capacity: 150. As the name suggests, it is near, round the corner of the National Museum. It's been there since 1885, one of the oldest places in town. With high ceilings, exquisite tiles high up and some original menu items — all in all, the menu is a good balance between modern cooking and traditional Hungarian killer dishes. The wine list also open in both directions. Pricing is OK.

ROBINSON *XIV. Városliget, Állatkert körút, on a small island on the lake, overlooking the right side of the Museum of Fine Arts and Restaurant Gundel. T: 142-3776.* Open: 12 a.m. to 3 p.m. and 6 p.m. to midnight. A very elegant place in a singular environment. Views to a fountain on a lake. Several rooms, all kinds of tables. Very smooth service, even on the somewhat less elegant open-air terrace. International menu, not very extensive. You shouldn't miss Robinson palacsinta, a sort of crépe stuffed with vanilla cream and fresh fruit salad.

SZINDBÁD *V. Markó utca 33. T: 132-2966.* Open: Noon to midnight, Saturday and Sunday: 6 p.m. to midnight. Takes its name from Krúdy's hero (see introduction to this section) and not from the Arabian Nights, which gives a hint to its culinary ambitions. A sensibly restricted menu á la carte, fully detailed, is a true delight. Excellent desserts and a good wine and spirit list. The atmospherical arches of the ceiling permit clear listening-in to every conversation in the room.

VADRÓZSA *II. Pentelei Molnár utca 15. T: 135-1118.* Open: 18-24. Closed on Mondays. Capacity: 100. The restaurant is housed in a little, elegant villa in the most fashionable "old money" neigbourhood in Buda: eggheads generally find the whole place a little too formal. The polyglott headwaiter likes to go over the limited, but fine menu and show you the raw ingredients. There is also a menu: without prices, to prevent you from going into petty calculations.

"SHIRTSLEEVE" GOURMET RESTAURANTS

To my mind it is these restaurants which are rejuvanating Hungarian cooking. Their menus generally list many dishes cooked in the manner of the last century and they make an effort to make use of ingredients which are fresh to hand and in season. "Shirtsleeve" indicates that they have no desire to overwhelm their guests by their ambiance. Service is straightforward and friendly. Cordon Bleu is not (usually) mis-spelled on their menus — a mark of their culinary ambitions. The early 90s saw the arrival of a different kind of shirtsleeve places, where the environment is glitzier, carefully designed by the best in town, and the menu combines traditional Hungarian menu with international items, with an occasional effort to offer vegetarian courses.

REMÍZ *II. Budakeszi út 5. T: 275-1396.* Open: 9 a.m. to midnight every day. The old fashioned evocative name stands for Tram Garage, a hint to a big one two-hundred metres away. There is a very visible landmark: the front of a yellow tramway from the interwar period, out of brick. A place where you can meet pretty everybody from the inner-Buda new middle-class, artists, business people and junior diplomats fom nearby embassies. Not a very touristic place. It has a nice garden, with a fountain, one that presents the "self-portrait of the artist as an acrobat" (the same one mentioned in the Budapest Bests of András Váradi, see pp. 202). The extensive menu offers Hungarian and international items. An informal place, I mean by dress code and behaviour expected. Very difficult to park, reservation is essential.

KÉHLI VENDÉGLŐ (Mrs Kéhli's Place) *III. Mókus utca 22. T: 188-6938.* Perhaps the only more or less genuine place left of the many that used to be patronized by the immortal gourmet writer, Gyula Krúdy. You can still see a plaque commemorating his table. His spirit is everywhere — in the menu, in the décor, in the witty inscriptions on the wall. The recent facelift fortunately didn't spoil the atmosphere (it used to be much smaller, dirtier and much cheaper). To include the cobblestoned gate area was a good idea, to flaunt the Gösser beer signs was not. The menu is a delight in itself (in several languages). If you want to try the famous scene in the film "Szindbád", you should order "Forró fazék velőscsonttal" (Hot pot with marrowbone), which is served in the cosy red pot that is used by impoverished old ladies. Other favourites (there is a full explanation in the menu): "Szindbád margitszigeti étke" (What Szindbád liked to eat on Margaret Island), and "Fidó Apó magyarkúti medvetalpa" (The Magyarkút Bear Sole of Uncle Fidó). Live accordion music. Miscellaneous music from a very cheap stereo rack — less than a perfect sight here.

BAGOLYVÁR (Owl Castle) *XIV. Állatkerti körút 3. T: 321-3550.* Part of the Gundel complex. Open: noon to midnight every day. After Gundel opened, adjecent Owl Castle building was left empty for a year. In the end it was turned into a theme restaurant: "Grandma's Homespun Cooking". It is an all-female operation, with a limited and daily changing menu. Tables and chairs of different form, the special choices on a plain blackboard. And ah! Some of the most beautiful waitresses in town, with some of the nicest, non-sexy smiles. As if the waitresses flaunted the proverbial dignity of the Hungarian peasant girls. A very nice place for a business dinner or a Sunday lunch with the kids. In Summer families with kids usually leave towards the zoo. Guests of all caste are invited to a free tour. Maybe they give away leftover food to the lions in turn, the roar of whom is often heard there. Reservation is advisable, especially if you are not a friend of the owner.

KISKAKUKK (Little Cuckoo) *XIII. Pozsonyi út 12. T: 132-1732.* Open: Noon to 11 p.m. noon to 4 p.m. on Sunday. Closed on Sunday in summer. On the Pest side of Margit híd, near the bridge. (See "Fifth Walk".) Has held its name for a good ten years. Menu specializes in game (with an Italian bias). Service can be fitful. And they have done something about their carpet and chairs — not enought yet. The redhaired proprietress, from a village near Pest, is said to be complaining that it is hardly worth going on with the lease, prices being what they are. That would be a great pity.

KISPIPA (Small Pipe) *VII. Akácfa utca 38. T: 142-2587.* Open: Noon to midnight, daily. Hidden away in a street running parallel with the Nagykörút. Fish swimming in their tank, forty-year-old posters on the wall, the charm didn't disappear, despite several facelifts that added more and more brass to the once shabby décor. The restaurant has its devoted regulars. Mr. Aubel, its proud proprietor, supervises his waiters and personally serves regulars, copes with accidents. He will cook anything to order which is not on the extensive menu. Advisable to book for lunch, essential for an evening meal. There are four-course "full dinners", which are worth a try.

KISBUDAGYÖNGYE (Small Pearl of Buda) *III. Kenyeres utca 34., T: 168-6402.* Open: 4 p.m. to midnight every day. Essential to book... Reborn out of a well known, shabby but charming place. The décor is a cross of the post-modern and the fin-de-siècle. The designer ransacked all the low quality antique shops and the Ecseri fleamarket. All the walls are panelled with sides and doors of cupboards, pieces of drawers; with hard wood of all kinds, tints and patterns. It all amounts to a very elegant and intimate atmosphere. Hungarian and international dishes. A nice, three-language menu, with very few misprints. The last time I was there, I enjoyed a pianist and a violinist. The latter looks like a 19th-century anarchist just back from Siberia. The place seems to be thirty years old — a real compliment in Budapest.

NÁNCSI NÉNI *II. Ördögárok út 80. T: 176-5809.* Open: Noon to 9 p.m. In Hungarian you do not tell it to the marines, you tell it to Auntie Náncsi. The lady in question was a simple, credulous countrywoman. The restaurant is in a charming district, quite far from the centre, called Hűvösvölgy — around 20 minutes by car. It has a pleasant garden and a formidable menu and it has a regular clientele who swear by it. Busy at all times so be prepared for a wait. Live music, menu in English and German.

SMALL RESTAURANTS *"Kisvendéglő" in Hungarian means a small dining area with room for up to 40-45 people, whose food is relatively cheap and which most often has a villagy feel to it (checkered table-cloths, candles, wine jugs). Although they may not pay too much attention to their furnishings and fittings, they most usually have a family atmosphere about them. In some places you are even expected to share your table if the place is full. With the advent of total privatization this is an endangered species. Everyone will be tempted to turn his/her just acquired place into a luxury establisment -- but sure to upgrade it.*

BOHÉMTANYA (Bohemian Den) *VI. Paulay Ede utca 6. T: 122-1453.* Open: Noon to p.m. daily. The sign above the door simply says "Söröző" — beerhouse. At the bar in the back there are always half a dozen customers having a beer while they wait. Only seats 52. Has large, well-cooked dishes and real beer-hall atmosphere. Deserves the loyalty it has from its regulars.

BOSZORKÁNYTANYA (Witch's Den) *III. Pacsirtamező utca 36. T: 168-9413.* Open: Noon to midnight, daily. Near the Buda end of Árpád híd, one of the friendliest small restaurants, run by the Bátkis. Air-conditioned, semielegant, with a TV-set and a huge white contraption for heating with a notice: "Forbidden to touch it". German-Hungarian, printed menu. The staff is very casual, swift and attentive. With a small drinkbar, with witches on top of the poles. Specialities: Treasure of Belzebub and the like.

CSARNOK (Market-Hall) *V. Hold utca 11. T: 112-2016.* Open: 9 a.m. to 10 p.m., Saturdays and Sundays closed. Close to the market (csarnok), this contains a few snugs in which you can eat and where you drink "real" (cheap and less fine) draught Kőbányai beer. Market stall-holders come here as well as a famous faculty member of the Department of Philosophy with her students. There is a rather uncomfortable terrace open in the summer. Specialities are lamb, mutton and marrowbone dishes.

CSENDES (The Quiet) *V. Múzeum körút 13., entrance from side-street. T: 117-3704.* Open: 12 p.m. to 10pm, closed Sundays. Quartier Latin atmosphere for this is a favoured meeting place of university students and alumni. Rather uncomfortable seats contribute to the "rustic" feel. Transylvanian and Slovak dishes usually on the menu — try them.

GÖRÖG TAVERNA (Greek Tavern) *VII. Csengery utca 24. T: 141-0772.* Open: Noon to 11 p.m., daily. Five minutes from the Nagykörút, neat, white, air-conditioned cellar. Two rooms, seven tables, for a maximum of forty people.Oil paintings (Greek peasants). Huge, Greek flag, out of silk. Soft Greek musaka — live music on Wednesday and Saturday. Bilingual menu.

HORGÁSZTANYA (Angler's Hut) *I. Fő utca 27. T: 201-0683.* Open: Noon to midnight daily. On the corner of a street parallel to the Buda bank, not far from Clark Ádám tér. The awkward combination of the fittings create the ambiance: a whisky advertisement, a fishing net hanging from the ceiling and a boat at the rear. The food has a country taste to it, the service can be a bit fitful and the foliage is rich.

KISBOJTÁR (Small Shepherd Boy) *XIII. Dagály utca 17. T: 129-5657.* Open: 12 a.m. to 11 p.m. Closed on Sunday. A museum piece of a restaurant that preserves the genuine coziness of the late fifties, early sixties. The small shepherd boy can be seen on an incredibly kitschy oil painting and the iron railings on the windows. Several rooms each with unforgettable design subtleties. A camp experience proper, to use the term established by Susan Sontag.

Food is delicious — all dishes represent Hungarian home cooking tradition. The head waitress is exceptionally warm and unobtrusive, speaks with a slight accent in Hungarian. She is of Slovakian origin. She also speaks German.

KIS ITÁLIA (Little Italy) *V. Szemere utca 22. T: 111-4646.* Open 11 a.m. to 9 p.m. Closed on Sundays. A very simple, reliable place just off Nagykörút, with about 8 tables. Quick and attentive service. Very few mistakes in the Italian menu. A small drinks counter. Their slogan: If you've been satisfied, come again, and recommend us to friends, if not, send your enemies. Moderate prices.

MAKKHETES (Seven of Clubs) *XII. Németvölgyi út 56. T: 155-7330.* Open: 11 a.m. to 8 p.m. daily. Named after a playing card — we call them "magyar", but they are of Swiss origin. Of this type of places, it tends to be one of the neglected ones. Nice, intimate family atmosphere and it is packed by local families for Sunday lunch. Service is cheerful and very fast — even when crowded. Good country cooking.

SPORT *XVI.(Rákosszentmihály), Csömöri út 198. T: 183-3364.* Open: 10 a.m. to 10 p.m. Closed on Monday and Tuesday. Anyone willing to make the pilgrimage out to this end of town is in for a pleasant surprise. One of Pest's best restaurants is located in what appears to be a shambly, tumble-down barn. Inside however it is an entirely different story, for the food has no connection with the place's exterior: well worth the 25 minute drive from the centre of town. Uncommonly rich selection of beer and wine. Specialities: Frogleg stew with gnocchi, Roast Duck with crepes filled with marrow, Beefsteak Nivernaise.

TÜKÖRY SÖRÖZŐ (Tüköry Beerbar) *V. Hold utca 15. T: 131-1931.* Open: 10 a.m. to midnight, closed Saturdays and Sundays and on all public holidays except August 20th. In the centre of Lipótváros and our "Second Walk". It can get almost unbearably hot in summer, even in the closed-in terrace. Inside are snugs and a long central table. Serves Dreher (Hungarian) draught beer. At noon it is full of clerks from the banks nearby. It can be full in the afternoon as well. One has the feeling that the customers always talk about business here. The décor is unbelievably shabby. On the walls you will find paper reproductions of a modern Hungarian painter just glued to the wall. The pony-tailed waitress has the nicest smile all over town. The food is plain Hungarian village cooking at its best.

PROBABLY THE BEST SALAD BAR It is to be found in a side street of the short part of a not very large Pest street, ridiculously called the "Pest Broadway" a salad bar specializing in raw "nuclear" salads and "falafel" which is chick-pea balls in Hebrew. You serve yourself and pay downstairs and can go upstairs and sit down. The whole place is small-scale, family-run and efficient. You can even wash your hands before or after eating.

The place is very near the Music Conservatory, so always full of nice, musical teenagers. The other day I saw a familiar adult face at the salad bar. He moved very slowly, as if he listened to some inward voices. He had a cap on, that's why it was difficult to recognize him. If you are fortunate, you can have a salad in the company of Miklós Perényi, the cello wizard. Have you heard his rendering of Rococo Variations by Tschaikovsky? If not yet, there is something substantially great ahead in your life. (VI. Paulay Ede utca, at Nagymező.)

THE KIFŐZDE: A GENRE OF ITS OWN *Called "kifőzde" in Hungarian, this is the sort of place where there are rarely more than 10 dishes available and where you would expect to find a stew of heart or of tripe or even of tongue — all cooked in the peasant style. Where there are tables, they are shared automatically. The kitchen is thinly partitioned off, but every comment can be heard. They get less busy at around two o'clock. Most of them close around four o'clock (unless stated otherwise). They tend to have a two-three week holiday in August. Below there are two examples, the only two that are here to stay — two Budapest institutions.*

KÁDÁR ÉTKEZDE *VII. Klauzál tér 9.* Open; 11.30 a.m. to 15.30 p.m., on weekdays. A charming, legendary establishment of the once heavily Jewish neighbourhood. With two soda water bottles on each table and celebrity photos on the wall (Mastroianni included). Jewish dishes on Friday.

KÉK IBOLYA *VII. Wesselényi utca 45.* On the corner of Nagykörút. Ibolya (or Violet in English) is not the energetic lady in the white smock, but her daughter. She does however speak excellent German.

AN APPENDIX: EXPENSIVE PLACES WITH GIPSY MUSIC FOR TOURISTS *The following places are not among my favourite ones. However, I can't help mentioning them in a book for tourists and travellers. Gipsy music is a highly problematic genre. My generation that has been taught genuine folk music from an early age somewhat unanimously sneers at this music that is often confused with Hungarian folk music all over Europe (Ferenc Liszt was no* *exception here). The pieces the bands play are called "magyar nóta" (Hungarian song) — a sugary, quasi-folkloristic song, originally written for the hundreds of thousands who migrated to Budapest. Later it was adopted by the upper classes as well. Nowadays it is rapidly losing its audience, even in the country. Twenty years ago there were about twenty thousand professional Gipsy musicians in Hungary, as opposed to two thousand today — living largely off the tourists. The classic Gipsy band originally consisted of no less than eight musicians: the "primás" (violin), the "kontrás" (second violin), the bass, the cymbalo-player, the clarinettist, the second "kontrás", the cellist and the second "primás". They are rarely seen in bands of more than four or five any more. Interestingly enough, a number of outstanding figures of Hungarian jazz come from Gipsy musician families (from the Lakatos–dynasty, among others). If you, Gentle Reader, are interested in genuine Gipsy (folk) music, you might buy two brilliant recordings of a band called "Kalyi Jag" (Black Flame). Also on CD.*

ALABÁRDOS *I. Országház utca 2.* T: 156-0851. Open: 6 to 12 p.m. (from 1 May to 15 September: 10 a.m. to midnight.) Closed on Sunday.

APOSTOLOK *V. Kígyó utca 4-6.* T: 118-3704. Open: 10 a.m. to midnight, daily.

ARANYHORDÓ *I. Tárnok utca 16.* T: 156-6765. Open: Noon to midnight, daily.

MARGITKERT *II. Margit utca 15.* T: 135-4791. Open: Noon to midnight, daily.

MÁRVÁNYMENYASSZONY *I. Márvány utca 6.* T: 175-3156. Open: 11 a.m. to midnight.

MÁTYÁS PINCE *V. Március 15. tér 7.* T: 118-1693. Open: 11 a.m. to 1 a.m.

MÉNES CSÁRDA *V. Apáczai Csere János utca 15.* T: 117-0803. Open: Noon to midnight, daily.

NEW YORK *VII. Erzsébet körút 9-11.* T: 122-3849. Open: 11.30 a.m. to midnight.

PEST-BUDA *I. Fortuna utca 3.* T: 156-9849. Open: 5 p.m. to 1 a.m., on Sunday: noon to midnight.

POSTAKOCSI *III. Fő tér 2.* T: 168-7801. Open: 11 a.m. to midnight, daily.

RÉGI ORSZÁGHÁZ *I. Országház utca 17.* T: 175-0650. Open: 11 a.m. to midnight, daily.

VASMACSKA *III. Laktanya utca 3-5.* T: 188-7123. Open: Noon to midnight. Closed on Sunday.

DRINKING WINE

or Anything Else, if you Have to*

In a beatiful essay entitled *Philosophy of Wine*, one of the most original Hungarian thinkers in this century, Béla Hamvas set up a classification of cultures according to their drinking customs: Hungary, of course, falls into the category of wine-drinking countries. When in Hungary, do as ... well, no, to be more honest than patriotic, I cannot simply advise you to do as most Hungarians do — 50 years of Really Existing Feudalism topped with unexpected and ill-advised fits of modernization did so much harm to the well over millennary Pannonian tradition** of vine growing, wine production and wine drinking that you had better be armed with some background information before buying or ordering your first bottle in Hungary. We will start by doing away with some widespread misconceptions about Hungarian wines.

FIVE UNTRUE STATEMENTS ABOUT HUNGARIAN WINES:

1. Hungarian wine, at its best, is a cheaper, and accordingly lower quality substitute for Australian, New Zealand, South African, etc. wines. This view is generally held by foreigners and is unfortunately reiterated in many wine guides, encyclopaedias, etc. It can be explained by disastrous marketing on the part of Hungarian wine producers and the Hungarian state that does not call sufficient attention to the traditions of Hungarian winemaking to be compared only with those of France, Italy, Germany, Spain or Portugal, nor to the very promising efforts made by many small winemakers and a few larger-scale wineries since 1991.

2. Hungarian wine is the best in the world. Full stop. The intimate conviction of most of my compatriots. This, along with some similar statements concerning various domains of life make up the logical counterpart of Hungarian defeatism.

3. Egri Bikavér (Bull's Blood) is the best Hungarian wine. Thanks to its captivating name, this red blend from the Eger region (there is also Szekszárdi Bikavér, often of superior quality: try Vesztergombi's) acquired a certain reputation (esp. in the US and Canada) as a cheap table wine, sold on the bottom shelves of supermarkets. At the same time, one of the most important ingredients of the traditional blend, a variety called Kadarka practically disappeared from the Eger wine region. Some vintners now consider replanting it to give back to their Bikavér the spicy aroma it was once distinguished by. At the moment there are some nice Bikavérs in the

---

* *This chapter has been fully rewritten by a friend of the author, András Egyedi, currently living and working in the Tokaj region.*

**The first significant vine plantations in the Roman province of Pannonia date back to the reign of the Emperor Probus (A.D. 276-282), a "martyr of wine" killed by his soldiers for making them work on wine plantations along the Danube and the Rhine.*

Eger region (Thummerer, G.I.A.), but for the time being wine makers (including the above-mentioned) tend to make other wines their top of the range product: typically single-variety Cabernet Sauvignon.

4. *There is so little real Tokaji wine produced in the Tokaj region that it is no use buying it: you are doomed to buy a fake bottle.* An old myth that has caused a lot of harm to this unique (and not so small!) wine region producing over almost 5,000 ha (12,350 acres) what Louis XIV of France called "the wine of kings, the king of wines": Tokaji Aszú. It is for its extraordinary quality and for its legendary reputation that Tokaji has in fact "baptised" different wines around the world. The most famous among these are probably Tokay d'Alsace (actually a Pinot Gris, a French variety widely cultivated also in Hungary and giving some very nice wines north of Lake Balaton under the name of Szürkebarát) and the Italian white varietal Tocai — both wines have nothing to do with Hungarian Tokaji and their confusing names will soon disappear from wine labels, but they are no fake Tokaji: they are different wines made from different varieties with different vinification methods. Slovak Tokaji is a different story: it cannot be considered fake either, since after WW I two villages traditionally belonging to the Tokaj wine region were annexed to Czechoslovakia and now are part of Slovakia, however it is not the real thing.

5. *Tokaji wines are "for women" because they are "too sweet".* No comment.

WHERE SHOULD I BUY WINE IN BUDAPEST?

Avoid buying wine in supermarkets or in the grocery shop round the corner. This general precept that might be corroborated by painful experiences from your own country, applies even more to Hungary where the first (very auspicious!) steps have just been made towards restoring our wine culture to its pre-war glory. Stick to the best wine shops that only sell wines from reliable producers and where the personnel is capable of giving you the necessary information on the wines they have on stock or even of advising you on matching wine with occasions, individual tastes or food. Here is a list of selected wine shops in Budapest.

1. THE BEST WINE SHOP IN TOWN:

Wine shop of the Budapest Bortársaság (Budapest Wine Society) *I. Batthyány utca 59., 5 minutes walk from Moszkva tér on the way up to Castle Hill, Tel./Fax: 212-2569, (06) 20 322 400.* — if you go there, don't miss the "habos mákos", a delicious cake with poppy seeds and meringue in nearby confectioner's "Bécsi Kapu" just around the corner in Ostrom utca. Open: Mon-Fri 10-20; Sat 10-18. In their functionally and tastefully furnished cellar wine shop (on leaving mind the steps though) Attila Tálos and his colleagues will guide you around the stunning complexity of Hungarian wine regions, grape varieties and the growing number of quality conscious wine producers in fluent English. Good choice of Hungarian wines from all interesting wine regions. Very reasonable prices. Free tastings on Saturdays between 2 and 5 p.m.

2. RUNNER UP

La Boutique des Vins *V. József Attila utca 12., 2 minutes walk from Vörösmarty tér. Tel.: 117-5919.* Open: Mon-Fri 10-28; Sat 10-15. The owner, ex-Gundel sommelier Malatinszky Csaba is an outstanding expert on Hungarian wines and if you find him in the shop, he will be glad to share his knowledge. His personnel is also competent. Good choice of Hungarian wines from all interesting wine regions but it is difficult to have an overview of what is actually on the shelves.

3. OTHER EXCELLENT WINE SHOPS:

Borház *VI. Jókai tér 7., off Andrássy út, near Oktogon. Tel.: 153-4849.* Open: Mon-Fri 10-20; Sat 10-18. A very pleasant shop, though you may not find the same variety nor the same degree of professionalism as in the above two wine shops. They still offer a remarkable choice at reasonable prices.

Demijohn *Cukor utca 4., 2 minutes walk from Ferenciek tere. Tel.: 118-4467; Fax: 118-6509.* Open: Mon-Fri 11.30-19.30; Sat 10-16. (Second shop with the same choice on the way up to Rózsadomb, at *Margit utca 27. Tel.: 325-0714*) One of the first quality wine shops in Budapest belongs to Interconsult Winery Neszmély. The choice is for the most part restricted to their own wines which, however, span various wine regions. (They also sell a number of French, Spanish, Italian, and New World wines, not necessarily the best though, which is understandable, if you know Hungarian import duty regulations.) In 1996 Interconsult's wine maker Kamocsay Ákos was elected East-European wine maker of the year in the UK.

Wine City *V. Párisi utca 1., off Váci utca. Tel.: 118-2683.* Open: Mon-Fri; Sat. Don't let the tourist trap atmosphere deceive you: the choice of wines is excellent. They also sell cheese.

Le Sommelier *V. Régiposta utca 14., off Váci utca. Tel.: 266-1314.* Open: Mon-Fri 9-20; Sat 9-14; Sun 11-17. (Second shop in the Budagyöngye Centre, *Szilágyi Erzsébet fasor 121. Tel.: 275-2194.*) Reasonable choice.

4. MORE WINE SHOPS IN ALPHABETICAL ORDER:

Bacchus Wine Shop
V. Váci utca 30.
Bor-Tár *XII, Böszörményi út 34/a.*
Corvinum-Gasztrovin
XII. Ugocsa utca 5.
Exkluzív Palackozott Italok
V. Régiposta utca 7-9.
Ex-Veritas *VI. Káldy Gy. utca 4.*
Goldvinter *III. Kolosy tér 5-6.*
Rea Wines and Antiquities
II. Lukács utca 1.
Tálentum *V. Bajcsy-Zs. út 66.*
Venyige Borház *IV. Szentimre u. 1.*
Vinarium *XXII. Dézsmaház utca 19/a.*

HUNGARIAN WINE REGIONS

The North-west
1. Sopron
2. Pannonhalma-Sokoró Foothills
3. Ászár-Neszmély
4. Mór 5. Etyek 6. Somló

Lake Balaton
7. Balatonmellék 8. Badacsony
9. Balatonfüred-Csopak
10. South-Balaton

The South-west
11. Villány-Siklós
12. Mecsek Foothills
13. Szekszárd

Great Plains
14. Hajós-Vaskút 15. Kiskunság
16. Csongrád

The North-east
17. Mátra Foothills 18. Eger
19. Bükk Foothills 20. Tokaj

THE CLIMATE AND THE LAND

The entire territory of Hungary is inside the vine-growing zone. This fact along with the special soil and climatic qualities of various regions explains why a small country like Hungary can boast twenty strictly delimited quality wine districts. In fact, one of the most amazing facts about Hungarian wines is their great variety: Hungary belongs to the few vine-growing countries in the world producing the entire range of classic wine styles including whites, rosés, reds and natural sweet wines (botrytis whites). These different wines are made from an impressive range of grape varieties characterized by a certain equilibrium between international* and local** varieties. Hungary is often considered as a white wine country — this opinion, though to some extent well-grounded, is at the very least complicated by a few wine districts (esp. Villány, but also Szekszárd, Eger, Sopron, and Hajós-Vaskút) producing mostly red wines of constantly improving quality. Lacking sufficient space to write on all twenty, we will only present less than half of our quality wine districts in alphabetical order.

LAKE BALATON

There are four completely distinct wine districts around Lake Balaton: Balatonfüred-Csopak, Badacsony, Balatonmellék on the north side, and Dél-Balaton on the south side. The three wine districts on the north produce almost exclusively white wines from Pinot Gris (Szürkebarát), Olaszrizling (Welschriesling), Kéknyelű (a local variety of the Badacsony district giving wines of amazing quality and elegance, which, however, could not avoid the fate of low-yielding varieties in a planned economy and almost completely disappeared), Chardonnay, and Sauvignon. These wines are usually marked by high acidity (esp. in Badacsony) beautifully counterbalanced by a rich, full-bodied texture. Viticulture in the North-Balaton districts suffered a lot from lakeside tourism during Communism and recovery is hindered by extremely high land prices and by complicated real estate conditions caused by the week-end cottages climbing up the hills where vine plantations date back to Roman times.

South-Balaton, though historically less important, has evolved into one of the most prominent wine districts in Hungary producing mostly whites (including sparklers) but also some remarkable red wines.

BEST PRODUCERS
Balatonfüred-Csopak: Figula Mihály, Csopakvin ***Badacsony:*** Badacsony Borászati Szövetkezet, Badacsonyi Pinceszövetkezet, Varga Kft. ***Balatonmellék:*** Kál-Vin Pincészet, Scheller Szőlőbirtok ***Dél-Balaton:*** Eifert és Légli, Légli Ottó, Szt. Donatus, Öregbaglas, BB Chapel Hill

EGER

It may be surprising that this wine region in the northern hills of Hungary produces more reds than whites. However, somewhat less full-bodied red wines are often distinguished by an elegance and refined com-

---

* *I.e. Cabernet Sauvignon, Cabernet Franc, Merlot, and Pinot Noir for reds; Chardonnay, Sauvignon blanc and Rhine Riesling for whites.*

** *By local, I do not only mean exclusively or originally Hungarian varieties, but also the typical varieties of Central Eastern Europe: Kadarka, Kékfrankos, Kékoportó, and Zweigelt for reds; Furmint, Hárslevelű, Welschriesling, Kéknyelű, Ezerjó, Juhfark, Leányka, Királyleányka, etc. for whites.*

plexity that is hard to find in wines with higher alcohol and tannin. Major varieties include Kékfrankos (Blaufränkisch), the Cabernets, Merlot, and Oportó (Blauer Portugieser) for reds (Kadarka might come back in a few years and experiments with Pinot Noir are to watch); Leányka, Királyleányka, Chardonnay, Pinot Gris (Szürkebarát) and Hárslevelű (esp. in Debrő) for whites.

In the shadow of the gigantic Egervin Winery (having some interesting vintages in old Bull's Blood testifying that this wine had seen better times before the "Bull's Blood project" started in 1979), it is a few small producers who have gone a long way in reviving quality-conscious viticulture and wine making.

BEST PRODUCERS Gál Tibor, Ostoros Bor, Thummerer Vilmos, as well as Egervin for old vintages.

SOMLÓ

The smallest and perhaps the most beautiful wine district in Hungary. The 500 hectares of vine plantation extend on the hillside below the basaltic columns called "organ pipes" forming the top of the hat-shaped volcanic hill. Somló produces some of the best traditional Hungarian dry whites that accompany marvellously typical, somewhat heavy Hungarian meals. A good Somló is a very acidic, "masculine" wine (legend has it that royal couples drank it on their wedding night to have a baby boy), unmistakably marked by the terroir: once you have tasted a Somló, you will always recognize wines from this region even if you don't care much about regularly brushing up on your olfactory memory. Somló is not the place to produce fashionable light whites distinguished by a pleasing varietal character (at least for a few months): whether you drink a Furmint, a Hárslevelű, a Juhfark (a local variety, virtually restricted to this region), or an Olaszrizling (Welschriesling) you will first of all drink a Somló. During Communism Somló wines were practically absent from the shops and they are still relatively rare because of the contrast between the reputation and the size of the region, but don't leave Hungary before you have tasted one.

BEST PRODUCERS Fekete Béla, Györgykovács Imre, Inhauser István.

BEST VINTAGES There are not enough vintages around to be choosy.

SZEKSZÁRD

along with Villány, is one of the most dynamically developing Hungarian wine regions. A growing number of quality-conscious wine makers are trying to combine modern vinification methods and traditions to produce some of the best reds in Hungary and also some delicious white wines. Szekszárd red wines are somewhere between the finesse and the richness of Eger and Villány reds respectively. Kadarka, a classic Hungarian variety, survived somewhat better quantity-oriented viticulture here than in Eger, but Szekszárdi Kadarka remains a rarity that you should taste in any case if you want to have an idea of traditional Hungarian red wines that go well with paprika based dishes. Major varieties include Cabernet Sauvignon, Cabernet Franc, Merlot, Kékfrankos, Kékoportó, used either for varietals or for the Szekszárdi Bikavér blend, more ancient than its Eger counterpart, even if for some reason the Hungarian state gave Eger exclusive rights to use the name in 1977. This is why until recently these wines were bottled under the Szekszárdi Óvörös label.

Even if Szekszárd is mostly associated with red wine, white wine production is slightly more important quantitatively, and Szekszárd now produces some delightful single-variety Chardonnays, Zöld Veltlinis (i.e. Austria's major variety called grüner Veltliner), and Királyleánykas.

BEST PRODUCERS
Aliscavin, Bátaapáti Kastélyborok, Heimann, Sárosdi, Vesztergombi, Vida.

TOKAJ A quasi-mythic wine region with completely original vinification methods and the world's oldest system of classified growths. Volcanic, mostly clay soil; a micro-climate characterized by a hot Summer and a long, sunny Autumn with morning fogs facilitating the development of botrytis cinerea, or noble rot; labyrinthine cellars providing a constant temperature of 10-12°C and a very high humidity; the survival of centennial traditions; and last but not least important investments due to a renewed interest of the international wine scene, all add up to produce one of the greatest wines of the world.

Only four varieties are authorized for the production of Tokaj wines*: Furmint, Hárslevelű, Yellow Muscat, and Oremus. The harvest begins late, traditionally on Simon-Juda Day, i.e. October 28th. If there are enough good quality Aszú-berries, i.e. if botrytis and sunshine have sufficiently desiccated a considerable part of the grapes, they are harvested separately, grape by grape, or selected immediately after the picking on large tables. The non-botrytised grapes are used to make the dry varietals Tokaji Furmint, Tokaji Hárslevelű, etc., part of which is used as base wine for the production of the sweet dessert wine called Tokaji Aszú. According to the traditional method first described in the 17th century, and which still gives the framework for Aszú production, 3 to 6 (occasionally 7) times 25 kg (the content of a "puttony", i.e. a hod originally used for the harvest) of raisin-like aszú-grapes crushed to form what is called aszú-paste are added to 136 l of base wine or must. The aszú-paste and the base wine/must (re)ferment together to give a product of approximately 12-13% Vol. of alcohol and a very high degree of residual (non-fermented) sugar, ranging from 60 g/l to over 180 g/l. Obviously, it is first of all the number of hods of aszú-berries that determines the concentration of the final product; thus Tokaji Aszús range from 3 puttonyos through 4, 5, and 6 puttonyos up to Aszú Eszencia, which is the equivalent of a 7 puttonyos (this term is never used). Tokaji Aszú Eszencia is not to be confused with Tokaji Eszencia, which is the free-run juice of exclusively the aszú-berries, racked off without pressing and giving a nectar of unequalled, almost honey-like concentration.

When aszú-grapes are not picked separately, the entire grape clusters including botrytised parts are vinified as a standard white wine to give Tokaji Szamorodni,** which can be dry (száraz) or sweet (édes), according to the proportion of non-selected aszú-berries in the crop. Aszú and

---

** *This word of Polish origin means "as it grew".*

* *Wines made from other varieties are very rare and must be sold under a different label: e.g. Zempléni Chardonnay.*

Szamorodni wines are matured in oak barrels (generally no new oak is used) for at least 2 (Szamorodni), 3 (Aszú 3-6 puttonyos), or 5 (Aszú Eszencia) years.

Since 1991 a number of important foreign investors including wine writer Hugh Johnson, Bordeaux baron Jean-Michel Cazes and the owners of the most famous Spanish bodega "Vega Sicilia" have created new wineries trying to combine ancient traditions with state-of-the-art technology to restore Tokaj wines to their glory, which was at its peak in the 18th century.

BEST PRODUCERS
Bodrog-Várhegy (Messzelátó Dűlő), Bodvin, Disznókő, Gergely Vince, Hétszőlő, Lauder-Láng, Megyer, Monyók József, Oremus, Pajzos, Royal Tokaji Wine Co., Szepsy István, Tokaji Kereskedőház (ex-state farm).

BEST ASZÚ VINTAGES 37(!!!), 40, 41, 56, 57, 59, 63, 68, 72(!!!), 75(!!!), 83, 88, 93(!!!), 95.

VILLÁNY-SIKLÓS

A two-faceted wine region, Villány perhaps producing the best red wines in Hungary, whereas Siklós is known for its white wines. This is the region where small private vintners responded the most rapidly and adequately to the new situation created by market economy and the collapse of the Soviet market which had favoured low-quality mass production. Villány has become the flagship of Hungarian quality wine making re-emerging since 1990. This is where stainless steel tanks and new oak barrels first became standard equipment in some wineries.

Villány reds are undoubtedly the most full-bodied in Hungary, usually characterised by high tannin, alcohol, and extract content. They are also the country's most suitable wines for maturation in new oak barrels. Top Villány vintners typically have a range of wines going from light reds and rosés made from the local varieties Kékoportó and Kékfrankos through blends of the latter with Cabernet or Merlot to more robust wines often based exclusively on the Bordeaux varieties.

BEST PRODUCERS
Bock József, Gere Attila, Gere Tamás, Polgár Zoltán, Tiffán Ede, different vintners under the "Le Sommelier" label. The ex-state farm now called Villányi Borászati Rt. also has some fine wines including older vintages.

GOOD AVAILABLE VINTAGES 87, 91, 92, 93, 95.

TWELVE BUDAPEST RESTAURANTS WITH A GOOD WINE SELECTION

Bel Canto, Café Kör, Chez Daniel, Fausto's, Fortuna, Gundel, Kacsa, Kisbudagyöngye, Légrádi Antique, LouLou, Múzeum, Náncsi Néni. (See details in the chapter "Eating Well".)

SOME INFERIOR PLACES — FOR THE SOCIAL EXPERIENCE *Unlike real wine-lovers, there are people in Budapest who do not rely on shops to indulge their passion, but buy from the producer by going direct to the vineyard. Then there are people who drop into the occasional wine-bar **borozó**, many of the best of which are supplied by wine growers' co-operatives. (There is another type of place called a **talponálló**, a wine counter, which is generally filthy and full of drunks.) However, the wine-bar here, unlike its counterpart in London or New York, is neither overpriced nor pretentious. Many a borozó has stand-up tables where customers take their wine at leisure, occasionally helping it down with* *slices of* **zsíros kenyér** *which they buy at the counter. (Try it: it is bread and pork dripping sprinkled with paprika, often topped with fresh onion slices.) In Hungary it is common to add soda to your wine. Our word for this is* **fröccs** *and there are five varieties of this spitzer.*

	wine	soda	meaning
kisfröccs	10cl	10cl	small spritzer
nagyfröccs	20cl	10cl	large spritzer
hosszúlépés	10cl	20cl	long step
házmester	30cl	20cl	janitor
viceházmester	20cl	30cl	under-janitor

The selection below took into account general ambiance as well as the quality of the wine served. They usually open at 9 a.m., but bear in mind that most of them close between 8 p.m. and 10 p.m.

SOME WINE BARS

Szarvas pince *I. Szarvas tér 2.* Expensive, beside the restaurant of the same name.

Hattyú *I. Hattyú utca 1.* Stands back off the bottom of Castle Hill. Cheap and cheerful.

Postakocsi borozó *III. Fő tér 2.* Expensive and favoured by tourists. Bar in form of coach, meals served.

Gresham borozó *V. Roosevelt tér 5.* See "Second Walk" for information on the building. Entry into bar is from Mérleg utca. Marble tables but not pricey.

Grinzingi *V. Veres Pálné utca 10.* Table and counter service. Hard-boiled eggs, sandwiches and salads, wine from the barrel. Middle price range and off the tourist track.

Rondella borozó *V. Régiposta utca 4.* Touristy and the prices are San Francisco.

Villány-Siklósi borozó *V. Gerlóczy utca 13.* Close to Deák tér. A wine-counter but serves wine from two interesting areas.

Tokaji borozó *VI. Andrássy út 20.* All the Tokaji wines, right beside the Opera House.

Móri borozó *XIII. Pozsonyi út 39.*

Tortilla borbár *XIII. Budai Nagy Antal utca 3.* Hungarian drinks and Spanish tortilla. Tiny figurine of Bacchus on the wall.

IF YOU HAVE TO: BEER AND BEER DRINKING It is only in the last dozen years or so that Hungary has become a beer drinking country. Now the figure has come up to about 100 litres per head per year, around four times the figure for wine. We have a preference for "világos", that is lager or light beers although "barna" (dark) beer is also brewed. (This latter tends to be sweetish to the English palate.) The beer most popular in the shops is Kőbányai Világos, the cheapest type, brewed in the Kőbánya district of Pest. This brewery is an old established one. The Kőbányai Brewery runs two beer halls of its own, serving what a native of Budapest considers as the only real beer on draught: the Sörcsárda on the brewery premises themselves and the Aranyászok in the inner city.

Three Kőbányai beers are sold in the shops: the Világos (pale), the Korona and the Jubileum. Look out also for the excellent Czech bottled beers such as Pilsner Urquell and Radeberger. Tuborg and Holsten are brewed here under licence. Beer sold in small 33cl bottles or cans is rather more expensive than that in the half litre bottles. All these bottled beers taste the better for being chilled.

Over the last few years, several foreign companies — mainly Austrian and German — have sponsored beer-houses selling their products.

Also, bear in mind: a true Hungarian never clinks his beer-mug.

IF YOU ABSOLUTELY HAVE TO: HUNGARIAN SPIRITS

The best known of Hungarian spirits is "barackpálinka", apricot brandy, which is perversely drunk as an aperitif, thus numbing the taste-buds well and truely. A variation is "óbarack", old apricot. The other fruit brandies are "cseresznye", cherry, "szilva", plum and "körte", pear: the brand of the latter called Vilmos Körte should be noted. The best cognac-type drink distilled here is Tokaji Borpárlat.

Tourists may often be offered a lethal concoction that was invented for their benefit a few decades back: "puszta-koktél", which is 3 parts apricot brandy to 2 parts Mecseki liqueur and to 3 parts Tokaji Szamorodni wine and all parts lethal.

All cafés and coffee-houses serve spirits in a mesaure of 5 cl called "féldeci" or "feles" (a half decilitre) and waiters tend to turn up their nose if asked for a kis (small) measure of spirits, this being "only" 3 cl. It is advisable to ask for a "kis szóda" or "kísérő", which will get you a glass of soda water. Mixers and ice are generally unknown. If you ask for a vodka and tonic you will get a glass of vodka and a glass of tonic.

Coctails have made some penetration in the larger hotels and a few of the places calling themselves "drinkbár", coctail bars, are recognizably such.

Another drink worth noting is Unicum, a dark brown liqueur containig 23 herbs and which has a passing resemblance to Underberg and Fernet Branca. (The old pre-war placards for Unicum are much sought after to decorate walls.) After decades of shortage, you can get it in practically every shop selling spirits. (Opt for the ones with red-white and green top if there is a choice.) The expat authors of the *Time Out Guide to Budapest* call it "The Hungarian National Accelerator". They also say that "it looks like an old style anarchist's bomb, and smells like a hospital corridor... It's vaguely sweet and minty, and bitter like Winter night." It made me wonder, why I like it. But I do.

CAFÉS AND BARS TO TRY HUNGARIAN SPIRITS

Angelica *I. Batthyány tér 7.* Open: 10 a.m. to 8 p.m. daily. Entrance a few steps below street level in an old house. Furnishings neo-Baroque. An old-fashioned, though not old place, ideal for discussing the meaning of life.

Café Pierrot *I. Fortuna utca 14.* Open: 5 p.m. to 1 a.m., Sundays 10 a.m. to 11 p.m. On the site of a six hundred-year-old baker's. Great lengths gone to in finding the Far Eastern fixtures. The pianist is eager to play your favourites. Music from 8 p.m. when the piano is uncovered.

Ruszwurm *I. Szentháromság utca 3.* Open:10 a.m. to 8 p.m. Closed on Wednesdays. A Baroque coffee-house dating from 1824, still with its ambiance intact. Its confectionary was so famous that couriers from Vienna were sent. Marvellous ice-creams too. It is swamped by tourists, although you may be able to get a table in its tiny salon between 2 and 3 on a Winter afternoon. Its famous speciality is its Linzer, given the name by an owner who shared a prison-cell with a man of that name in the aftermath of the 1848–1849 War of Independence.

Miniatűr presszó *II. Rózsahegy utca 1.* Open: 7 p.m. to 3 a.m. Closed Sundays. A genuine Pest place, though in Buda, with red silk décor, intact from the sixties. Not anybody is let into the inner room. Full of aged burghers, bohemians, and couples wildly in love. Service is old-fashioned and very attentive. Music from 9 onwards, by a real classy Budapest pianist.

Csendes drink *V. Múzeum körút 13.* Open: 12 p.m. to 8 p.m., closed Sunday. Entry from side street.

Galéria drink bár *V. Vitkovics Mihály utca 6.* Open: 11 a.m. to midnight daily. Pleasant fin de siè-cle bar. Pottery and pictures on display are for sale. Remarkably nice and friendly barmaids, not for sale but innovative mixers.

Café Gerbaud *V. Vörösmarty tér 7.* Open: Main hall 9 a.m. to 9 p.m. daily. Side-room 7 a.m. to 9 p.m. Discussed in the "Introduction to the Walks", the great monument to the old coffee-house life. Due to huge number of foreign visitors, service can be fit-ful. If an elderly lady in a blue smock comes to the table and reaches for your coat, do not be alarmed — she is the cloakroom attendant.

John Bull *V. Apáczai Csere János utca 17.* An English pub — as real and expensive as its location suggests. In the middle of the tourist reservation, opposite the back of Forum Hotel.

Mumm Champagne bár *V. Kristóf tér 8.* A beautiful tapestry shows the whereabouts of Otard county (adjacent to Cognac). Drinks of the same brand. Possibly the most expensive place in town.

Pertu drink *V. Váci utca 39.* American cocktails — has made the Manhattan stylish.

Café Művész *VI. Andrássy út 29.* Open: 8 a.m. to 8 p.m., Saturday 10 a.m. to 8 p.m., closed Sunday. Mirrors, statues paintings surround the rather elderly regulars who sit over their papers. The terrace is plesant though a little noisy. The chairs are chained up at evening — in order not to be stolen. For more, see "Walk Four".

Picasso Point *VI. Hajós utca 31.* Open: 9 a.m. — 2.30 a.m. Mon-Thu, Sun, 9 a.m. — 4 a.m. Fri-Sat. Still large, still popular, still "in", but not anymore the only one where one must be seen every Friday at least for a short time. Less expats, more younger crowd. Generally, a quieter place, with more Hungarians downstairs. The urge to drop in for some food to Marquis de Salade round the cor-ner is still a good idea.

Café Incognito *VI. Liszt Ferenc tér 3. T: 267-0239.* Open 10 a.m. to midnight Mon-Fri, noon to mid-night Sat, Sun. Obviously the trendiest café in Budapest in the Spring of 97. Revived Liszt Ferenc Square. Students, expats, yuppies, also musicians from the nearby Music Academy. Overpriced Heineken from draught, and tables of all shapes and kinds. I like the series of funny pictograms by the door: what not to bring in. Also the signs on the two toilet doors: "Zsuzsi" and "Rudi",

respectively. Guess where you should go.
Paris, Texas IX. Ráday utca 22. T: 218-0570. Open 10 a.m. to 2 p.m. Mon-Fri, 4 p.m. to 2 p.m. Sat-Sun.

BUDAPEST BESTS : : BUDAPEST BESTS : : BUDAPEST BESTS

András Váradi, Biochemist, Collector of Watches, Fleamarket Freak

For over 12 years I have been going to the Ecseri fleamarket now, each Saturday morning. I get up brutally early — I prefer getting there before 7 o'clock. During the last four or five years my interest more or less focused on old mechanical wristwatches. Roughly by the same time I became a really advanced addict: I can be happy now even if I leave the market empty-handed.

"How much discount would you give from the half of your price?" is an age-old Ecseri fleamarket witticism, still often overheard. Here are some thumb rules, for your use:

Don't ask for a price unless you really want to buy the stuff. • *Always decide the maximum you are willing to pay.* • *Be a Man (even if you are a woman), and stick to this maximum.* • *Don't Let Yourself Be Tricked: if you are asked about the price, return the ball right away. Or offer the half of your maximum. Or try one third.* • *It is forbidden to interfere. If the piece is in somebody else's hand, wait until he/she puts it down.*

Practically *everybody is a character* in the fleamarket, except for the Noisy Tourists With Too Much Money. A man in his early fifties come here every Saturday and sells old Hungarian "peasant glasses", — wine and brandy-bottles from the 18th and 19th century. On weekdays he is a murder squad detective. And there is a remarkable highschool teacher of physics who sells old telephones and vintage radios.

The most prominent obsessed fleamarket-goer is certainly a somewhat small, bearded man in his late forties, with a small golden earring in his left ear and with ponytails, almost always in boots: professor of Academy of Arts and Crafts Vladimir ("Jani") Péter, a silversmith, designer of the Wladis jewelry. He is a very attentive listener at large: but not here. Hardly notices friends, he is so much immersed in scanning "the stuff". (A mere pile of junk for the uninitiated.)

Eating at the Fleamarket is no gourmet occasion. In front of small buffets people are enjoying the traditional ultra high cholesterol "diet": juicy sausages, grilled pork ribs, smoked knuckles with all the skin on, blood pudding or tripe stew. It is like a *real time* educational video on the theme "Why Hungarians Die So Early?" I only eat sweets there.

A last piece of advice. Never go there with the idea of any definite article to buy. That very object won't pop up that day. Have fun and buy whatever you want, but if you happen to find a nice wristwatch, please, leave it for me. I am coming on Saturday to catch it.

ART TO SEE, ART TO BUY

A First Swallow in the Gallery Scene "The only good artists are the ones already dead" (only dead Indians are good Indians) — the age-old Budapest art dealers' witticism seems to have lost some of its validity in the Spring of 1995 when the first glitzy New York-style gallery opened in downtown Budapest, between the river and the touristy part of Váci utca. The vernissages of this new gallery are equally popular with the overage sector of Hungarian yuppies and the egghead society — that little that remained from the good old days.

The gallery represents some artists who tend to paint huge, colourful sensuous canvases. The couple that established the gallery must know all too well that their investment will not easily come out from the red in the next hundred years. It is actually run by one of the owners, an exceptionally elegant lady in her mid (late?) thirties — the gallery bears the earlier name of her family, an Irish name. Her husband, the other owner is a successful real estate dealer — always present at the evening openings (perhaps so late to make him able to attend) flaunting his unorthodox dress code. He somehow (some day) looks a sort of cross between a future market broker and a rock opera set designer.

With the opening of this gallery contemporary Hungarian art inevitably began its long march towards being chic one day.

Dovin Gallery (V. Galamb utca 6. Open 10–18, Sat 11–14.)

And the Second About the same time Design Center Budapest, (a small publicly owned agency that recommended designers and services to businesses, held exhibitions and operated a wonderful small library) had to close down, a new, three-level shop opened in a somewhat unlikely place: in Theresa Town, an impoverished area, true, only 300 metres east from downtown.

In the shop and gallery there was everything from copies of Mackintosh and Rietveld through classic Breuer to recent Philip Starck chairs and tables. Over the corner there is a spacious design studio, where they are said to have frequent visitors from the Russian nouveau riche, who come to order furniture both for their homes and their new office buildings.

Then they opened their second gallery, at a more predictable address, in the southern section of Váci utca (just before it was converted into a pedestrian zone), in the basement of the New City Hall, which is a hundred-year-old fine Beaux Arts palace. This was cold-bloodedly designed to be a tool of owner Miklós Vincze's vision: to match latest international design with recent Hungarian fine art — and lure his clients who buy recent furniture into buying some paintings, just to go with the furniture.

The space is highly original, capitalizing on the brick vaults, and the random tubes — things that are impossible to hide anyway. The name of the gallery is coined from the name of the two owners: VAM = Vincze Anna and Miklós. (**VAM Design 1.** VI. Király utca 20., corner Káldy Gyula, **VAM Design 2:** V. Váci utca 64.)

BY FAR THE BEST IN SZENTENDRE Szentendre is the proverbial out-of Budapest destination for tourists, and also for travellers, who avoid the museum devoted to ceramist Margit Kovács, the one-time innovator in the thirties, later over-adorned Grand Dame of Kitsch. The serious traveller can find a great amount of great art, by artists hitherto unknown to him. Mr Erdész and his recently enlarged gallery, in one of the nicest inner courtyards of Szentendre is a revelation both for those who have always admired, and those who haven't heard about early 20th-century painting. Sándor Bortnyik and Lajos Vajda are the two fortes of the gallery, a dozen other names. Here you can have a close and intimate look at them, in an unusual atmosphere.

Erdész Galéria (Szentendre, Bercsényi utca 4. T: 0626 317–925).

THE STATE AS SANTA CLAUS Just like in literature, the advent of liberty favoured the very good and the very bad artists in Hungary. The really bulky middle part, in between the two extremities, the overall majority found itself frustrated, poor and with his/her career somewhat questioned.

From the early 80s a new generation emerged — a much more market-oriented one that had already seen the modern museums of Europe, (some of them even of America), could speak languages, if not brilliantly. A little later they capitalized on that somewhat artificial, politically oriented interest in Hungarian art — that wonderful half a decade in the second half of the eighties.

But thousands had to learn that they were becoming more and more week-end artists. They are art teachers, civil servants, paste-up artists at illustrated papers, graphic designers **in the first place.**

The once almighty Fine Arts Fund, that used to buy pictures from hundreds of artists on a weekly basis, in the meantime lost its monopolies, and most of its marketable assets. Its duty to pay pension to old artists remained there, without sufficient sources of income. It was turned into a quasi foundation, a purse, into which the state has to put money from year to year. It still has some of its galleries, selling a very mixed, commercial stock, indeed.

Magyar Alkotóművészeti Közalapítvány ("Public Foundation for Creative Artists"): VI. Báthori utca 10.

(One of the surviving **"Képcsarnok" Galleries**: VI. Teréz körút 11.)

A FORMERLY REALLY FAVOURED ARTIST Few contemporary Hungarian artists could live up to see a museum solely devoted to their work. Imre Varga, maverick septuagenarian sculptor is one of the few. It was a long way to reach that status for the artist, so much liked by the general public, and so much sneered at by quite a few fellow artists.

For a decade or so, he was treated like a pariah, in the fifties and early sixties: the sculptor came from a landowner family, and as a young man he was even a fighter pilot in the Hungarian army, during the Second World War.

Later on, during the first "thaw" he let himself lure into the role of "conspicuously-non-party-member-favoured artist", trusting fate and good luck that he can influence things for the better on the way ahead. So in the end he was "elected" even to be an MP in that parody of Parliament, which had four sessions a year, each a maximum of 3 days, one every season.

There was a year when he was said to use about 75 per cent of the capacity of the one and only bronze statue foundry in Hungary. He slowly fit into the cookie-cutter-mould of the proverbial great Hungarian sculptor, who is known all over Europe, who blends tradition and modernity, who was often interviewed on TV. He has no less than 300 works accomplished and erected, a rare feat. His undoubted chef d'oeuvre is the Wallenberg monument, which is in a tucked away part of Buda, because in 1986 it needed considerable bravery to commemorate the Swedish diplomat, who saved tens of thousands of Jews, and vanished finally in the end in the Gulag.

With the advent of democracy Mr Varga again became a sort of a pariah, being accused of having been a sort of collaborator. He mainly works for Germany now, but recently a Bartók statue of his was erected in Brussels. He spends time in the museum devoted to his works, a wise old man still of imposing presence, over six feet, ultra-short silver hair, like a retired four–star general of the US Air Force. Speaks German and French well, not English, as far as I know.

Imre Varga Collection (III. Laktanya utca 7.)

ARTIST-WATCHING, BUDAPEST Artists live everywhere around the country. If you want to be sure to spot them, you can go to at least two places in Budapest, to purpose-built colonies. The bigger one of the two is in outer Joseph Town, a hundred metres from Népstadion (People's Stadium) underground station. Built before World War I, it consists of about three dozen homes of varying sizes, all with a studio — some very big. In between there is a garden, for common use. There is one fence around the colony with an iron gate that is never locked. The style is sometimes loosely labelled as National Romanticism. A lot of woodwork is used, complicated latticed roofs, and raw stone on the outside, especially near the bottom. It is a lovely place, even after some major alterations happened, not always with the necessary expertise, so to speak. The right to live here was theoretically granted to artists, not to their widows or their offsprings. But few of them ever left. Unfinished statues are all around the place, even some finished totalitarian work of "art", by the one-time dreaded dean of the Academy of Fine Arts. There lives a famous Hungarian prose writer turned film director, with his sculptor wife, and a brilliant illustrator with an interest in Oriental art. It is definitely worth the walk.

The other one is a nice art nouveau block of flats, with studios, a hundred metres from elegant Gellért Hotel, somewhat up the hill. The one you have already seen if you haven't skipped "Walk Three", one that was built in 1903. A typical tenant here is the couple, both painters, who launched a successful career in graphic design. They work a lot, as participants in the rat race. So they leave early, and get back home late. The husband gets away for three weeks once or twice a year, to a Summer artists' colony in

Kecskemét, about a hundred kilometres south of Budapest. During that time he does not want to hear about business. Even switches off his cellular phone. Or at least its ringer.

Százados út Artists' Colony (VIII. Százados út 3–13.), **Block of Flats with Studios** (XI. Kelenhegyi út 12–14.)

ARTIST-WATCHING, NORTHWEST HUNGARY

Lake Balaton, the "Hungarian Sea" is a naff place on the whole. But not the relatively untouched villages north of it, roughly between Veszprém and Tapolca, one of the most attractive part of Hungary, admired for its volcanic hills. The fashion to buy Summer homes and studios started some fifteen years ago, when there where more and more abandoned homes in these villages. The craze spread from a village called Kapolcs, where composer István Márta and friends organize the annual "Valley of Arts" festival with hundreds of smaller events (mid-June/mid-July) on the fringe. (Not held in 1997, for some reason.) By now several dozens of better-known painters have studios there, but also writers and actors. (György Konrád has a wonderful house in a village called Hegymagas.) Traditionalist painter/semi professional hussar Győző Somogyi moved permanently to a village called Salföld and gathered quite a herd of different animals. His house is a frequent destination of pilgrimage by glowing-eyed egghead students, dreaming of "unspoilt life".

The last outpost is a shore resort called Szigliget, where there is a Writers' "Creative Center" (a relic of past times – even the name), a big, yellow, dilapidated complex in a big estate, once belonging to an aristocratic family. An offspring, cult figure/writer Péter Esterházy traditionally spends three weeks there (with some of his four kids) in the beginning of August, always with the same bunch of friends — writers, musicians and artists. It is no small privilege to be invited there, even for a visit.

Szigligeti Alkotóház — Szigliget Creative Center, Veszprém County.

CONTEMPORARY GALLERIES: PROBABLY THE TWELVE BEST

Artpool VI. Liszt Ferenc tér 10. T: 121–0883. e–mail: artpool@artpool.hu

Bartók 32 XI. Bartók Béla út 32. T: 186–9038

Bolt Galéria VIII. Leonardo da Vinci utca 40. T: 324-7769

Dovin V. Galamb utca 6. T: 118–3673

Erdész Galéria Szentendre, Bercsényi utca 4. T: 0626 317–925

Galéria 56 V. Falk Miksa utca 7. T: 269–2529

Körmendi Galéria II. Nagybányai út 25. T: 176–2110

Hans Knoll VI. Liszt Ferenc tér 10. First Floor. T: 121–1556

Pandora Galéria VIII. Népszínház utca 42. T: 113–4927

Stúdió 1900 XIII. Balzac utca 30. T: 129–5553

Várfok 14 I. Várfok utca 14. T: 115–2165

Vam Design 2 V. Váci utca 64. T: 118–1594

BUYING ARTWORK During the last two or three decades most quality artwork was sold straight by the artists, from their studios, to friends and collectors. If you are a collector, you should go to a gallery and look around, and ask them to organize a visit to the artist. This is worth the margin. In the galleries you can leaf through catalogues and colour transparencies, and you are helped with formalities — you need a permission to take out artwork from the country, to save embarrassing moments at the border.

The gallery world is still a small one in Hungary, friendliness, jealousy and pickiness is characteristic of it at the same time. It is worth visiting some artists, through some galleries, and see that somewhat ancient, retarded, unspoilt way of life they lead: artists, daydreamers, critics of society, craftspeople at the same time. So much different from the stars of the Western hemisphere.

It might be a good prelude to considering to buy Hungarian art to visit the recently opened Contemporary Museum of Art, (if you happened to have missed it during "Walk One".) Imagine that you can visit any of the artists that are exhibited here, through practically any of the gallerists mentioned above.

NAME-DROPPING: ART TO LIVE WITH Here is a list of my favourites, a highly subjective listing. I know many artists, and I try to avoid offending them by emphasizing that the following list is not about their artistic greatness, but about their friendliness and decorative value. There are others, who are great for museums or for real collectors (who will hardly rely on my advanced amateur advice, concerning what to buy.)

In my home there are two paintings by **Gábor Karátson**, the writer, painter and green advocate, Oriental thinker. He is a living legend, a man in his early sixties, with long silver hair, who practically never sells his artwork, he rather faces the difficulties to pay his electricity bills. I especially like his oil paintings from the seventies that have picturesque titles like the one that hangs in my living room: "Borg hits the ball during serving in the 1974 Monte Carlo Open Tournament", and his illustrations to Goethe's Faust. Obviously, he is not represented by any of the gallerists, but any of them can contact him.

Károly Kelemen paints large, sensual canvases, full of bright colours, that since the mid-eighties always include some teddy-bears. He loves to paraphrase some classics of Picasso. He is a large, ever-smiling man, very easygoing, like a giant teddy-bear, who rarely says no to one more glass of drink.

László Fehér is a rare case when the man in the street, Hungarian art critic gurus and the international gallery world agrees and universally acclaims an artist. Fehér has intensive, mainly large canvases, often with a white, outlined little boy against a black backdrop. And his other favourite colour is yellow. I don't think you have enough cash here with you to buy a picture. And only certain versions of American Express lets you to withdraw the amount in question.

Being his godfather, I have long been biased towards the art of **István Orosz**, at least since I proposed him a Greek pseudonym ΟΥΤΙΣ (say: "ooh-tis") which means Nobody in Greek, that was Odysseus pretended to be called, when the Cyclops, the one-eyed giant inquired. (So when blinded and howled, and asked by fellow-giants who had hurt him, he thundered: "Nobody hurt me! Nobody hurt me".) István is an obvious follower of

M.C. Escher, the Dutch graphic artist, and much more. Resurrecter of the medieval genre "anamorphosis", cartoon film director, and highly successful poster-designer. In my flat there are some of his brilliant, illusionist etchings that echo his eternal attraction to Classical Antiquity and to Piranesi. He isn't represented by galleries, as far as I know. (Lives in Budakeszi, a suburb of Budapest about 20 kilometres to the west.)

I mentioned **Győző Somogyi**, the Salföld hermit above. Until about ten years ago he only made bitter black-and-white prints that provided a sort of x-ray of impoverished Hungary sinking into an intellectual mediocrity and torpor. Then he decided to switch to painting colourful, large canvases, historical scenes. He became obsessed with military heroism. He is also active as an illustrator of books on the history of Hussars. You might meet some of his original drawings made for these books.

I also own some work by my friend and co-author of this book, painter/illustrator **András Felvidéki**, who helped me a lot to open my eye up to the subtleties of Budapest architecture and its urban fabric. They are etchings showing Budapest details and imaginary, symbolic scenes, unmistakably Budapest ones. During the last couple of years he began to paint scenes from the city, trolley bus interiors, a lit-up telephone booth at night, a couple kissing on a bench in the old underground, etc. He is a solitary figure, involved in teaching art students, who had a brief adventure with contributing high-quality design for some computer game you might be playing with at home.

Another Six Names I Would Buy, Had I Sold An Unexpectedly High Number of Copies of The Present Book: Imre Bak, Ákos Birkás, István Mácsai (an old master, who has always loved the city), Károly Pollacsek, Tamás Soós, Erzsébet Vojnich.

GOING OUT

BUDAPEST AS A MUSEUM
Most of Budapest is still a big open-air museum. So going out for a walk, to whatever direction, it can be most enjoyable, if you look out for adventures.

There is a curious backward quality in most of the streets outside the tourist reservation, within the green belt and the pre-fab "suburbia". You can walk into most blocks unhindered and watch people come and go on gangways. People live in closely knit communities, sometimes terrorized by newcomers, who do not care about rules more or less respected by most of the tenants. Budapest is still a pretty much unsegregated city. You still cannot tell what kind of people live behind a certain façade. If you bought the present book back home, in the Tattered Cover in Denver, or Powell's in Portland, or Kramerbooks in WDC, or the Triangle in London, or the Atheneum Boekhandel in Amsterdam, and read the Crash Course in your very armchair at home, then you have your pair of binoculars with you here. If not, you can still buy a cheap pair at one of the fleamarkets. Then you can start your fieldwork in "applied people-watching". You should have a close look at Budapest balconies. Most people store things on balconies, are oblivious of the fact that this is not hidden from the eyes of others. The balcony of a family is as telltale a sign of their values and tastes, as their rubbish. But easier to have a look at it.

Of course the very rich have already left, but in the urban jungle of quickly gentrifying Pest there are tens of thousands of middle class people who like it there. Especially that after the parking revolution local people can park free.

That is the situation in Pest, the big open-air museum, where I have lived all my life. After all, "nothing ever happens in Buda".

THE SMALL MUSEUM EXPERIENCE
In Budapest museums, big or small, we find old underpaid ladies as attendants. But in the small ones one often finds a peculiar, and very pleasant, small-town quality, a sort of personal pride on the part of the attendants, who go out of their way to show you the collection. A unique character, one can only experience it, outside Budapest, perhaps in London, in the Soane's Museum.

While the big museum means alienation for the attendant, and perhaps job unsecurity, in the small one it means indispensability and family. And for the visitor it almost always gives something extra. A nice example is the

STAMP MUSEUM (*VII. Hársfa utca 47.*) This small museum is really a big one — one of the biggest of its kind in the world. It is housed in a classic modern building from the late twenties: a huge ministry block in a small, impoverished side street. As a matter of fact it is on the line of "the most unfinished avenue" in Budapest. It was planned in the twenties, but it was never realized except for a big arch at the beginning and the first hundred metres. (VII. Madách Imre út, beginning at Madách square).

The permanent exhibition of about eleven million stamps is exhibited in quite an ingenuous way, what otherwise would need the whole building, is stored in 3200 pull-out metal frames, quite a modern concept, uniting storing and exhibiting. They are shown by country and continent. There are also temporary exhibitions, when they show designs, counterfeits, prizes.

Hungarian stamps are still painfully picturesque and painfully obsolete from the graphic point of view. The state has always used a heavy hand in deciding what to publish a stamp about, at least since the museum existed, since 1930. (As a matter of fact, since 1918.) In the Dark Fifties too many stamps were published so that they ruined the collector's market. In the late fifties the Post Office had to pass a ridiculous decision: to prevent stamps values to fall below face value, they declared that any Hungarian stamp issued since 1946, i.e. the forint era, can be used to pay the postage.

The Post Office has been given a facelift recently, with a corporate identity designed by the same British design company that redesigned the Royal Mail image. That should affect stamps soon. Perhaps the officials deciding about stamp designs should visit the Art Pool mail-art collection in VI. Liszt Ferenc tér 10.

AN OVERSIZE SMALL MUSEUM: THERMAE MAIORES — THE BIG BATH Most Budapest people do not know about the Big Bath, they simply drive over it on the flyover leading on M11 toward Szentendre and the Danube Bend. The Bath, the small piece of which was unearthed as early as in 1778(!) is, in the mind of many of us, Budapest freaks, nothing less than the symbol of a changed attitude towards the city.

At its heyday, in the first part of the 3rd century, the Roman settlement in North Buda, called Aquincum, had at least 10-12 thousand inhabitants, a really sizable town those days. There has been a big museum since 1892 that has showed the public the very extensive remnants of the center of the civilian town "the municipium". (III. Szentendrei út 139., open from Spring to Autumn.)

The area in the immediate neighbourhood of Óbuda or Old Buda was bull-dozed in the mid- and late seventies, and the most awful ten-story pre-fab buildings were erected by the hundred. In 1981, when the pillars of the flyover were dug, they hit a part of the Big Bath, just in the place where some of the experts expected it. And now it was impossible to go on with the building, and bury the ruins forever, as some construction lobbyists possibly wanted to. They redesigned the pillars almost overnight, and excavated the sight, and designed a quite unique underground passage which crisscrosses around the open-air museum.

The Bath was really huge, even in modern standards: 120x140 metres. There were all kinds of pools, hot, lukewarm and cold, the hot heated from underneath, through a network of pipelines, by hot air. In the underground passage there are dozens of replica statues and tablets and big glass-covered tableaux that tell the public about the history of the bath. The glass seems to be a problem with the younger generation. The more liberal the society became in the early eighties, the more glasses were broken here. The authorities should experiment with enameled, graffiti-resistant signs. Do they exist at all?

12 OTHER GREAT SMALL MUSEUMS

The Underground Museum (in the Deák tér subway) the carriage Emperor Franz Joseph I travelled on in 1896, when he opened the line.)
György Ráth Museum, Chinese art downstairs, Japanese upstairs (VI. Gorkij fasor 12.)
Pál Molnár C. Collection a charming family establishment of the artist who was much influenced by Art Déco.
Telefónia Museum the old, mechanical central of the Castle District. (I. Úri utca 49.)
"Golden Eagle" Pharmacy Museum (I. Tárnok utca 18.)
Lutheran Museum a former school, where Sándor Petőfi, the great poet was a slightly problematic schoolkid, and now retired priests show you around (V. Deák tér 4.)

Music History Museum (I. Táncsics Mihály utca 7.),
Jewish Museum in the Great Synagogue (VII. Dohány utca 2.),
The Imre Varga Collection the representative sculptor of the seventies: he is often around. (III. Laktanya utca 7.), its stylish prints from the thirties (XI. Ménesi út 65.)
Vasarely Museum for those who fancy the pop-art master (III. Szentlélek tér 1.)
Museum of Electrotechnology in a massive, elegant art deco building, in the heart of the former Jewish District (VII. Kazinczy utca 21.)
Gizi Bajor Actors' Museum great for émigré eggheads, who usually remember childhood performances better than anyone. (XII. Stromfeld Aurél út 16.)

INFORMATION ON GOING OUT — NOT TO MUSEUMS You'll perhaps forgive me for not stressing the obvious. You can find information in the first place in the two competing English-speaking weeklies — both have excellent listings, and they are ever improving their readability and reliability. This competition is especially strong in movie listings. *Budapest Sun*'s film guide is an excellent grid, with the movie theaters across, and the days down. *Budapest Week* at the time of going to press changed its format, it is called "Now Playing — Pull Out Film Guide". It gives ratings, relatively well written summaries (miles away, though, from their apparent role model, London Time Out).

Of the booklets you are likely to be bombarded with, the Budapest companion volume of *Where Magazine* (Where in Budapest) is quite low-key and reliable.

Below I have compiled "Twelve Obvious Places to Go Out", and twelve more adventurous destinations. But I can't produce an invitation for a Hungarian home, I mean I can't invite everyone to my very own home. (There were times, when I attempted that. Especially, when we moved to Leopold Town, and quite incidentally, we found ourselves on the route of Walk Two, and I often met readers of mine, scrutinizing the rooftop ornaments of the immortal Post Office Savings Bank. This practice was then discontinued, succumbing to a more than symbolic pressure from my wife.)

GOING TO A HUNGARIAN HOME would beat most of my ideas below. As a matter of fact, it is relatively easy to be invited to a Hungarian home. As to how to elicit an invitation there is only one good advice: always forewarn the friends of the friends of the friends of your close friends, whose phone number was reluctantly given to you. Call them in advance that you'll come, even better if you write in advance. Most Budapest professional people (not only eggheads) tend to have at least one extra job, so it might not be easy to devote to you two evenings while you are in Budapest. They also have a busy social life.

If you want a guarateed non-invitation(?), call them while you are in Budapest, give them a very short notice.

On the day you arrived, offer them an invitation to some luxury/moderately-priced chic restaurant (See "Eating Well"). When you talk to them over the phone, give them five or six ideas, remarking, that they were reported to be a known gourmet couple/person in town. (They will be flattered and your invitation to their home got an inch nearer.)

You might offer to expand the invitation to some of their friends for that first meeting. That might make it easier for them, (they can include some people with whom a meeting was long overdue). Your local contacts will be grateful, and it is unlikely that they will let you pay the friends' bill. If, finally invited, you can mention again that you would be delighted to meet some other friends of them.

GOING IN Once you are invited, you can relax, and be as inquisitive as you wish. "You don't mind if I look round, do you", is a question that is considered a natural one, but it is rarely heard, since the hosts will almost definitely show you around. You will probably see many more books in the homes of Hungarian professionals than in the homes of European or American counterparts. And it can be embarrassing, how independent it can be in Hungary a high IQ, wit on one hand, and good taste on the other. You can see incredibly low quality, naff furniture (especially lamps!), and neglected, broken parts in an intellectually exuberant, vibrant home.

The naffest part of a home (if you like that kind of inverted, camp enjoyment) is often the balcony. It is rarely shown, unless you ask, what I often do, when I inspect homes where I am first (sometimes also last) invited to: "Can I enjoy the panorama for a moment?"

And I can't withhold a reluctant warning: in some élite intellectual homes you might be confronted to the toilet cleanliness you do not regularly meet, if not on movie screens. If you know what I mean.

TWELVE OBVIOUS PLACES TO GO OUT IN BUDAPEST

The Music Academy: A major concert in the Great Hall.

The Music Academy: Graduation concert in the Small Hall (a bouquet of roses needed).

A Vernissage in Műcsarnok (Exhibition Hall).

Gundel: Taking your time. Meeting friends at the bar at seven, sitting down to Table 8 at nine, finishing the evening at the cellar.

Watching A Hungarian Movie in the rented room of Odeon Art Video, (8 seats).

The Opera House: "Cosi Fan Tutte", then dinner at Bel Canto Restaurant.

Genuine folk dance evening in the National Theatre (as a spectator).

Genuine operetta in the Municipal Operetta Theatre ("The Tschardash Princess").
Organ concert in Matthias Church: Bach and Liszt, by the organist of the Notre Dame, or a rising Hungarian star.
Friday evening in the Great Synagogue.
Shakespeare or **Kleist** in Katona József Színház.
Shakespeare or **Kleist** in Új Színház.

TWELVE ADVENTUROUS EVENINGS OUT

People-watching in Picasso Point Corner of Hajós and Ó utca.
Alternative Theatre Event: Watching the audience.
Dance House Event in the Almássy tér Community Center (spectator- or participatory).
Reading "Paul Street Boys" by Ferenc Molnár in the National Library (closes at 9 p.m.), if you can't find it in a bookshop.
The Municipal Circus: Splitting the interest between the show and its spectators.
Gay Cabaret in Angel Bar.
Evening Lecture in Collegium Budapest, on some scholarly subject (have a nap before in the afternoon, it can be very heavy and long).
Wichmann's: brooding over the meaning of life.
International Soccer Event in Kétballábas Pub, with Hungarian fans (definitely not for the faint-hearted).
Open-air Concert: Vajdahunyad or Martonvásár (the latter on M1, devoted exclusively to Beethoven).
Watching the award-winning Hungarian film at the Filmszemle (Film Review) in early February (Corvin Budapest Film Palace).
Egghead party at iconoclastic

poet/playwright/essayist in his lavish home on the riverfront, overlooking both Inner City Parish Church and Erzsébet híd and Gellért-hegy. Practically every New Year's Eve.

TWELVE HUNGARIAN FILMS NOT TO MISS

During the Summer months some cinemas and clubs show recent Hungarian films with English subtitles. (Most of them can also be rented from Mokép Videotéka.) The following ones are not to be missed:
Miklós Jancsó: Confrontation ("Fényes szelek", 1969). A historical parable telling a story about the "revolutionary guardists" of the late forties, who start to disrupt the ancien régime with gusto, until they themselves are pushed off the scene. (Original title "Shining Winds".)
Péter Bacsó: The Witness ("A tanú", 1969). A hilarious comedy on the Hungary of the early fifties, when the authorities experimented even with growing cotton and lemons. Premiered only in 1979. ("... a satirical comedy worthy to rank with Schweik" — *The Times*, London, 18. 2. 1982.)
Zoltán Huszárik: Szindbád (1971). A sensuous, poetic film on the last days of an ageing hedonist, based on the writings of Gyula Krúdy, chronicler of small town fin de siècle. An exceptionally successful common effort of director, cameraman, composer and actor. See also the introduction to "Eating Well". ("A striking tour de force of visual technique and metaphysical imagery" — *Films and Filming*. Dec. 1981.)
Gyula Gazdag: The Whistling Cobblestone ("A sípoló macskakő", 1972). A philosophical satire set in a Summer student work

camp — on the perspectives of the post-68 generation. A feature film of documentarist technique. Amateur cast, black and white. ("...high-spirited and sly satire of government incompetence..." — *Village Voice*, 29. 10. 1979.)

Pál Sándor: Football of the Good Old Days ("Régi idők focija", 1973). A very funny and moderately sentimental film about an impoverished laundry owner, who keeps on sponsoring a football team in the Budapest of the twenties (during the first low ebb of Hungarian football), because "There must be a team!". Starring Dezső Garas, the great comedian.

András Jeles: Little Valentino ("A kis Valentino", 1979). A young man runs away with some ten thousand forints and loiters through some of the most pessimistic Budapest neighbourhoods. A malicious, depressing, though delightful film on values in the late seventies. Tells a lot about this city. (Black and white, amateur cast.)

Gábor Bódy: Psyché (1980). A two-part, spectacular film epic, an intellectual, somewhat esoteric movie "relating" the adventures of a fictitious poetess from the 1770s up to now. The greatest effort of the avantgard film-maker (1946-86) on the origins of new-wave point of view. ("...a chronicle of seduction and depravity... in the experimental, avantgard vein." — *Variety*, New York, 13.5.1981.)

István Szabó: Mephisto (1981). A two-part, well-made, spectacular movie piece on the life of an actor in the Germany during the first half of the 20th century, on the limits of cooperation between the gifted and the powerful. Starring Klaus Maria Brandauer. (An Oscar-winning film based on the novel of Klaus Mann.)

János Rózsa: Kiss, Mummy ("Csók, anyu", 1986). The days of an upper middle class family, in the witty, somewhat sentimental vein of recent American cinema. Provides insider's knowledge on present-day Hungary. In the role of the overworked, amoral father the all-round personality of Hungarian film and cinema, Róbert Koltai.

Bereményi Géza: Eldorádó (1988). A very funny and vivid story of a market vendor and his struggle to survive in the dark fifties, his love for his grandson. Excellent fun plus authentic acting, even startling music. The story ends in 1956. Starring Károly Eperjes, a marvellous actor — a kind of Depardieu of the Hungarian cinema.

János Szász: Woyzeck (1992). A black-and-white rendering of the Büchner classic, transferred to unspecified time in the 20th century. Excellent, breathtaking acting, dense, tense apocalyptic atmosphere all along. Also highly original photography. Known all over the world.

Péter Gothár: Vaska (1996). "A fairy tale from the Gulag." A hilariously funny tragi-comedy, shot entirely in St. Petersburg, mostly, with Russian actors. With a lot of Russian text left untranslated in the Hungarian version — for Hungarian eggheads, who spent a decade struggling with Russian. A film with a beginning, a middle and an end. The English version is available on video now.

A Note on the Dance House Movement

The end of the last century saw a large number of people moving up to the capital; here they cherished their folksongs for a while but rarely passed them on the next generation. the middle class favoured (as they still do) a type of folk-music-like romantic songs, called "Hungarian songs". (They are analogous to "Loch Lomond" in its connection to real Scottish folk-music.) Then around 1970, quite out of the blue, two young musicians, Ferenc Sebő and Béla Halmos, brought the real thing into fashion overnight. This music is still alive around the village of Szék in Transylvania, in a part of Romania which used to belong to Hungary. It was not only folk-music that became trendy at that time, traditional dancing also captured the imagination of the young. Many gathered in "dance-houses" week after week to dance to live Transylvanian music, to learn new dances and to enjoy the melodies. Anyone could join at any time and newcomers were taught the already mastered dances. Soon dance-houses for children also appeared. A one-day/one night national dance-house festival takes place every year in the Budapest Sports Hall, as part of the Budapest Spring Festival, where folk musicians and dancers come together from all over the country and thousands of people dance together. These occasions are usually accompanied by a busy market of folk crafts. Dance-houses have a unique atmosphere — the devotees regard each other as members of a large family. This rising interest in folk-music is reflected in a number of records.

It is a rewarding, quite unexpected experience to attend a dance-house session. Something you haven't heard about, and might fall in love with, on the spot.

READING: ON THE SPOT AND TAKE AWAY

LIBRARIES *had a special significance in keeping free thinking alive in Hungary. They were a link to the past, and also to the free world. Big libraries regularly ordered basic works of social sciences, and they were accessible to all university students. That was an intrinsic characteristic of Hungarian mild totalitarianism: it more or less let expertise develop — just did not use it; or very little of it.*

But unlike Russia, where unwanted books were only referred to in a special catalogue — accessible only to reliable comrades, anything like that was unthinkable in Hungary. There were two telltale letters stamped on the catalogue card of a couple of hundred openly anti-Communist books in English, or by émigré Hungarian presses: Z.A.: "closed material". But they were not so closed: any professor was willing to sign a request for a student: and they became available.

I only once heard about a shameful trick that affected the given level of freedom of information: in the periodicals department of Gorkhy Library (see below) Time magazine and Newsweek were on the shelves — but certain issues somehow did not find their way there. Of course the ones with politically sensitive features. But early next year they put back the issues where they belonged. In the bound volumes none of them are missing.

On the other hand, the Library of the Academy was the cradle of the dissident movement. They helped everyone with inter-library change: first they tried the Uppsala University Library, if they did not have the book there, they were willing to contact a US library. As far as I was concerned, Uppsala had everything.

NATIONAL "SZÉCHÉNYI" LIBRARY (*Royal Castle, Wing F, i.e. the huge part overlooking Buda. There is a special lift from Dózsa György tér, which provides the easiest access. T: 175-7533. Open: Monday 13-21, Tuesday to Saturday 9-21.*) In my student years the National Library — which bears the name of the father of the "Greatest Hungarian", István Széchenyi, whom you can see on the 5000 forint bill — was housed in the National Museum building. (*VIII. Múzeum körút 14-16.*) One had to walk through long corridors with Roman tombstones on both sides. Inside there were high ceilings, creaky linoleum floors and elderly readers frowning on every hiss. I went there often, since they had everything. The National Library since than moved to the Royal Castle. Huge and pompous, without being elegant. In the main reading room there is natural light from above. It is between the glass roof and the false ceiling where the small electric carriages come and go — I always feel myself a railwayman with defective hearing when I am there. Still, a singularly appropriate place to spend a whole day and sink into your work. There is a computerized catalogue which is very difficult to use — you should leave behind your computer routines you picked up in recent years, amidst tears.

LIBRARY OF THE ACADEMY OF SCIENCES AND LETTERS (*V. Arany János utca 1. Open: Monday to Friday 9-20, Saturday 9-17.*) Until before the renovation, the library was housed on the ground floor of the famous monument building, (1862-65), to the left of the main entrance. The Reading

Room was just like in the sixties of the last century, oil paintings of donators, famous scholars and writers on the walls. There were only 38 seats, out of which four were reserved for academicians — who hardly ever came. It only slowly dawned on me that the library, where I went every day, almost religiously, was the hub of the dissident movement.

Since then the library was moved to the adjacent building. The reading room is on the first floor, checking in is complicated. Sooner or later you find yourself standing in front of a lady in her seventies, who allots you a seat number, based on rank, or record of readership, or simply on sympathy. The quietest seats are near the smoking area. The smaller the number, the better the seat. It's a modern library with hundreds of seats, with mildly posh, tailor-made furniture. Now you don't have to wait two days for certain books you want, the floor does not creak, there are computers, still... You know what I mean.

PARLIAMENT LIBRARY *(V. Kossuth tér 1-3. T: 112-0600. Open: Monday to Thursday: 9-19.45, Friday: 9-14, Saturday 9-18.)* Inside it is the "Cross between a Gothic Church and a Turkish Bath", as a great 20th-century poet put his opinion about the building (1887-1904). As a student I sometimes went there. As a student I found out that the beautifully leather-bound volumes all around the gigantic Reading Room are the US Congress Papers. But when I wanted to use them they turned out to be not processed at all: I was given a ladder (sic!) to have a look. (Nevertheless, I succeeded.)

The Library is still beautiful, (it can spare you a touristic visit to the rest of the building) but still makes one sleepy. There is still no catalogue of the US Congress Papers. But there are some new, computerized services. The other major change is the purpose of the building around. It is used for its original purpose, again.

BUDAPEST PUBLIC LIBRARY, AKA. CENTRAL "SZABÓ ERVIN" LIBRARY *(VIII. Szabó Ervin tér 1., off Kálvin tér. T: 138-4933. Complicated hours: Monday, Tuesday and Friday 9-20, closed on Wednesday, Saturday 9-17, Sunday 9-13.)* A lovely, traditional place, with a superb periodicals room with oak panelling up to the roof, plus incredible chandeliers. You should first visit the cloakroom in the basement. Apart from the usual Budapest notices (what to do and what not to do) there is a pleasing sentence from a great 19th-century poet, Arany: "Oh, what a burdensome life / Dressing and undressing every morning and night". You should ascend the great staircase to come to the first floor, to the catalogue, the Main Reading Room, the Budapest Collection and the Periodicals Room. While waiting for the books I want to borrow, I love browsing the new acquisitions. A great place to be.

UNIVERSITY LIBRARY *(V. Ferenciek tere 6. T: 266-4634. Open: Monday 11-19, Tuesday to Friday 8-20, Saturday 8-18.)* Originally established in 1561, the collection moved to Buda Castle in 1777. It has been here since this building was completed in 1876. It was seriously damaged when the underground was built under it, in the 1970s. Renovation has just been finished. The Main Reading Room, on the first floor, traditionally the place where medical students spend all their lives, has an awesome, cathedral-like quality. That's where students feel that they will never be able to remember all that stuff by exam day.

Among the invaluable treasures there are 171 codices, among them 11 of the famous Corvinas, from the legendary library of King Matthias Corvinus (reigned 1458-1490.) They also have a Greek gospel from the 11th century. And subscribe to over 3000 foreign periodicals.

CENTRAL FOREIGN LANGUAGE LIBRARY or as popularly still called "The Gorkhy" (V. Molnár utca 7. Open: 9-20, every other Saturday: 9-5, Monday: 14-20.) The place used to belong to the YMCA before the war, the only hint of which is to be found under the doormat at the front door: SALVE. After "the changes" (the previous ones) it became a Russian language library, but from the early sixties it began to collect literature in a dozen or so foreign languages. The Reading Room on the first floor was redecorated some three or four times in the last fifteen years. Except for the name and the disappearance of the statue of Gorky, hardly anything changed by now. The typical noise is the not easily recognizable sound of the pigeons that walk on the glass roof. A somewhat stocky, unshaven, curly-haired man, about forty, reading proofs or translating some Durrell or David Lodge book, one of the funniest persons in town, a very good friend of mine is often there on Wednesday afternoons. He loves to talk to foreign eggheads, in his superior English.

SO MANY BOOKS! Friends of mine from Western Europe remark with surprise on the number of books in peoples' homes here in Budapest. Because of a high level of state subsidy, books were very cheap compared to many others in the seventies and early eighties. In 1989 the monopoly held by several state publishers went and some 400 (!) small publishers sprang up. Anyone can publish a book in Hungary. Books are sold in all sorts of places, including the streets, pre-destrian subways and supermarkets — which is quite a recent development, too.

TWELVE GOOD BOOKS — NON-FICTION

Lukács, John: Budapest 1900. (A Historical Portrait of a City and Its Culture.) *Weidenfeld and Nicholson, New York, 1988.* An intimate and engaging story — an unusual one. Budapest experienced a remarkable "exfoliation" at the third third of the last century. It was one of the most promising metropolitan centres of Europe, both expansion-wise and exuberance-wise. This is a scholarly, yet very readable book, by a Budapest born American historian. Not on sale in Budapest. (Try at the CEU–shop; see below.)

Budapest, anno... *Corvina, 1996.* This is a selection of the work of György Klösz, court photographer. A major photographer of the nineteenth century and his work which provides many scenes that have changed little since, together with many contemporary advertisements, too. Klösz worked with glass plates as negatives, hence the fantastic details. Some of his great picures, covered with graffiti: in the subway passage under Elizabeth Bridge.

Gundel's Hungarian Cookbook *Corvina, 1997.* The name Gundel is to Budapest as Sacher is to Vienna and Horcher to Madrid. Károly Gundel first published this book in 1934 and it has since gone through more than 30 editions. He is the great figure in Hungarian cooking. The two of his thirteen children who followed in his footsteps have complied this present edition.

István Örkény: One Minute Stories *Corvina, 1997.* Translated by Judith Sollosy. A selection from a cult book, by the master of Hungarian grotesque. The hilariously funny miniature stories give a deep insight of the Hungarian psyche, a funny and sorry picture, full of irony, cynicism and occasional self-hatred. A very good present to buy. A book very well known for all Hungarian graduates.

Kosztolányi Dezső: Darker Muses (Nero) *Corvina, 1990.* A historical novel by the great master of twentieth-century Hungarian prose.

Ferenc Molnár: The Paul Street Boys *Corvina, 1994.* The juvenile classic, known by all in Italy, Poland, and other countries, published for the first time in English since 1927. A funny, moving story, enjoyable for kids and grownups alike.

Gerő, András: Heroes' Square, Budapest (Hungary's History in Stone and Bronze.) *Corvina, 1990.* A fascinating story of a monument about Hungarian history. About how it was designed and built, how it was changed by the specific regimes that happened to rule in Hungary. Very well written, with superb colour and black-and-white pictures. Also in German.

Csontváry album *Corvina, 1994.* The stunning great original of Hungarian art was like a gigantic comet. Sudden inspiration led him to take up art as an adult and the results, enormous bewitching canvesses, are to be seen in the Nemzeti Galéria, and in the Csontváry Múzeum in the town of Pécs. See our "First Walk". Better still, see the paintings.

TWELVE GOOD BOOKSHOPS

Bookshops are generally open on weekdays between 10 a.m. and 6 p.m., Saturdays 9 a.m. to 1 p.m. In the list that follows, opening hours are only given when they differ from these. During the Book Week at the end of May / beginning of June, the stalls that sprout up everywhere trade on Sundays too.

Bookshop at the Central European University (CEU) *V. Nádor utca 9, on the streetfront. T: 327-3096.* Open 9 a.m. to 6 p.m. Mon-Fri, 2 p.m. to 5 p.m. on Sat. A very serious academic bookshop that does not exclude good readings, though with a limited selection of Hungarian related subjects, literature included. Operated, together with nearby Bestsellers Bookshop by Budapest legend Tony Lang, who immigrated to the land of his ancestors to start a bookshop here. He had to learn the language, which he did brilliantly. See "Bestsellers" in Crash Course, pp. 11. Obviously, the full range of Central European University Press books.

Corvina *V. Kossuth Lajos utca 6.* Fair selection of Hungarian books in foreign languages to the left on entry, sheet music and records to the right. In the unbearably busy thorougfare, where you can't park. You can also buy the books of my publisher, with a discount in a more pleasant environment, in Vörösmarty tér (2nd storey), in the ugliest of the ugly office blocks, on the first floor. The ugly ad is seen from the square.

Erkel *VII. Erzsébet körút 52.* Opposite Royal Hotel, with three display rooms. Large selection of sheet music and records too. The latter are on first floor and a stiff cardboard record sleeve is happily supplied on request to protect purchases. Catalogue available.

Fókusz *VII. Rákóczi út 14.* Occupying two large floors, this is the biggest bookshop in the country. Maps, records and Hungarian books in translation all available. Remaindered books are to be found on the first floor. If they haven't rearranged the stock, what they often do. Not as large and pleasant as Barnes and Noble, though, anywhere in the US, or Powell's.

Helikon *VI. Bajcsy-Zsilinszky Endre út, corner Hajós utca.* A large, lavishly decorated, recently opened, two-level bookshop, owned by the publishing house of the same name, one that is owned by an Investment Fund. That investment is obviously a very long term one. The American-Hungarian CEO must have had Rizzoli of New York in mind. Experts say, that in this part of the town no business ever flourished this century. We'll see. Large selection of Hungarian and foreign books, a small café in the basement. Also CD-ROMS.

Kódex *V. Honvéd utca 5.* Not far from Parliament and on our "Second Walk", this large, well-designed bookshop has two floors. The upper floor stocks in many foreign languages.

Láng Téka *XIII. Pozsonyi út 9.* It's also a video rental outlet, that's why it closes so late. Also records and cassettes. Open until 11 p.m. every day.

Le Pont *I. Fő utca 17,* inside Institut Français, hours of business adjusted consequently. A very funny coincidence, operated by the Pont Bookshop people. The word has a different meaning in French. ("point" in Hungarian, "bridge" in French.) By far the largest selection in Hungary, of course, and they order anything for you. Ground floor, to the left.

Litea *I. Hess Adndrás tér 4.* Opposite Hotel Hilton — in the courtyard. The name comes from the merge of two words: Literature + Tea, both available there, a really choice selection of both. A singularly pleasant, recently built pavilion. A full range of foreign language Hungarian books. Catalogues. They also send books abroad: above 800 forints worth no mailing costs. Ice tea. Irish Coffee. Grog. Portuguese tea.

Osiris Könyvesház *V. Veres Pálné utca 4-6. Corner of Curia utca. T: 266-4999.* That is an unlikely place in such an expensive area. The most egghead of the egghead bookshops. They operate a minority publications reading room, a small café, a book club, and a showroom. A singularly pleasant place, not yet discovered by the expatriate community. Just go in, sit down, read anything. They should have the two English-speaking egghead quarterlies: *The Hungarian Quarterly,* and the *Budapest Review of Books.* On the inside and outside of the back page you are likely to find my column on Budapest.

Pont *V. Mérleg utca 6.* This is a clearcut egghead bookshop, one that rents its space from the Alliance of Free Democrats, aka. the egghead party. (Headquarters upstairs.) All kinds of fiction and non-fiction. They operate a book-club, too. Now, that the party is a member of the ruling coalition, there are fewer MPs browsing here. Still a pleasant, overcrowded place. Good advice is free and abundant here. In the same building a pleasant, cheap restaurant, called Mérleg (Scales), after the name of the street.

SECOND HAND AND ANTIQUARIAN BOOKS *The division of these two genres has happened (again) fairly recently. For decades, the best shop, characteristically, was called "Központi Antikvárium" (Central Antiquarian Bookshop) — in this shop the two activities, some ten years ago, separated so much, that they actually cut the shop into two. (V. Múzeum körút 15. T: 117-3514.)*

OLD AND RARE BOOKS

Borda *(as aready mentioned in your Crash Course: VII. Madách Imre tér 5. II. floor, only Tuesday and Thursday afternoon, otherwise by special appointment, T: 142-2086).* 50 metres from Deák tér, where the three underground lines meet, in a red brick twin bulding, that was designed to be the beginning of a new avenue, to lead from here to City Park, as planned in the twenties.

Forgács *(V. Stollár Béla utca 8., T: 111-6874)*, pleasant, small shop in a silent side street, near the Parliament. Open until 7 p.m., also Saturday afternoon, until 4 p.m. Strong in architecture and bibliophile German and English editions, plus Hungarian fiction in German and English, especially the non-Hungarian editions. Also small objects. Great service and paper bags.

Kárpáti és Szőnyi *(V. Szent István körút 3., T: 111-6431)*, a small, crowded, well-stocked shop on the noisier end of Nagykörút, at the Pest end of Margaret bridge. Old books and prints at the back of the shop. They also give away a carefully compiled, but poorly produced small list and map of all the second-hand shops in Budapest.

Kollin *(V. Bajcsy-Zsilinszky Endre út 34., upstairs, T: 111-9023., at Arany János utca underground.)* Accessible through a second-hand bookshop called "Nyugat". Kollin opens at 2 p.m. ad closes at 5.30 p.m. Specializes in old German travel books; there is an amazing collection of the classic Baedeker editions, also some volumes in English. Very elegant and well-informed.

Font *(VI. Andrássy út 56., T: 132-1646, near Octogon, the eight-sided square, there is this small shop with a Paris Left Bank atmosphere, run by too bearded friends. Strong in old art books and eccentric postcards. Don't forget the upstairs part. A complete Köchel-list has been longing for a new owner there. Aren't you the one?*

Ex Libris *(V. Kálmán Imre utca 16.)* is strong in Judaica and old cinema posters.

Honterus *(V. Múzeum körút 35.)*, is strong in old maps and prints.

Horváth *(VI. Andrássy út 76.)*, takes pride in a large collection of antique authors (also scholarly and critical editions).

SOME FURTHER SHOPS, WITH A MISCELLANEOUS STOCK

Bibliotéka *VI. Andrássy út 2. T: 131-5132.*
Óbuda *III. Lajos utca 49/b. T: 188-7332.*
Ráth Mór *II. Margit körút 44. T: 201-6793.*
Uránia *VIII. Népszínház utca 23. T: 114-2050.*
Zenei Antikvárium — Second Hand Music Bookshop *V. Múzeum körút 17.* Virtually opposite the Nemzeti Múzeum, with a huge selection of books on music and of sheet music. Occasionally amazing older East-European scores and records in good condition are to be found.

HOW DIFFICULT IT IS TO EXPLAIN IT IN PORTLAND, OREGON...

Gentle Reader,

I know it far too well that the word "egghead" is an obsolete one, inherited from the times of President Kennedy's siege of Washington. It is a borrowing which is fuelled with an audacious, vain idea: if I use the word often enough, I will be able to bring it back from the dead. Moreover: though most often I omit the word "Budapest", as a matter of fact I always refer to certain "Budapest eggheads".

This lecture would like to provide some introspection into a very special world in a very special town. To share the findings of my long and laborious discoveries with you.

It is often asked what — if any — real benefits of the totalitarian regime went down the drains with the changes of Eastern Europe. There haven't been many, needless to say. The far too much money spent on high culture had the awful background of censorship: in two ways. Individual authors and publishers' lists were censored, and on the other way round, whole layers of consumer culture were kept away from the people. They were more or less forced to read better quality things than they actually wanted. That's how it could happen that "Absolon! Absolon!" by William Faulkner was printed and sold in no less than 140,000 copies in Hungary (translated by the present President of the Republic), in the late 70s. Who read all those copies, one might ask. Very few people, of course. Hungary has never been a country of eggheads. But books were cheap, i.e. subsidized by everyone, also by the semi-illiterate miner, who never read anything, not even comics. (True, one of his kids might have been tempted to read books... an endless argument. Also, miners were much better paid than teachers and even doctors...)

In this mildly cruel, utterly frustrating but mild totalitarian Hungarian society almost everything was hazy and dreamlike, not only books, but life in general was cheap. There the Budapest egghead as a species grew up, ambitionless, letter-hungry, gadget-happy, slightly privileged, with more and more contacts to the West, cosmopolitan, womanising, drinking semi-heavily, knowing that no real responsibilities will ever be bestowed on him.

"Sub poena crescit palma" — (under burden the palmtree grows) this is a Latin saying that was often cited in Budapest among intellectuals, who wanted to explain the unexplainable: why, amidst frustration and general torpor the mild totalitarian regime of the 1970s and 80s was a sort of intellectual and literary Golden Age. Today, with the burden gone, Budapest is even more of an intellectually invigorating and colourful place, with beautiful, long-established libraries, rich classical music life and bristling student cafés. While the museum scene suffers from scarce funds, the alternative and marginal art scene has grown enormously. The art cinema network almost equals that of Paris and New York. Earlier there was one hopeless obstacle for a foreign egghead: Hungarian language, a not even Indo-European, originally Asian tongue.* Now, with most students speaking English, with several English-speaking weeklies in the city, information is no longer a problem here. All this amounts to something like an egghead paradise.

A decade ago Budapest seemed to most visiting eggheads as a nice Roman province— some time after the Romans left. Now they return and rejoice: the Romans are back.

Sorry, they are not right. This lecture would like to prove nothing less that we have been the Romans all along.

The Budapest egghead is an intellectual who was trained in a country where free thinking was confined to a reservatum of eggheads, where political pressure forced eggheads to become a member of a very closely-knit society, where the members were going to live a life without any real responsibilities, outside the family or their own spiritual circle. Critical spirit has become one of their forte, an uncompromising, sweeping, easy-going critical spirit. Egghead society used to be much wider than any intellectual society in any given metropolis in Europe. Students and young adults of all interests, stripped of normal career prospects, who would otherwise browse the stock exchange rates, and looking for adventure chances there, or working hard for an exotic holiday, or a sports car, or a state-of-the-art hi-fi-equipment, were reading hard-to-read latest American fiction translated into Hungarian and discussing the findings of muckraking Hungarian sociologists, who were given the money to do the surveys which were then shelved in a room of the Communist Party headquarters. Budapest was a special place: the expertise was here, just policy makers did not use it. Life was relatively cheap, everything was subsidized: even electricity and gas and rents. Oil was traded from the Soviet Union through some shady barter transactions. Food was cheap, books were cheap, an egghead could live on very little money. He could even buy some booze for the week-end party cum intellectual salon.

The typical egghead had some small job at a publisher or at a university or one or other think tank of the Academy of Sciences or a theatre, or a language school, but was involved in some odd job — translating a long book of social science for a publisher, and many of them were involved in the underground press, from the early eighties on. But there existed the most improbable jobs — a key underground fighter, now the Mayor of Budapest worked in a department of some Party-run institute, where he commissioned translations of works of contemporary social sciences — for the use of comrades who wanted scholarly titles, but could not read in English or German. So this egghead lived on that work, and could pay his egghead friends a lot of money. Another egghead, a writer, while writing his own books, among them the hilariously funny "1985", a sequel to the Orwell classic, officially still unpublished, was translating Soviet war novels — into a tape recorder, and not really looked at the typed version again.

They worked a lot, but with varying intensity, working and leisure time was one big bulk, inseparable from each other. Random meetings in the street, in a library, at lunch could give the day a turn. As an archaic soci-

---

* Hans Magnus Enzensberger, a frequent visitor in the Budapest egghead scene in the late seventies, early eighties, once complained that Budapest is the only place in Europe where he can't decipher the word "pharmacy" in signs. True, true: it is called "gyógyszertár".

ety, news passed from mouth to mouth. National sports was to read between the lines. There were Them and Us, Them being the compromising intellectuals, with some power or other, the ones we looked down on. It was a highly interesting world full of information, misinformation, love intrigue and pure scandal. The walls of possibilities were pushed forward and backwards an inch all the time. The system could not be more liberal than that. Nobody expected any real change in our life, especially not after 1981 in Poland.

The Budapest egghead could not have influence on anything, so he developed a sense of universal interest. They could not change anything, so they wanted to change everything. They tended to become jacks of all trades and even masters of everything. Most of them developed eccentric traits. They grew interested in the minutiae of railway timetables, of sports records of long ago, of football team lists of particular matches and so on. One put together makeshift furniture to his very modest second home, the other was writing on hi-fi-equipment, the third was collecting antique typewriters, the fourth old stationery. But almost all of them were collecting the past. Some of them kept on returning to Transylvania, looking for Hungarian roots, ransacking the lofts, taking home parts of looms and oxcart accessories. The better-informed also tended to be enthusiastic for the contemporary avantguard, more specifically concept art, with its long documentation on the imagined artwork, mostly ideas substituting art proper.

Inside the typical egghead the citoyen and the bohemian was wrestling all the time. A real bohemian and the shell of a citoyen. The latter was a set of rules inherited and/or read in books. A citoyen that had no other salary but what he earned. A citoyen with no property, just the pride and self-consciousness, some "gesunkenes kulturgut", conjured alive. It's so interesting to see that some eggheads can fill that formerly empty shell. Maybe all of them could, but few have the chance…

Egghead society hinged very much on informal, clandestine information: everything that is "not available in books". It was important to know people in person — that was the source of knowledge, much more than books, and much much more than the media, which was not at all. Studying the canon had some very archaic, even peripatetic character. You followed Socrates to the cafeteria of the Library of the Academy, and listened to his 20-minute lecture on a current issue, or on the contrary, on some eternal aspect of the arts. This egghead civilization tended to be a verbal, face-to-face communication, archaic in this respect. Thus, much less alienated.

Not only verbal, of course. After that 20-minute lecture one spent days in the same library, to read those books mentioned…

Archaic, human, verbal, metaphoric, funny, proud of itself, gossipy, idiosynchratic, experimental, self-destructive, enviably vigorous, friendly to talent. All that.

Of course, little of it is spotted now in Budapest — egghead society as it was.

But the scenery is still here. And most of the people are still here. Turned middle-aged. Still unusually witty and original and creative with an unexpected twist here and there. Let's have a sudden sample of Budapest egghead society right away.

RUNNING AMOK IN BUDAPEST EGGHEAD SOCIETY
An Imaginary Journey through the City Hour by Hour

But first, a couple of keynote remarks about

GLOOM AND CHANGES No doubt, Budapest has become younger, more contemporary, more sophisticated, faster-paced, but also more segregated, in all the senses of the word, more scandal-ridden, more commercial and also more commonplace. There are bigger and bigger contrasts in wealth, in ambition, in the way people look at each other. Eggheads tend to find it more difficult to follow what has been happening all around in bigger and bigger concentric circles, as if they needed a replacement lens into their eyes: one with a wider angle. They were conditioned to live a different kind of life.

Is Budapest still that intellectually invigorating and exuberant and turbulent place what it used to be in the last decade of the mild totalitarian régime, what recently even included some optimism and hope for the future, during the glorious years of transition? Most observers agree that it is and it isn't any more. Gloom is spreading and protruding in and out of most minds, moreover: disillusion.

Here is a worthy task for a factfinding tour: Is there any damage so far in the minds? "If not, how much?"

The generation of eggheads that so much wanted change, seems a bit taken aback that changes don't seem to stop. Things are not what they seemed at first. Liberty seemed to destroy high culture in the first place, but later it turned out to decentralize and multiply it. It has become gradually more and more impossible to have an overview of what is happening. That constant rearrangement of all the factors of the layers of the eggheads' lives that makes many of them tired and worried. They hoped to withdraw into their beloved ebony towers. After the thrill of 89 and 90 they hoped not to read daily papers much. They hoped Hungary to be the exception, with sulphurous notions forever in the bottle.

7 A.M.: A SWIM IN GELLÉRT BATH If I were you, and had no friend who shares his/her big apartement downtown with me, I wouldn't listen to syren voices and stay anywhere else, but in Gellért Hotel. As an artist friend keeps telling me, it is a big, white, self-cleaning gem, a sort of retarded art-nouveau building, erected during WW I. There is direct access to the bath via an elevator. First, swim indoors in the small pool, and examine the stained glass windows. Then go outside: so early in the morning there is hardly anyone in the bath. I am sorry, but I don't think that it is possible to persuade anyone to go and swim and talk to you so early in the Gellért.

9 A.M.: CAFÉ GUSTO WITH FERENC BODOR The café is a first swallow: the first real and new café in living memory. There is a pleasant street terrace: inside it is small, but intimate, with brown furniture that does not look brand new. What really gives the charm and flavour and personality of the place is a big oil painting of Augusto Piave. He is said to have been a café owner somewhere in Northern Italy, and the ancestor of one of the owners. A sort of the "patron saint" of this place.

Tall, bearded, cross-eyed Ferenc Bodor, chief librarian of the Academy of Arts and Crafts, director of nearby Tölgyfa Gallery (belonging to the same school), city historian and gallery director, a romantic figure, is a sort of a knight of the bygone days. He loves the that retarded, naff Budapest, that distorted café world of his childhood, where (few) underground philosophers shared the dingy tables with other underdogs of society and the cheap drinks specially unwatered for them. He recently published a slim volume on Budapest espressos, with some very evocative photos and descriptions. Beware, most of the places were closed and /or redecorated while the book printed. So ask him for an updated list of places to visit. Though some people think it is better to know these places through Bodor's adjectives, and not let reality destroy the indirect impressions.

Try to grill him about new, favourable developments in Budapest, and what made him buy a computer, the last out of the egghheads. (II. Frankel Leó utca 24.)

11 A.M.: LUKÁCS BATH, WITH GERGELY BIKÁCSY This run-down, open air bath, amidst hundred year old trees and hundreds of small, thanksgiving tablets, used to be the hotbed of free thought, a kind of a witty intellectual salon, even in the Darkest Fifties. The last of the mohicans, who could hardly see the highest days of the place, spends almost all his days here, from spring to autumn, eccentric film critic and short story and porn-epic writer, bald, white-bearded, muttering Gergely Bikácsy, aka. Tamás Glauziusz. He is a French egghead, theoretician of the French New Wave, and lover of Paris, vacillating between Paris and Budapest all his adult life. He feels that he made the bad decisions all the time. He would like to be at both places, at the same time, all the time. It's no use asking him about gloom, since he is the gloomiest of all Budapest eggheads. "Could you find a publisher for your porn epic yet?" could be a good question to unleash him. The epic follows the legend of the Holy Grail: the most indecent, most parodistic work of travesty since Apollinaire and Bataille. He is also famous for his novel "A Tomboy in the Shaded Lane", which is a cruelly sincere rendering of his own love story, with the characters taken from the national classic early 19th-century tragedy: "Bánk bán" which made the piece hilariously funny. His pseudonym Tamás Glauziusz refers to a character in a play and the film based on it: Uncle Glauziusz was a good-hearted accountant of the good old days who doesn't understand new intrigue in cruel, new times, nevertheless serves his new masters. Typically Budapest egghead manners. (II. Frankel Leó utca 25-27.)

1. P.M. LUNCH WITH ADAM NÁDASDY AT MERLIN Merlin Theatre is a 2 and a half year old institution, within the City Hall complex, from the mid-XVIIIth century, originally an old soldiers' home. Merlin is an independent building from early this century: now a drama school and host theatre for visiting productions. Also an English-speaking theatre in the summer. The restaurant (and jazz club at night) was meant to be elagant, expensive and profitable, to sponsor the other activities.

Instead, it became a sort of cross between an avantgarde café and a city hall canteen. The latter at noontime, the former especially in the afternoon. Ask

Adam to point out the hub and mastermind behind the "venture", actor-director-manager Tamás Jordán. He and wife/co-visionary/actress (recently excelled as Petra von Kant in the Fassbinder play) run the Merlin Drama school, presently in the second year. They hope to keep them together and turn them into a permanent company.

Adam, the arch-egghead of Budapest, some 18 month ago, won a dinner for two, as First Prize at the annual Poetry Championship (on Twelfth Night). He is a scholar, poet and wit, iconoclastic university lecturer in English linguistics, innovative university administrator and coloumnist of the Hungarian BUKSZ magazine. He can be best enjoyed during one of his lectures, or on stage or at home. Unfortunately for you, he is just moving, you can't see his natural habitat, a mixture high class art, thousands of books and low-tech, naff equipment.

You should read his "egghead manifesto" "The Name of the Captive", in the very first issue of BOOKS, Winter 1991), and ask what happened since. Ask about gloom in him, about his university reform, about changes. You can ask him in English, German, Italian or French. He is much less eloquent in Russian, Polish or Persian.

He is not tall, has a round face, grey hair and beard, generally speaking, a bit stockier than he would like to be. Uses Wordperfect (DOS-version). Would like to have a phonetic symbol set within this software. Couldn't get it even in England. Could you help him, do you think? (V. Gerlóczy utca 4.)

3 P.M. CAFÉ NEW YORK WITH THE EDITORS OF "2000"

The once foremost literary café tends to be deserted nowadays: the building upstairs, a sort of former Fleet Street itself, has been emptied: it's on sale. It's 99 years old and big — it has past and future. The editors of 2000 gather in the gallery, they literally but not figuratively look down on the ground floor, where tourists video each other, and to the luxury restaurant called Deep Water, where occasional, wayword travellers and nouveau riche tycoons have lunch, mistaking it for a gourmet place.

By three all the editors are there, except for those who happen to be in London or Firenze or Vilnius or St Petersburg or at the University Council in Budapest, and the one who is permanently stationed in Vienna. After 3 o' clock only promising young, hitherto not published poets risk a visit. The editors, seven in numbers, form a brotherhood of love and hatred. They have loud quarrells over publications, not necessarily here, in front of the authors.

And I am also there, often in deep conversation with our overqualified secretary, a retired, Russian-born lady, research fellow in literature, or Aunt Irene, the "literary toilet attendant", who always reads our paper, but doesn't let us pay if we happen to use her institution. But if you come to leave a manuscript with us, don't expect a very quick answer. There is no editor in chief — a blessing and a curse. One of the curses: slow decisions. (VII. Erzsébet körút 9-11., only on Thursday, otherwise by special commission.)

5 P.M. THE COURTYARD OF "THE NEST" WITH MIKLÓS VAJDA

Miklós Vajda is the "last literary gentleman", the editor of *The Hungarian Quarterly*, a government sponsored quality journal, also the translator of maybe as many as a hundred plays, from the English. He looks and behaves gentlemanlike, has read everything, old and new, and has lived a remarkably colourful life. Son of a wealthy upper-middle class family, was grown up pocketing extra adoration from the first wife of his father, the greatest actress on Hungarian stage. Later went through awful things he has yet to write in a mémoire. He has a singularly unbiased opinion about life and literature today. Of course, ask him about gloom, about Hungarian literature in English. Try to grill him as much as to mention one (just one) Hungarian novel in English that is a must for visiting eggheads.

The "Nest" or Fészek is an artists' club established in 1903, one that has always retained some self-government or other, but has become increasingly naff in the eyes of the younger generation, perhaps because of the leadership padded with "favoured" artists. The restaurant, recently leased by the wife of a successful Budapest restaurateur, is different. It does not really belong to the club.

Miklós is the left figure in the legendary painting "Three Editors" from the fifties (This is for the Advanced Egghead Tour, for next Summer). (VII. Kertész utca 36.)

7 P.M. A BEER OR TWO (OR THREE) WITH FERENC TAKÁCS AT WINSTON'S, AN ENGLISH PUB Takács is perhaps the most curious crop of that intellectual orchard that Budapest has been in the last twenty years. Gargantuan, rebellious, scholarly, ambitionless, (though newlywed), he is the storyteller champion and the Joyce-and-Eliot lecturer at Budapest University. His English is phenomenal, rich in idiom and meta-language features. He even translated *The Transporters* of Péter Esterházy, the paradigmatic contemporary writer into English: short, but impossibly difficult and metaphoric. Cynical to the utmost, or so he pretends, he does his best to camouflage his larger than life vanity with flaunting his ego. A brilliant mind and stylist, published an allusion-hint first chapter of a Gargantuan novel. Turning mid-forty, he seems to begin longing for everything: power, fame in the eye of the man in the street. Be careful with your questions: he always contradicts, whatever you state. Just ask. "Was life in the Kádár era really sweet?" could be a good start with him. He seems to pay attention but to himself — he is a very attentive listener, actually. (VI. Jókai tér 4.)

9 P.M. SEMI-FORMAL DINNER WITH THE EDITORS OF HUNGARIAN BUKSZ MAGAZINE This should preferably take place in the home of one of them, possibly in István Rév's flat, in a dreamlike Buda villa, because then you can take a glance at the middle-aged-egghead-style at its best. Second choice is Mr Klaniczay's home, the third is Gundel's, a small gala room upstairs.

Most of them are longtime friends since undergraduate years. This is a closely knit brotherhood with a shared vision of quality and right and wrong. They seem to believe in scholarly life and scholarship in general. They indulge in being independent and sarcastic, cruel and devastating if necessary. They are smart to the utmost, workaholic and cantankerous, according to many. An independent power centre, even know how to enjoy life (yes, maybe all of them). You should test the gloom theory and their beliefs, you should ask if Hungary is big enough for the theoretical possibility of independent opinion in every question. And whether they ever published an unconditionally praising review of a book. And whether any one of their readers ever realized that the design of their title page logo changes by season (the way the sun shines from different directions), respectively... (XII. Virányos út 16., if the first choice.)

11 P.M. PICASSO POINT WITH JÁNOS CSILLAG Currently the most fashionable intellectual café, can be the starting point of the night tour, to put the dot on the "i". János Csillag is the lifestyle editor of *Hungarian Orange*, the Village-Voice and Rolling Stones-like weekly, that sticks out from Hungarian Press as a sore thumb, mind you, a tasty one. János, maximum 26, or looks so, knows everything from the Budapest night, even updated every day, by the pooled experience of the paper. I have no idea where he wants you to take, maybe to Nincs Pardon, or to Hold. Ask him. No use to ask him about gloom. He is too busy to be gloomy, a new breed of cross between an extroverted egghead and a yuppie with just emptied credit card. Though the paper is not related by the Young Democrats' Party any more, most of the Orange guys think this Parliament term has yielded only gloom, was a nightmare for them. But they can wait. ... Oh, yes. And ask him to tell the story of the name of the paper. And also ask him to let you go not much later than midnight.

AFTER MIDNIGHT, POSSIBLY ALONE ON LIBERTY BRIDGE I bet you will not ponder about answers to questions of theoretical kind. The only exception maybe: "Hey, civic boosterism, so profuse in Budapest in the last couple of years, is becoming scarcer nowadays... But not gone. Not all, anyway..."

The night lights of the city, trying to gather the stamina needed to crawl to bed. Try harder, you will overcome. Some day.

MORE REMARKS ON THE ORIGINS OF EGGHEAD SOCIETY The real egghead enjoyed his way of life, reading a lot, discussing a lot, partying a lot, also working a lot, but rarely meeting a deadline, seeing the outcome of their work rarely, late or never. Knowing everybody who counts, never hoping to arrive to Rhodus where they can really jump. He or she was an intellectual, eminent (or at least promising) in something, but his (her) intellect was more developed than his counterpart in a free society. One had the feeling that the Budapest egghead used a higher proportion of his/her brain than the ones in the ideal position — over there. Also the Budapest egghead could and did make the most improbable connections between his pieces of information. To put it short — he/she is an artist as well, apart from being a scholar (at least a budding one).

Also the Budapest egghead made an effort to explain everything. He did it wit gusto. He either supposed that everybody is well aware of the basic principles of his field or carefully and evocatively explained them to the interested fellow eggheads — especially to younger egghead ladies.

Some egghead-inclined persons some time or other grew tired of talking and revelling and tried doing something: going to teach to a small village for a year or two, to start a club for Gypsies somewhere in the outskirts of Budapest, some activity barely tolerated. There was a continuous spectre of eggheads, former eggheads, doers, former-doers-just-dropped-out persons, artists, girls of demi-monde, even young, serious scholars, deprived of their due position, and of course writers banned or rarely published. It was a colourful society of about a thousand people, the hotbed of political, intellectual and artistic dissent. This transitional existence forced people to form their own opinion. It worked against the stereotypes. You never know who do you sit adjacent to at a party: a great, trend-setting philosopher of international rank, a rich dentist, an avant-garde pope with his unlikely, fragile companion, or the beautiful, "enfante terrible" youngest daughter of the greatest psychologist of the day, the hero of 1956.

PRIVILEGES Privileges were of many kinds: politicians, or retired politicians as parents, who could arrange a privileged bank loan for to buy a small flat in a modern housing estate, relatives in Britain, where one could pass the Summers, access to one of the private children's camps, especially the one in a village called Bánk, where a substantial part of the egghead society knew each other from.

Some of the privileges were natural, inherited ones, from middle-class parents, simple privileges that meant a big home library, a nice home in Buda, grandparents who spoke languages. Among the fathers were a painter working as a journalist, a writer, died long ago, an opera director and great educator, a great historian, who could use his power, always even-handedly. But the typical family was some slight privilege: a not known, relatively affluent father. The general director of a food wholesale company, a head of a small film studio, even small business people. Then there were the kids of déclassé families, with very old aunts and nice vases and china sets in the cupboards. But now, remembering the good old days, I realize, that at least half of them was of first generation intellectuals — in many cases with parents also college educated in evening courses in the fifties, or none at all.

Many of these kids sort of summarized the ambitions of the family to rise: also, these kids somehow got to the amazing aura of free thinking. Most of them totally lost intellectual contact with their parents, who desperately wanted to fit the cookie-cutter mould of the mild totalitarian regime of the late sixties, early seventies. But once they were in the egghead society, they became privileged overnight: they had access to information one needed to outwit the Communist regime. In everyday matters, I mean. In housing regulations, in getting odd jobs, how to get a social housing flat or a telephone line, or maybe just keep it. The egghead has become the member of one huge credit card system of favours. Where you could have some help from some fellow-egghead. Information meant a lot in that archaic mild totalitarian society. But of course you mustn't have overdrawn your credit — not to become a pariah.

A GLASS HOUSE THREATENED Living in the egghead society, in this glass house of pseudo-existence was nice and frustrating, intellectually very invigorating. This human tapestry sort of served as a highly scenic backdrop for that Golden Age in literature and film. Both ended, when the ground began to tremble: politics started to be more interesting. With the advent of liberty normal chances emerged for the eggheads, to start new careers, somewhat late in life: to become multimillionaire businessmen, or nationally known politicians. The latter happened en masse: something singular happened in 1988-89: an egghead party was formed and it almost won the national elections. It has just undergone the painful process of getting rid of egghead characteristics.

Being an egghead now is totally anachronistic. Still, occasionally, can be charming. Come and see and experience it.

BUDAPEST BESTS : : BUDAPEST BESTS : : BUDAPEST BESTS

István Rév, Historian, Maverick Political Scientist, True Son of Buda

By taking a 91 bus from the Vígszínház and, after it winds its way up *Rózsadomb*, by getting off in the quietness of Áfonya utca to a stroll up to the József-hegy look-out point on the very top of Rózsadomb, a truly charming view is to be had. In clear weather, looking north, not only all the Danube bridges and the hills lying beyond the city but the contours of the Carpathians themselves can be seen. A clear view all round is blocked only to the south-east by two boorish houses that obscure the hill known as Svábhegy. In the house that ruins one of the city's finest views, on Józsefhegy, lives A-J-, who at the time he moved in was responsible for the city's development and planning.

At the beginning of the century, Rózsadomb was essentially a place of parks, vineyards, gardens and kitchen gardens; it was between the too wars that building started here. Out of the noisy city there mainly came upper and middle-class citizens to build their detached houses and their rented-off villas of various sizes. After WWII, Rózsadomb became the quarter for the déclassé: wives of arms manufacturers who painted scarves, of business magnates who became daily helps, widows of distillery proprietors who survived by giving German lessons, barons reduced to smuggling codices, chairmen of foundations, retrained as carpenters. Here they all lived in seized and expropriated houses, that used to be their own.

During the fifties Communist functionaries began moving into the vacant expropriated villas. On the streets of the hill could be seen the Chevrolets from before the war and the Soviet makes brought immediately after the war, the Zims, the Zils, the Pobyedas. After 1956 János Kádár, the dictator himself came to live at number 19-23 Cserje utca at the foot of the József-hegy look-out tower. For 33 years he stood at the helm of the country and the Party... It is because of him that it is still difficult to reach the vantage point by car, the streets being one-way and filled with no halting signs.

From the mid-sixties, as constraints on the real estate market if not on the country began to be relaxed, the *nouveaux riches* who had made their fortunes in the "second economy" began to appear on the hill. Their dull apartment houses gradually gave way to suburban villas copied from West German magazines, and to Disneyland dreamhouses.

To a Central European Beverly Hills.

THE INGREDIENTS

An Index to Budapest – a Reading in Itself

BUDAPEST BESTS : : BUDAPEST BESTS : : BUDAPEST BESTS

Pál Schiffer, Trend-setting Documentary Film Director, Drop-out from a Dynasty of Politicians, One of the Most Intensive Admirers of the Female Sex in Central Europe

I have many a favourite cinemas in Budapest. Being a film director, it has been an intriguing task for me to decide whether I prefer making a movie or watching it. Nevertheless, I am risking the statement: my favourite cinema in Budapest is the "Décsi" (deh-tshi).

You might assume, that you are likely to find this name in one of the programme listings. Alas, you can't. No cinema bears this name today — just like street names, cinema names kept on changing in Budapest, especially during major political changes.

The Décsi is called "Művész" (l'Artiste) these days, though for a time it used to be called "Új Tükör" (New Mirror, after a weekly magazine). The original name goes back to a certain family name, that of the owner. The humble author of the present lines had the privilege to know old Mr Décsi in person, who, together with his entire family, happened to live in a flat just above the cinema, retaining an old tradition of crafts- and business people, that of living above the business.

In the Décsi there used to be some balcony seats, and small loggias, and lavish gilded plaster decorations, as it was the fashion of the early twenties. It was a typical "cinema with bell sound", since five minutes before the end of every performance a bell was rung, as a signal: it was high time for couples to start to compose themselves. I clearly remember, that a couple of years back I failed to lure my senior gentleman father to that cinema (then already called "Művész"), to watch a Nikita Mihalkov movie.

"Where is it on?" he asked.
"In the Művész" I replied in an unsuspicious way.
"Which one is that?" he asked.

I came to my senses, remembering from my essential Péter Lengyel (p. 150. — *The Editor*) that a true Budapest gentleman remembers only one name per Budapest street, never mind how many times its name is changed... And it's valid for cinemas, too. So I added:

"Well, you know... the Décsi."

He objected, angrily:

"One does not go there. This is a cinema with a bell!..." And he really did not come there, though I insisted that they stopped ringing the bell decades ago.

Changing movie names did make the life of the serious movie buff a hell, indeed. Atrium was built in the 30s, it later became May 1 (guess when), now it is Atrium again. Royal Apollo was Red Star for a trifle forty years, now it regained its original name (might be pulled down soon.) The one-time Forum was rechristened as Puskin — and it is still called Puskin up to the time this book went to press. City became Toldi. (It is still a mystery, why this cinema got its new name from a legendary hero of the Hungarian Middle Ages, who was best known for its bodily strength...) And so on.

These days Művész is the "flagship" of the Budapest art movie network. (Most of the network is maintained by the City of Budapest, but there are some that belong to studios, and one is operated by the Film Archives.) There is hardly anything like that in Europe, — it obviously rivals Paris and London: such a variety of titles, so often, according to such a reliably recurrent pattern...

No more gilded plaster ornaments, no more plush and velvet any more, but there is air-conditioning and Dolby, and there are 20-25 films a week on, in five rooms now, called Chaplin, Bunuel, Tarkovsky, Huszárik and Bódy, respectively. (The last two names reminds the Budapest moviego-ers of two outstanding Hungarian moviemakers, both died young — the last very young.) A couple of years back the director of the British Film Institute could hardly believe me when I mentioned him that there is a cinema in Budapest, where one can see no less than 5 films of Peter Greenaway within a week. I meant the Művész, needless to say.

So Gentle Traveller, if you feel the urge to watch a film by Mihalkov, or Hartley, or Kusturica, or Jarmusch or Jarman, or Menzel, or Kieslowsky, or Wang (or the like), it is Művész you should come to... Don't panic, unlike many cinemas in Budapest, there are no dubbed films shown here. Just subtitles. And a lovely café to sit in. Called Café Fellini.

(Művész cinema, VI. Teréz körút 30.)

Dear Reader,

I am really interested in your opinion.
Both about the book itself, and also your
on the spot experiences here.
So please, detach this page and send it back to me.
You can also e-mail me: torok@datanet.hu.

Your Invisible Host: *András*

To: András Török

Budapest
Perczel Mór utca 4.
Hungary

H-1054

Dear András,

I found your book

I missed the following

I found the following things inaccurate

I can add from my experience:

My name:

My Sex and Age

My Address (Optional)

My E-Mail:

Date of My Visit

Printed on 100 g Biancoprint paper
manufactured in the Dunaújváros Paper-mill

Printed in Hungary